Selected Books by Bobbie Reed

Bible Learning Activities (with Rex Johnson)
Building Strong People (with John Westfall)
Christian Family Activities for One-Parent Families
Creative Bible Learning—Adult (with M. Marlowe)
Creative Bible Learning—Youth (with C. E. Reed)
Dear Lord, I Can't Do It All!
Developing a Single Adult Ministry
How to Have a Healthy Family Even in Stressful Times
I Didn't Plan to Be a Single Parent
Learn to Risk
Life after Divorce
Listen to the Heart
Longing for a Child
Making the Most of Single Life
Merging Families
Ministry with Single Adults Today
Pleasing You Is Destroying Me
Prescription for a Broken Heart
Single Mothers Raising Sons
Single on Sunday
Stepfamilies: Living in Christian Harmony
Surviving Your Child's Dating Years
The Single Adult Journey
The Single Parent Journey
Too Close, Too Soon (with Jim Talley)
501 Practical Ways to Teach Your Children Values

BAKER HANDBOOK
OF *Single Parent*
MINISTRY

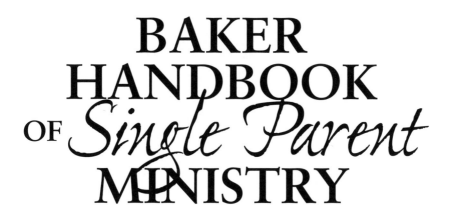

Bobbie Reed, *Editor*
Foreword by **Lynda Hunter**

Baker Books
A Division of Baker Book House Co
Grand Rapids, Michigan 49516

Published by Baker Books
a division of Baker Book House Company
P.O. Box 6287, Grand Rapids, MI 49516-6287

Printed in the United States of America

Library of Congress Cataloging-in-Publication Data

Baker handbook of single parent ministry / Bobbie Reed, editor : foreword by Lynda Hunter.
     p.   cm.
     Includes bibliographical references.
     ISBN 0-8010-9052-0 (cloth)
     1. Church work with single parents. I. Reed, Bobbie.
     BV4438.7.B35   1998
     259'.1—dc21   98-3800

The stories are real. In some cases, individuals' names have been changed and their circumstances altered to protect their privacy. Where real names are used, verbal permission was given.

For current information about all releases from Baker Book House, visit our web site:
http://www.bakerbooks.com

Contents

Foreword

LYNDA HUNTER

When I was a child, one of my favorite desserts was warm blackberry dumplings served over ice cream. The trouble with blackberry dumplings, however, was that Mom couldn't make them without blackberries, which grew on prickly bushes in the most chigger-infested part of the woods. As much as I liked the dessert, I hated picking the berries.

I remember one day when my mother loaded the pails and buckets into the back of our old Ford station wagon and sent me off with my dad to pick blackberries. Pretending I didn't like the popular family dessert failed to get me out of the task. We had been given permission to pick on someone else's property where the berries grew in profusion, and so I went to pick berries.

Although we made an early start, the sun burned down on my head, and my dark hair intensified the heat. I stooped, tugged, bent, and stretched to reach the biggest and best berries. After a couple of hours, I was pleased to note that I had a full bucket and decided to take a break and sample some of the fruits of my efforts. Standing on top of a small knoll, I put the last handful of blackberries into the bucket, which was fastened with a belt around my waist.

All of a sudden, without warning, the bottom gave way, and all the berries I had gathered went rolling down the hill. It was a horrible feeling to see everything I had worked for slipping away from me. Instead of taking the break I had planned, I ran, slipped, and slid down the bank trying to salvage as much of the fruit as I could.

Several years later, I had a similar experience as an adult. After graduating from high school I went to college, earned a degree, landed a teaching position, and agreed to marry the man I loved. I had worked hard, and my life was full. I was very happy.

We had a beautiful November wedding. Two years later our first daughter, Ashley, was born, and two years after that another daughter, Courtney. But while I was expecting my third child, the bottom dropped out of my life. My husband left. Like the blackberries I had watched roll down the hill, everything I had worked so hard to build was slipping away from me. The fruits of years of hard work were dispersed; some were lost and forever gone. I began picking up the pieces and salvaging what I could from my life. It was then I made a full commitment to make Jesus Christ the Lord of my life, and that made all the difference.

I have been a single mom now for twelve years. During that time I have met countless courageous moms and dads from different ethnic, educational, and economic walks of life who are parenting alone. They are divorced, widowed, or never married. They are sometimes heartbreakingly young—still children themselves. They are sometimes older—grandparents taking in grandchildren and beginning the parenting process again.

Our journeys to the job of being single parents are different. We each have our own stories about the day the bottom dropped out of our lives. But we share a common goal to train up our children in the way they should go (Prov. 22:6), and we have direct access to the power of the Holy Spirit to assist us in our task. Our hope lies in realizing that we are not alone. We have each other, and we have the Lord.

The authors in this book have joined in sharing their expertise and experiences about single parenting and ministering with single parents. May their ideas assist you in helping the single parents in your ministry pick up the spilled fruits in their lives and make delicious "desserts" for their families.

Lynda Hunter, Ed.D., is the founding editor of Single-Parent Family *magazine at Focus on the Family. She is the single mother of two daughters and one son, ages fifteen, thirteen, and eleven. Lynda holds a doctorate in curriculum from the University of Cincinnati, and she taught at Miami University of Ohio. She is beginning a syndicated newspaper column for single parents through Focus on the Family, and her books* Single Moments *(Colorado Springs: Focus on the Family, 1977) and* Parenting On Your Own *(New York: HarperCollins, 1997) are available in Christian bookstores. Lynda is a popular speaker on family issues.*

INTRODUCTION

Embracing Single Parents with God's Love

BOBBIE REED

Every church, regardless of size, needs a ministry with single adults. If there is even one single parent in the congregation or community near the church, the need cannot be denied. Like the shepherd who left the ninety-nine sheep in a safe place and went out looking for the one lost sheep (Matt. 18:12–14), pastors must focus not only on the two-parent families in the church but also on caring for the one-parent families.

The type of ministry provided for single parents will vary from church to church depending on the size of the congregation and the number of single parent families in the church or community. At a minimum, the church family must come to understand the challenges faced by single parents including the never married, the widowed, the divorced, those with custody and those without, and the married spouse who essentially functions as a single parent due to the absence of the other parent.

The ten chapters in part 1 of this book will give you an overview of life as a single parent and suggest ways in which the church can demonstrate love and acceptance through understanding of and responding to the needs of single parents. As James points out, simple mental recognition of a truth is not enough; responsive action is required (James 1:22–25).

Responding to the needs of single parents begins on an individual level as members of the body of Christ reach out to one another in love. One way to increase the church's understanding of the challenges of single parenting is to invite a single parent to give a personal testimony relating the story of his or her family and God's faithfulness in times of need. In this way members come to see a single parent as a person and not just another special interest group within the church.

Part 2 of this book has four chapters that address the challenges faced by children who live in one-parent families. I found Cheryl Macoy's discussion of living in a single parent family a wonderful tribute to her mother's faith and determination to succeed (see chap. 12). This chapter also can be very encouraging to church members and single parents because it proves that children raised in a single parent home are not necessarily doomed to failure, dysfunctional lives, or maladjustment. Single parent families can be and often are very healthy and blessed by God.

For churches that are ready to consider developing a formal ministry with single parents, part 3 of this book provides fourteen chapters that focus on individual types of ministry from caring to sharing, from support to instruction, and from parenting partnerships to mentoring for the children. Your church may begin a ministry in any one of these areas and then increase the ministry options as the needs develop and as leaders come forward.

Many of the ministry options are not costly in terms of finances, but they do have investment price tags in terms of time, energy, and personal commitment. It is not necessary, or even desirable, that all of these ministry options be provided for single parents by nonsingle parents or pastors. Single parents can organize and lead most of these programs for themselves, but they need the recognition and support of the church. As you will notice when reading this book, ministry with single parents is actually an integrated process involving married couples, other single adults, pastors, children, and other single parents.

If your church does not have a specific ministry with single parents, then this book is for you. It is a great beginning, a gift from many leaders of ministries across the United States, a pooling of their best ideas. If your church already has a ministry with single parents, perhaps you will find not only affirmation for what you are doing but also new ideas for expanding your current ministry.

Many years ago when I became a single again, and a single parent, there was no ministry in the church to which I could turn for support, assistance, understanding, or affirmation. I sometimes stumbled as I tried to find my way and experienced secret doubts and fears about my abilities to raise two sons alone. I was heartsick when there were problems with my sons, and I convinced myself it was all my fault. I prayed that God would give me wisdom and guidance to make the right decisions. But I felt so alone. What I wouldn't have given to have known a few other Christian single parents who could have reassured and encouraged me with their stories and helped me with reality checks.

My healing started after months of being alone, when I inadvertently overheard another parent complain to a friend that she was so frustrated with her kids that morning that she "could kill them." I was both horrified and relieved. I had thought I was the only parent who had ever reached the end of the rope.

Don't let the single parents in your church suffer the isolation, the sense of alienation, the fears, and the loss of self-esteem that I (and many other single parents) went through. Open up your arms and embrace them with God's love. You will be richer for the experience.

May God bless your ministry with single parents.

Part 1

THE CHALLENGES
OF SINGLE PARENTING

1

Facing Life as a Single Parent

ARVIN GOWENS

A television commercial that aired during the Atlanta Olympics posed, "How much does the world weigh?" The reply was, "Ask a single mom." It could also have been, "Ask a single dad." The weight of the world often seems to rest on the shoulders of single parents. The responsibility of raising children alone is great.

Single parents have male children, female children, or both. Challenges confront single fathers and mothers regardless of the gender or age of their children. Betty, a single mother, said about raising a teenage son and daughter, "All the issues are the same as with a two-parent family but magnified!" It is that magnification of issues that single parents have the privilege and the responsibility to manage.

Being a single again adult is a challenging experience. Being a single parent adds a special dimension to the experience. Therefore, single parents need all the resourcefulness and adaptability that can be mustered. There are demands for time, attention, energy, wits, humor, patience, and finances. Balancing the needs of children, employment, community, church, and self places heavy requirements on the single parent. Such demands upon the single father or mother may cause him or her to feel sharply the need for help from a second parent. Asked to describe her experience with single parenting, Betty, who has successfully raised two teenagers, replied in two words, "Very difficult."

In a time when raising children in any circumstances may indeed be very difficult, single parents have many challenging tasks confronting them. However, most of these parents do very well with those tasks. Great rewards of parenthood are theirs as they raise their children.

Before writing this chapter, I interviewed five single parents—both men and women, churchgoers and nonchurchgoers—who spoke directly about these tasks, difficulties, and rewards. I used their input to supplement my research and knowledge. What follows is a blending of both.

Parents as Teachers

Parents are the first teachers of their children. Long before arriving at school age, children learn a lot about values, faith, God, church, the Bible, and right and wrong from their parents (especially if the parents are Christians). God's early instruction was for parents to continually teach their children as they walk and talk together throughout the day (see Deut. 6:7–9; Eph. 6:4).

When taking care of the day-to-day tasks of living, single parents must not forget to be teachers. And the most important teaching topics are those that are spiritual. Sharing a personal faith, helping children come to know God, and encouraging Scripture memorization are all terrific teaching goals for single parents.

What is different in the single parent family equation is that there is one less adult to do all of the "adult" tasks. The temptation is to pay more attention to the urgent needs (food, clothing, cleaning, etc.) than to the activities that seem to have less tangible results. The reality is that goals such as family devotions and Scripture memorization have eternal consequences and are therefore more important.

Single Mothers Raising Sons

A single mother parenting a son without the help of a father often finds that she is dealing with a "little man." Inside that little man may be all the difficulties in understanding and communicating that she saw in the big man who is no longer around. A boy twelve years old or older may feel his role is to be the head of the household, the strong one. As such he may try to protect Mom and discipline the younger children for her. As the caretaker, he will want to take an authoritative role over the household. He may also believe he must fulfill the traditional male role model of showing no emotion and becoming the decision maker.

A challenge for the single mother in this situation is to maintain her own, consistent authority in the household and yet allow this young son the flexibility and room to develop. The mothers interviewed reported that they had difficulty relating to the suddenly almost-grown-up male ego of their now protector sons. Mothering one who acts as though he is the provider is a complicated task. Because boys often take after their fathers, single moms may find themselves facing some of the same male issues (e.g., procrastination, continuously watching televised sports, strewing clothes around the house) they believed they had left behind when they and their spouses parted. Now these traits are present in the sons they have the responsibility of nurturing and parenting.

Physical growth of the sons can complicate the issue of authority. One single mother said, "At age fourteen, my son was bigger and taller than I." At the police department where I serve as chaplain, we received three separate calls in one evening for assistance from distraught women; all were single mothers of teenage boys. In all three cases the women were actually afraid for their physical safety because of the sons' physical aggression and attacks. These mothers had failed to find a way to gain the proper order of authority over their physically dominant sons.

Even when the single mother has the appropriate authority, she may still be uncomfortable doing unfamiliar "guy stuff" with her son. Showing up at sports events is time consuming, and dealing with male competitiveness and understanding the intricacies of a particular sport can be a challenge. Trying to be a cheering, encouraging mom in the midst of a bunch of loud, boisterous, aggressive dads is not easy for most single mothers. So, an alternative for single moms is to find Christian men who will be good role models for their sons. Even if the father has visitation rights, other role models are often needed to fill in the time or teaching gaps.

Finding male role models requires effort on the part of single mothers. Male coaches can be good role models for boys, and it is even better when a role model can be found within the Christian community. The church can genuinely assist single mothers raising sons by actively involving men in children's and youth ministries. Some churches have male-female teaching teams for children, which is a wonderful idea. Men can lead children's choirs, supervise work days, work in the church nursery, lead a weeknight boys' club, or coach a church sports league.

Single Fathers Raising Daughters

Little girls and their dads make good partners. However, things may change as the girls mature. As Mike said about raising his two daughters, "Everything was okay until boys came along." Maturity also brings emotional and physical changes that can be overwhelming for single fathers like Mike.

Single fathers have discovered the first and perhaps most important skill in raising their developing daughters is communication. By starting early to establish open lines of communication and have frank discussions, many single fathers find they are able to handle the issues of menstruation, breast development, and adolescent changes. "Even so," says Mike, "gender topics do come up that require the single dad to involve women." Many single fathers find the help of a trusted woman to be invaluable. The women the fathers choose to assist with such discussions can also serve as excellent role models for daughters being raised by single fathers.

The Ex-Spouse and Raising Children

The ex-spouse of the single father or mother can have a profound effect (either positive or negative) on the efforts of raising children. During my interviews with five single parents, each expressed definite influences from his or her former spouse. In each instance, the ex-spouse made at least some positive contribution to the parenting process. Each of the former spouses also contributed in a negative fashion to the parenting process.

When custody visits are amicable between the two parents, the custodial single parent may receive a great deal of help with the children from the ex-spouse. Many single fathers and mothers are quite adept at recognizing and utilizing the positive contributions their ex-spouse can provide. The two parents may agree on very little between themselves as individuals and yet be able to coparent effectively.

Coparenting provides a needed break for the custodial parent, and this personal renewal enhances one's parenting skills. It also can be beneficial to have the other parent around to deal with children in matters unique to their gender. The noncustodial father with a son or mother with a daughter may be able to help handle tough or uncomfortable, gender-specific areas. Wise is the single parent who avoids influencing the children in a negative manner toward the other parent and who coparents effectively.

Sometimes, however, the impact the noncustodial parent has on the parenting process is negative. Imagine one single mother's frustration with the attitudes her teenage son picked up from his father's promiscuous live-in relationships. In another family, the noncustodial father consistently withholds monetary support and uses it as a weapon of manipulation over the single mother. The destructive nature of such behavior makes coparenting very difficult and creates undeserved hardship for the children.

The church can assist single parents by teaching that forgiveness is a key factor in maintaining an ongoing relationship with a former spouse. Sometimes there is little to forgive; in other cases the need approximates the "seventy times seven" Jesus spoke of to Peter (Matt. 18:21–22).

Other Adults and Raising Children

Single fathers and mothers seem to be alone in the task of raising their children, and in a real sense they are. Mike, however, realizes, "You can't do it alone. You must have support from others." The skillful single parent seeks out and enlists the resources of adults who can contribute both to the children and to the parent.

Single parents in the apartment complex where Bill lives have established a network to provide care for their children. They agree on who will provide transportation to and from school each day and carpool. In the afternoon the children walk home together and go to a prearranged apartment to stay with one of the single parents until the other parents get home.

Members of the extended family also can provide help and resources to the single parent. The parents interviewed reported grandparents to be good baby-sitters, travel companions, and recreation buddies. In more than one instance, significant financial assistance came from grandparents. One sister-in-law served as a counselor and friend helping a single father explain the onset of puberty to his daughter.

The extended family helps establish consistency in the familial relationships of the children in a single parent home. This is true of the single mom who was never married to and does not have contact with her child's father. In the face of divorce or death of a parent and the loss of a significant family member (a parent), the familiar faces and relationships of the extended family members help stabilize the children's lives. Through compassion, understanding, love, and acceptance, these family members play an important role in the lives of both the single parent and the children.

The Church and Raising Children

There are many excellent resources available to single fathers and mothers in those churches that have a concern for ministry to single parent families. Of the single parents interviewed, those who sought it found ample assistance available in the church.

Divorce recovery ministries are instrumental in bringing divorced persons to healthy coping levels emotionally. Their children benefited from sessions for children of divorced parents. The entire family gained the advantage of a positive outlook and self-esteem. Most significantly, they were reminded that they needed sincere faith, trust, and confidence that God had not abandoned their families or the individuals in their families because of the breakup of the marriages.

Single parents can find their network of support expanded greatly through the resources of the church. Children's workers, youth pastors, pastors, counselors, and committed Christian individuals are excellent sources of nurture, care, and training. As one single parent emphasized, knowing who these persons are and having an acquaintance with them is but one step. Single parents then purposely must establish rapport between caregivers and the children so they know each other and feel comfortable with each other. Real benefit comes through such relationships.

Some single fathers and mothers attend churches that are not as rich in resources as others. The programs may be lacking, or they may exist without the sophistication of larger ministries. Specific staff members listed above may not be available. Yet many of these churches still can provide nurture, love, and concern for single parents and their children. Churches that successfully embrace, love, and accept single parent families can provide an avenue for God to work in the lives of single parents raising children.

The church as the body of Christ has a responsibility to care for one another (read the Book of 1 John). Caring for each other is one way to demonstrate the love of God at work in our lives. The church needs to actively initiate ways to reach out to single parents and minister to them.

Discipline Issues

"I'm it!" That is the concise statement of one single mother regarding how discipline gets done in her home. Another said, "I must do it all." There is no one in the home on whom to fall back. Regardless of how tired or stressed one gets, single fathers and mothers have to set the standards for discipline. Then they have to maintain those standards. There is no opportunity to walk away and say to the other parent in the room, "You handle this." There is no other parent present.

Discipline requires balance. Standards must be set and boundaries defined. Flexibility is also required, however. Balance is easiest to accomplish when there is more than one person giving input to the process, but single parents must work through issues alone.

Raising children is on-the-job training; single parents are both students and instructors. If they have headaches, they still must discipline when necessary. If single parents are not sure of the best solution to the discipline problem, they still must select an approach. If the approach they chose fails or is not adequate, single parents must try again. If the boundaries break apart, they must be reconstructed by the single parents. When discipline in the home is out of balance, the single parent must right the balance.

Discipline takes time. Yet time is not available in sufficient quantities to the single father or mother because so many other things take up the available time and energy. There is often little left for additional problems. However, the single parent must find time because time spent listening, reinforcing, communicating, discussing, and sharing helps reduce the number of discipline crises. The single parent must learn to juggle time and use time wisely in order to give good help to children.

The Best of Times and the Worst of Times

Single fathers and mothers sometimes have terrific struggles in their parenting experiences. There are also wonderful rewards in raising children alone. The parents interviewed were extremely optimistic about their success in raising children.

However, there are rough spots in the new family structure. One mother found it necessary to guard against establishing a buddy-pal relationship in place of the mother-daughter relationship that will be much more beneficial to both parties. This mom discovered she had expected the child to take on too much adult-level emotional responsibility as a sounding board. What the teenager needed was a mother to help her through her years of growth and development, not another pal.

The single parents reported that their relationships with their children became stronger after divorce. Mike, a single father, confessed that while married his priority had been his job. In fact, this contributed to the breakup of his marriage. He had left parenting and relationship building up to his now ex-spouse. Since becoming a single parent of two daughters, he has realigned his priorities and placed the well-being of his children ahead of his work commitments.

This type of selfless giving on the part of single parents to their children is evident in other ways. The best aspect of single parenting according to one mother is the "closeness that comes from investing myself with my kids. I've become everything I can to them." The satisfaction of watching the children grow and develop personally is worth all the struggle to these parents.

Asked to describe the best times and the most difficult times in single parenting, men and women tended to stress different aspects. Women noted building closeness and intimacy with their children as the best times. They emphasized meeting the needs of the children and did not dwell on their own needs as much. Men, on the other hand, stressed the relationships they build with the children, but they also pointed to the difficulties they personally experience from divorce.

The worst aspect of single parenting according to one father is his own feelings of inadequacy and frustration, especially in raising his daughter alone. For another single father, his main difficulty is his change of lifestyle. He went from a four-bedroom house with a pool to sharing a one-bedroom apartment with two children. His family income dropped from $72,000 to $17,000, and he lost a position of leadership in his church. "I have lost who I am. The responsibility of parenting, work, and attending church leaves me no time, energy, or resources to build a life of my own. I feel totally alone."

Pressed to express the positive side of single parenting, this same father said his favorite aspect is the time he spends together with his girls: "Even doing the small stuff, I have the opportunity to be involved in every part of their lives." This father, who has one high school senior and one twenty-two-year-old daughter who recently married, softened his tone of voice as he recalled the joys of watching his daughters grow up.

A single mother said, "The best times for me were when I saw God at work in my children's lives and watched them respond."

Oh, yes, it is worth it all—even if it sometimes hurts or is lonely.

Rev. Arvin Gowens is the single adult pastor at First Southern Baptist Church in Fountain Valley, California. He has been a single adult growth consultant for the California Baptist Convention and served for sixteen years as an associate pastor and minister with single adults. He has an M.Div. from Golden Gate Baptist Seminary.

2

Being a Never Married Parent

NORM YUKERS

hy do you call your dad 'Papa'?" Melody asked her friend Julie at a recent church picnic. Both girls were five years old, and the man Julie called "Papa" was actually her grandfather.

"That's not my dad!" Julie responded.

"Where's your dad then?" Melody asked.

Julie replied, "I don't have a dad."

"Oh," Melody replied casually. Then both girls continued playing without any further discussion.

Has it become so commonplace for children to respond, "I don't have a dad," or, "My dad doesn't live with us," that other children just play on as if nothing odd has been said? I am afraid the answer is *yes*. It is true that circumstances sometimes require women to raise children without a father, but should this be just another lifestyle option?

Julie's mom made a choice. Becoming pregnant by a man she did not love left her two options: enter into a marriage that probably wouldn't last or become a statistic—a never married mom. Julie's mom never for an instant considered abortion as a choice, and Julie will spend a lifetime being thankful.

Who Are the Never Married Parents?

Many women in the United States who are not married are having children. Some women conceive through sexual encounters, while others are impregnated through scientific advances that allow women never to come into physical contact with the biological father. Some single women become mothers through adoption. A portion of these are through normal adoption proceedings in or outside of the country, while others adopt or assume the parenting role because a family member could not or would not care for the child/children.

It has been reported that as many as four out of ten unmarried women in their thirties have had children outside of marriage.[1] Another report states as many as 32 percent of the children born in the United States today are born to a woman who is unmarried.[2] If you couple this statistic with another that suggests 30 percent of children in the United States live with a single parent, you can quickly grasp the need for a single parent ministry as well as ministry to the children of single parents.

In an issue of *Single Adult Ministries Journal,* it was reported that *Glamour* magazine asked "single moms by choice" to describe the highs and lows of their experience. Fully one half expressed serious regrets.[3] The article went on to say it is difficult for children to grow up deprived of a precious thing—a father.

Let's look at a few stories that illustrate the different types of never married single parents. All of these stories have one main thing in common—they are real. (All of the names have been changed to protect their privacy.) Most of these examples are about single moms, because they are the overwhelming majority of single, never married, custodial parents.

Single Parent because of Intercourse

Susan was born in the inner city of a large metropolitan area in the southeastern United States. Her mother was concerned that she would be drawn into trouble by those around her, so she enrolled Susan in a swimming program at the local YMCA. Susan proved to be a naturally gifted athlete and won gold medals at several swim meets. Then a young man in Susan's neighborhood convinced her that the pleasure of sexual sin was more important than winning swim meets. Now, still unmarried and the mother of two children by different fathers, Susan can only dream of what might have been.

Many never married girls and women choose to become sexually active and run the risk of an unplanned pregnancy. Others deliberately become sexually active in order to have a child. It seems that our culture has begun to adopt social mores that Christians reject. Some of these beliefs include:

It's all right to become sexually active in order to have a child.
It is natural for single adults to become sexually active.
The father's role in parenting is minimal.
Single men cannot be held responsible for accepting parenting duties.
Men are unnecessary.

As a church, our first obligation is to take a firm stand for what is right. No longer can we fail to address the issue of sex outside marriage. We must clearly communicate that premarital sex is wrong. In this day and age when it is illegal to pray before a football game, it is perfectly legal and acceptable to pass out condoms at the pep rally.

The singles minister and the youth minister must teach abstinence, even though once a person has become sexually active it is difficult to stop. We must be able to create a safe environment where accountability can be established. People today want to know right from wrong, and we must teach that God has a standard of chastity and purity. Although we can be forgiven when we sin, we need to choose not to sin.

When teaching God's plan, a great place to start is Genesis 1:27–28, "So God created man in his own image, in the image of God he created him; male and female he created them. God blessed them and said to them, 'Be fruitful and increase in number.'" Matthew 15:4 says, "For God said, 'Honor your father and mother.'" We can infer from these verses that God intended men and women to conceive and raise children together.

Obviously God's plan is not always followed, and like any other area of life in which we fail to measure up to the plan, God forgives through grace. We also must show grace and forgiveness to those in our ministries who are never married parents (see Eph. 4:32). If the never married parents have not yet been restored to fellowship and reconciled with God, then it is also our task to assist them in this process (see Gal. 6:1).

In the case of the unplanned result of a sexual encounter, we must applaud the decision not to abort. But our God-given responsibility goes much further. Helping the single adult properly decide to keep the child or offer him or her for adoption is paramount, but this counseling must be provided by a trained individual in a safe environment. Encouraging single adults to marry for the sake of the child is certainly not always wise counsel, because these marriages do not have the best success rate and thus could lead to later feelings of abandonment and rejection for both parent and child.

Single Parent because of Abandonment

Ingrid was a lovely young woman who was a flight attendant by profession. She chose a lifestyle option that is common in the United States—cohabitation. Ingrid's job transferred her to another city, and her roommate, Sam, planned to join her in a couple of months.

Alone in new surroundings and a strange city, Ingrid found herself at loose ends and decided to visit a nearby church. Two nights after that a couple of single adults dropped by for a follow-up visit. Ingrid was so excited to have visitors that she shared about herself and Sam. She also told the visitors she had just discovered she was pregnant. She was sure that when Sam heard about the baby, he would be eager to get married.

The single adults who visited Ingrid refrained from responding in a judgmental manner and reassured Ingrid that she was very welcome in their single adult ministry. In the next few weeks as Ingrid attended the single adult ministry meetings, classes, and functions, she realized she needed to make a faith decision to accept Christ as her Savior, and she did. This made her even more anxious for Sam to join her so she could share her newfound faith with him. However, when Sam arrived, he was not ready to accept a changed Ingrid or her faith, and so he left her. What a test for a new Christian and expectant mother.

Although most people who decide to become sexually active do so of their own free will, the decision to remain an unmarried parent is not always within their control.

Those who have children because they became sexually active voluntarily may still encounter issues if/when their sexual partners do not stay around to assist during the pregnancy or to coparent. Many a single mom would willingly marry the father of her child, if only he would ask. On the other hand, some of the fathers are unavailable for marriage—they are already married to someone else! There is the final group of single moms who say, "I made one mistake getting involved with the guy, and I'm not going to compound it by making another and marrying him!" The challenge is to minister to these single parents (and their children) even if we cannot approve of how they became pregnant.

Some never married parents did not even make a choice to have sexual intercourse. These are the women who become pregnant because they were raped either by a stranger or a date. These single parents who decide to keep and rear the child often have to deal with the additional pain of emotional and psychological trauma and require extra care and love from the community of believers. It is our calling and commandment to take onto ourselves the burdens of others with loving concern (Gal. 6:2). This is because when one of the family is hurting, the entire family hurts (see 1 Cor. 12:12–26).

Single Parent by Adoption

Marylyn was very active in her single adult ministry and had a genuine burden for foreign missions. She gladly accepted an opportunity to lead a team of single adults on a two-week trip to Romania. On the first day in Romania, she was introduced to a young orphaned girl. Both of this young girl's parents had been killed in the recent turmoil in that country.

Even after leaving the country Marylyn thought constantly of the little Romanian girl, and eventually she began the long process of adopting her. After two years of continual work, Marylyn was granted a miracle—permission to adopt her little Alexandra. Suddenly, Marylyn found herself moved from leader in the single adult ministry to participant in the single parent ministry.

Some may question whether or not single adults should be allowed to adopt children, because this places children into a home with only one parent. However, while it is ideal to have two parents to rear a child, it is better to have one loving parent rather than none. James tells us that it is a sign of genuine Christianity to care for the orphans (James 1:27). So until there are sufficient married couples who will take in the orphans of the world, how can it be wrong to allow single adults to step into the gap?

When single adults come to you to discuss the possibility of adopting a child, be prepared to help them seek God's guidance in the matter. If the motivation is to provide nurture and care to a child who has been orphaned, abandoned, or neglected, and God leads a single adult to adopt that child, then offer your support. Then be sure to marshal assistance from within the single adult ministry and the church at large for the new family.

Single Parent through Technology

Linda was a seriously career-minded single adult in her late thirties. She wasn't in a dating relationship, and she believed the prospects of starting one in the near future were slim. Everyone who knew Linda said she would be a great mother. Linda's own mother continually commented that her ambitions to be a grandmother were going unfulfilled. Also, Linda could hear her biological clock ticking away her chances to fulfill her friends' and mother's visions of her and her own maternal desires.

Linda did not choose to become sexually active in order to have a child; she remained chaste in that regard. Instead, in ultimate frustration, she chose consumerism (buying what she hadn't achieved), visited a sperm bank, and arranged to become pregnant.

A slightly different version of this story is that of Rita, a professing lesbian, who made a commitment to Sally to be her lifelong partner in a lesbian relationship. They desired to have Rita give birth to a child and to raise that child just as any other couple might. So they arranged for Rita to be artificially inseminated.

In an early 1990s episode of *Empty Nest,* the older daughter, Barbara, wants to have a child. She discusses sperm banks with her dad. "Why should I obligate a guy for the rest of his life when I only need him for less than an hour?" she says. And to this many girls and women in America answered, "Amen."

Because women today can become pregnant without having sexual intercourse with a man, parenting has become an option for more single women. Leaders of single adult ministries need to be prepared to offer wise counsel to women who question whether or not this option is for them. One approach is to help them explore the reasons they wish to have a child. Some reasons are healthy; others are unhealthy.

Many single adults struggle with feelings of inadequacy, low self-esteem, loneliness, being unloved, and inferiority. They often are jealous or envious of what appears to be the perfect picture (husband, wife, and 2.2 children). Too many times a child appears to be an answer to these negative feelings. Speaking preventively, the singles ministry must teach on these issues and provide biblical answers. All of us, single or married, must find our completion and wholeness in God, not in other people, not even in our own children (see Col. 2:9–10).

Harold Ivan Smith says, "A struggle for the single, especially the childless single, is, will I be remembered?"[4] Harold goes on to discuss the sense of significance in a family context. Heritage and lineage are concerns for those without children, but having children outside of marriage is not the answer to questions about significance, meaning, and purpose.

Other reasons women want children include:

to enjoy them
to love them
to create another person
to have companionship
to have grandchildren

to fulfill a personal fantasy
to feel whole
to become a family
to justify one's existence
to take charge of one's options
to have help when one gets old
to meet the expectations of others
to show how good a parent one can be
to be all that one can be
to experience parenting
to follow the command to "be fruitful and increase
    in number" (Gen. 1:28)
to receive blessings from God (Ps. 127:3–5)

As leaders we can help single women evaluate their reasons for wanting a child so desperately. Invite them to pray carefully over their decision and to seek God's guidance.

One thing leaders can do to assist the single woman considering becoming pregnant through technology is to help her think through the challenges she will face as a never married mother. Invite her to interview other single mothers to fully understand the issues she would face as a parent on her own. Encourage her to evaluate the financial responsibilities and her ability to provide for these. Suggest that there are other ways to meet one's need for children such as adopting, working with children, mentoring other people's children, or sharing a home with a single parent family. However, chances are that if the person is determined to have a child of her own, you may not be able to influence the decision.

Single Parent without Custody

Margie decided early in her pregnancy to give her baby up for adoption because she recognized she was not ready to be a single parent. She was only eighteen and just out of high school. She had no job experience or special training. Her prospects of obtaining an immediate job that would pay enough for her to afford child care were poor. After much agonizing soul searching, Margie was sure the best decision she could make for her child was to allow a

Christian family to adopt him or her. Although at the last minute she almost changed her mind, Margie did relinquish her newborn son. Margie cried for several days whenever she thought of her son.

When Paul's girlfriend, Tanya, discovered she was pregnant, Paul suggested they get married and raise the child. However, Tanya did not feel their relationship was one that would survive marriage, so she broke up with Paul. When the baby came, Tanya moved in with her mother, who helped her raise the little girl. Tanya would not allow Paul to visit his daughter or assume a father's role. Paul grieved the loss of a daughter he never knew.

Both Margie and Paul were never married single parents, even though they did not have custody of their children. There may be Margies or Pauls in your single adult ministry who carry inside the pain of having a child they cannot raise or visit. You may never know about this pain because the secret may never be shared openly. But as leaders we need to be sensitive to the fact that some of the single adults in our ministries may need healing from their private sufferings. One way to care for people such as Margie or Paul is to pray that God will grant inner peace and healing for each of the single adults with whom you minister.

Ministering to the Never Married Parent

There are some unique issues involved when ministering to never married parents. First, there are often feelings of guilt, shame, and embarrassment on the part of never married parents who became pregnant because of sexual intercourse. Accepting these parents and children in your ministry is an important way of sharing God's unconditional love (see Eph. 1:6). Acknowledging that these negative feelings are the result of not living according to the divine plan for one's life does not have to be judgmental. Instead, approach this as a teaching opportunity to point individuals in the direction of obedience to God's plan for holiness and purity.

A second and very important issue in ministering to never married parents is helping them develop parenting skills. The never married parent is usually a woman (although there are cases of never married men having custody of their own child or adopting a child), and most have little contact with the father of the child. Only a very few receive financial support from the other parent. So the never married parent must fulfill the roles of both father and mother as much as possible. As leaders, we can provide parenting classes, seminars, or workshops that will help single parents become effective in their roles. (Of course these classes may be attended by all single parents whether or not they were previously married.)

A third issue is that children tend to form their impressions of a heavenly Father through their contacts with their earthly dad. When a child has little or no contact with a father, the impressions of God are often distorted. Some children are fortunate that a grandfather or other male family member provides that male influence. Other children are not so fortunate, and the church must recognize this need and provide ways to help meet it. Psalm 68:5 says God is the "father to the fatherless," and it is the church's responsibility to teach and show this truth.

Another issue of which leaders need to be aware is the impact on a fatherless child whose mother is dating. If never married single parents allow or encourage a dating partner to assume the role of the absent parent and the relationship breaks off, the children tend to feel rejected and abandoned by the only father they have known. Therefore, never married parents need to be cautioned about not assigning the father's role to a dating partner or allowing that role to be assumed until there is a genuine commitment to making the relationship a permanent one through marriage.

As those of us ministering to single adults attempt to deal with these issues facing never married parents, let us remember one basic truth: Jesus died for each of us. None of us make the right choices all of the time, but forgiveness is available for each of us when we ask for it (1 John 1:9). As ministers and leaders of a flock of God's prized sheep, let us constantly pray for the ability to see our flock as God himself sees them. In summary let's remember:

There are many types of never married parents.
Some are unmarried because of the choice of a partner.
Some became single parents as a result of poor choices.
Some may need to deal with forgiveness issues.

Some may struggle with personal significance issues.
All need instruction on godly parenting skills.
All need a safe environment to grow and mature.
Their children are in need of the same things.

According to a recent *USA Today* article, 43 percent of Americans are concerned about the number of children born to single parents.[5] Unfortunately, most people look to someone else or the government to do something about the problem. That is not an acceptable solution. An amoral agency like the federal government cannot become a moral force.

We, the church, and more specifically, the leaders in single adult ministries, must guide single adults and their children into making moral choices that are pleasing to God. Because God created the human race with a free will, we become stewards of our decision-making opportunities. God provided us with the inspired Scriptures to assist us in learning how best to live our lives and how to follow the divine plan for us. Let's band together and make a difference in the lives God has entrusted to us.

Rev. Norm Yukers is the minister with single adults at Rehoboth Baptist Church in Atlanta, Georgia. He served on the board of directors for the Network of Single Adult Leaders and chaired the board for a period of three years.

3

Surviving a Divorce with Children

BARBARA E. GEORGE

*T*he traditional family ("till death do us part") may be a dying breed, but many of us were raised in one. Women were expected to manage a home, love a husband, and raise responsible children. Men were expected to find a good job and support the home, wife, and children. It was a plan that had been in effect for several thousand years, and it seemed a reasonable one—biblical actually. Yet it may be a plan that our grandchildren and great-grandchildren will only read about in history or sociology books.

Divorce happens—to the rich, the poor, the educated, the uneducated, the powerful, the powerless, the churched, the unchurched, those who haven't a clue that it is coming, and those who have been mentally walking away from their marriages for some time. It happens to our neighbors, our friends, and our relatives. Sometimes, it happens to us.

Going through a divorce can feel like riding a train that is out of control. You try holding fast to your seat while everything you know about life, marriage, family, love, God, and faith comes crashing down from the baggage compartment onto your head. Virtually everything seems to get broken, jettisoned out the window, or rendered useless.

My mother taught me how to be a traditional wife, as she had been taught by her mother. It worked for her. I tried it. It didn't work for me. My train was not only on a track with numerous curves that threw me from side to side, causing me to bump my head, but it was also out of control. The engineer had obviously jumped off, and the kids were hiding under the seats in utter confusion. Just when I thought I couldn't stand it another minute, we entered a long, dark tunnel. I began to scream.

At that point, I had two options, as do all single parents: Jump off and end it all, or stop screaming long enough to hear a still, small voice say, "And surely I am with you always" (Matt. 28:20). I realized I had to decide whether I believed God was in the engine car and well aware of what was happening to our family. I chose to believe that God was in control. For me, Philippians 1:6 became an essential verse: "Being confident of this, that he who began a good work in you will carry it on to completion until the day of Christ Jesus." I clung to the promise that God who began the good work in me wasn't about to desert me in my hour of greatest need.

There are many who scream, "Not this! Not now! Oh, God, please not me!" But after a period of weeping, wailing, pleading, and bargaining, at some point one wakes up and admits, "Okay, it happened. Now what? How long am I going to let my past destroy my present and future, and more importantly, the present and future of my children?" As leaders of single adult ministries, we need to convince divorced single parents that there *is* life after divorce—the meaningful, abundant life God desires for each of us (John 10:10).

When my husband left, I wanted to die. I asked God to take me home because I knew there was no way I could go on living. Left with a house I couldn't afford, three acres of grass to mow, no marketable skills, and three precious children, I didn't have a clue where to begin to rebuild my life. My oldest daughter was thirteen going on eighteen, my son was eleven and now the only man in the house, and my youngest daughter was five. She sat on my lap and said, "I don't understand." The tragedy was that none of us did.

The Single Parent Job

Parenting as a single adult is the most important and also the most difficult job a person can tackle. Few of those who have the job filled out a "Single Parent Job Application" form. A comparison of the duties and responsibilities involved with the incentive package that comes with the job would daunt the most courageous. Of all the jobs in the marketplace, single parenting never comes up as a career choice when high school and college plans are being discussed with mom and dad. This job offers a 168-hour work week, no merit raises, no paid health or life insurance premiums, no paid holidays or vacations, no pension or retirement packages, and not even reimbursement for out-of-pocket expenses. Who in their right mind would ask for such a job?

Each day seems to bring new challenges. As one single parent wrote:

> No money, sick children, no food, a broken-down vehicle, children failing school, counselors, pastors, loneliness, having to move, runaway children, stolen checks, rejection, friend of the court, social services, police, desperateness, lawyers, . . . judges, . . . custody battles, child support, alimony, visitations, referees, tears, hurts, and oh so much pain—will it ever stop?[1]

In spite of this frightful description, each day in America almost three thousand children find their parents have accepted the job of being a single parent.[2] Most single heads of households have some things in common: twenty-four-hour responsibility, awesome aloneness when it comes to making major decisions, and concern for the economic, emotional, physical, and spiritual well-being of themselves and their children. Usually single parents have two full-time jobs, one in and one out of the home. In addition to the practical tasks involved, there are numerous emotional issues to deal with: the loss of a spouse, the loss of married status, the fear of not being able to survive, and the mental anguish of what could have been or should have been, to name just a few.

Concerns of the Divorced Single Parent

Divorced single parents face all of the challenges of single parenting as well as dealing with some issues unique to the divorced home. They face the shame and embarrassment of failure, the pain of rejection, the negative attitudes of church members who believe prayer would have prevented the divorce, and the rejection of former friends who stay away because they believe that divorce is contagious. Also feelings of inadequacy, incompetence, and low self-worth are often experienced in the aftermath of a divorce. There are those who, in ignorance, refer to divorced single parent families as "broken," implying that they need to be fixed. The remedy is generally believed to be another marriage. (Yet experts agree that remarriage is not what a newly divorced person needs.)

Negative Attitudes in the Church

I remember years ago when my church presented a need for greeters before each worship service. As a single parent and full-time office manager, my schedule was extremely full. But wanting to contribute to my church in some way, I figured it wouldn't be too difficult to arrive fifteen minutes early and shake hands with other parishioners. When I approached the proper person with my offer, however, she smiled, patted my hand, and said, "Thank you, but no. We really prefer to keep the family image here. You understand, don't you?" I smiled back, mumbled something, went home, and cried.

I had not only lost my identify as a wife, I was now no longer a *proper* church member. It is easy to question your self-worth when you discover that if you are no longer a "Mrs.," you are no longer qualified even to shake a few hands.

As leaders of single adult ministries, we have an opportunity to ensure that when divorced single parents come to our churches, they are made to feel welcome and given opportunities to contribute along with all of the other members.

Is your church or ministry helping divorced single parents change their attitudes about their situations? Are the parents encouraged to pray not only *for* their kids but also *with* them? Are they invited to join in your family-oriented activities? Do families offer to watch single parent family children on a regular basis to provide much needed respite? On "Father and Son Night," do men ask the boys being raised by single moms to attend with them? Being avoided by church members adds to the already full bucket of pain that a divorced single parent carries. When asked why they shy away from the divorced, many parishioners respond, "I don't know what to do, so I do nothing," or, "I am afraid of doing the wrong thing, so I do nothing." If they truly want to extend the hand of Christian love, all anyone has to do is ask themselves, "What would I do if the spouse had died?" Then go and do likewise.

Loss of Self-Esteem

Some people make their marriage their whole focus in life, so their self-esteem is wrapped up in being someone's spouse. When their marriages end, they may find themselves asking, "If I am not somebody's spouse, who am I?" Jim Smoke, the creator of Divorce Recovery Workshops, has had many single again people tell him they are lost and just want to be married again so they will know who they are. How sad. Knowing who you are should not depend upon being married or single. Identity starts with oneself. As Jim says, "If you don't know who you are as a single-again person, you may never know who you are as a remarried person."[3]

As leaders, we need to assist divorced single parents in recognizing they have a complete identity of their own and do not need to live with poor self-esteem.

Relationships with the Ex-Spouse

A large part of the emotional upheaval a divorced single parent deals with is the ongoing association with the former spouse. Rarely is a divorce neat, clean, and tidy. When two wounded individuals are trying to sort out their own lives, work through their negative emotions, and develop a different relationship with each other, they often do not get along very well. There are many issues that affect the relationship: visitation, child support, alimony, shared expenses for major items such as braces or medical bills, new dating partners, and differing values.

A single parent support group can be very helpful for newly divorced single parents who want to develop working relationships with their former spouses. As other members commiserate and share what has been successful for them, the newcomer can feel that someone understands and that there are options that work.

Response of the Children

Children are often caught in the middle of parental differences and usually have a lot of questions. They ask,

> "Why does Mommy cry when I tell her what I did with Dad?"
> "How come Dad has a room for me filled with toys, and at Mom's I sleep on the couch?"
> "If Dad says he will pick me up at six o'clock and doesn't show up, does that mean I did something bad?"
> "How come Dad takes me to Disneyland, and Mom only takes me to the park?"
> "Why are Mom and Dad always screaming at each other? Why can't they just be friends like before?"

As innocent victims, the children are often the most confused. Divorced single parents must strive not to put their children in the middle of their anger with an ex-spouse. Teaching about anger and forgiveness is one way to minister to divorced single parents.

Emotional Leftovers

The stigma of the *divorced* label is another challenge divorced single parents face. Those who are widowed are respected and honored in their loss. In their cases, the good can be remembered and the bad put to rest. To be divorced, however, is another matter. Because the former spouse lives on, his or her strengths and weaknesses continue to be a part of one's life.

For those who have not been divorced, it is easy to believe that divorced people really didn't try hard enough, are selfish and uncommitted, lack faith, have a dysfunctional background, drink or do drugs, or have no morals. Until it happens to you, it is easy to quip, "God hates divorce. The church hates divorce" (cf. Mal. 2:16). Getting closer to the issue, however, you discover that "nobody hates divorce quite as much as the divorced do."[4]

Scott Peck began his book with the simple statement, "Life is difficult."[5] Almost two thousand years earlier, Jesus knew this and said that in life we would have trials and tribulations (John 16:33). Although this applies to everyone, it seems to be the life verse for divorced single parents.

The emotional baggage that comes with a divorce is often harder to handle than the practical issues of survival. Since admitting failure is difficult for most people, some stuff their pain inside as one would sweep things under the carpet and hope no one will notice. Unfortunately, most things swept under the carpet eventually stink.

Gary Richmond says that when people are weighed down by heavy emotional baggage, they find that challenging tasks become even more difficult to handle.[6] When all of one's energy is spent on past struggles or the *what ifs,* one has little energy left for loving and raising children. Some of the things Richmond encourages divorced single parents to watch for, guard against, and deal with include self-pity, guilt, shame, anger, envy, fear, and frustration.

Self-pity. Marsi Beauchamp explains, "To heal more quickly you must 'act' yourself into new feelings—not 'feel' yourself into actions."[7] People who are moaning "poor me" years after a divorce are not fun to be with and never mature as Christ intends.

Guilt and shame. These are two of the saddest pieces of baggage divorced single parents carry. They need to receive forgiveness, grace, and mercy and get on with their lives.

Anger. Although anger is a normal response to a loss, *prolonged* anger will destroy a person and a family. Anger and hatred will sap one's strength and keep one from doing good. Anger needs to be expressed in a safe place (such as a support group), confessed to God, and let go.

Envy. Some single parents are envious when they see others buying, building, traveling, and having fun. Many think that 99 percent of their problems would be solved if they just had more money. But when we read about the struggles of the rich and famous, we should realize money cannot be the answer. Envy and jealousy are a waste of precious time.

Fear. While single adults often have the fear of always being alone, single parents have a fear of *never* being alone. Or they fear that they aren't smart enough, wise enough, or strong enough to do the job. They may be fearful of ever trusting or having an intimate relationship again. Yet God has not given us a spirit of fear (2 Tim. 1:7). Allowing fear to control us is not trusting in the faithfulness of God.

Frustration. There are many frustrations in a divorced single parent's life: not enough money, time, energy, love, or self to go around. One single parent shared her frustration of not finding time each day to do the three things she wanted most: exercise, devotions, and relaxation. The solution is to change the schedule, lower the expectations to realistic levels, leave a little more dust, and discover what is really important.

As leaders we can recognize when some of the single parents have fallen into one of these pitfalls and be ready to assist them back on the right track.

Personal Attitudes

Nothing robs the joys of today like the worries of tomorrow. One's personal attitude is very important to being a successful single parent. When one finally stops screaming, "God, I can't raise these children by myself!" one may hear a gentle voice say, "I know." For God is there for each single parent and ready to help with the parenting process.

Some divorced single parents believe their family is irreparably dysfunctional because there has been a divorce. However, Carolyn Koons reports that the healthy adjustment of children to a divorce is related to the quality of the parenting and not the number of parents in the home.[8] It is important that as leaders we ensure that single parent families are not negatively stereotyped.

I Can Do It!

The knowledge that single parenting can be done well is both a positive and negative for divorced single parents. Those who really want what is best and are doing their best for their children will stand up and cheer at this information. But those who have been hiding behind excuses such as, "He'd be doing better in school if his father were here," or "She'd take better care of herself and the house if her mother were here to show her how," or "It's because we don't have enough money that the kids are messed up," will find this information discouraging. After all, it's easy to blame someone else and circumstances for problem behavior and hard to take responsibility for it.

Divorced single parents can be successful. Ray Maloney gives ten ways to turn out terrific kids. Four of these include: love them, listen to them, make God a part of their lives, and let them go.[9] It doesn't take two parents to do these things; one parent can do all of them. It will take time and energy (precious commodities to a single parent), but it is worth the effort. Good parenting is harder than bad parenting, but parenting is our most important job.

Depend on God

If we will stand in the presence of God for even ten minutes each day, we can be transformed. God can change our hopes and dreams, take away our fears and loneliness, change our attitudes, teach us about victorious living, share the responsibility for the children, and be trusted with the past, present, and future. God made us and has promised to love us and never leave us (see Ps. 139:13–14; Jer. 31:3; Matt. 28:19–20).

How can we refuse help from a God like that? We can't. And we can't succeed on our own (see John 15:5).

God is able, willing, wanting, and waiting to speak to each of us at any given moment of any given day. I used to be very suspicious, however, of people who would report what God had said to them. Then the Almighty spoke to me. I don't know how many times God had tried before, but on a sunny day in July 1980, I received my first divine single parenting tip, loud and clear. That day God chose to speak through my youngest daughter, Ann. I was nineteen months into my role as a single mom and, to put it mildly, I was not a happy camper. And I found plenty of opportunities to let God know! That day the Lord spoke and took my attitude, my complaints, and my tears and turned them around 180 degrees.

Ann, then age six, came to me and asked, "Can I get the mail?" No big deal, right? Except our mailbox wasn't attached to our house. To get the mail, she would have to walk down our 350-foot driveway and cross the street lined with trees. She would be out of my sight then. In addition, we lived on a country road where cars, motorcycles, horses, and tractors traveled at any speed they chose. Knowing that letting go couldn't wait until my children were eighteen, I said, "Yes," and then included a dozen warnings.

Sometime later I asked my oldest daughter if she had seen Ann. My stomach was immediately in my throat when she reminded me that Ann had gone to get the mail. I flew out the front door and ran until I could see Ann. She appeared to be all right but was just standing across the street next to the mailbox.

I calmed down a bit and went to see what had happened. Ann's arms were full of mud-splattered mail. Bit by bit her story came out. She had managed to get all the mail by straddling the mud puddle in front of the box, but when she turned to come back to the house, a piece of mail dropped into the puddle. When she bent over to pick it up, another piece dropped in, and so on and so on. When she realized she couldn't fix it on her own, she decided to stand there and wait for me. Ann looked into my eyes with great love and trust and said, "I knew you'd come." I was overwhelmed with her trust in me. I had tried so hard to be the perfect parent and once again had failed by forgetting all about her. I hugged her, mud and all, and we started back to the house.

Halfway across the yard, I encountered an invisible, yet very real, brick wall. I stopped dead in my tracks (as one must do when encountering brick walls) and heard God say, "Let's do that again, Barbara. You feel like you are standing next to a very large mud puddle. All your hopes, dreams, and plans for being a wife and mother have fallen from your arms and are covered with mud. For just a few minutes I would like you to be the child, and I'll be the perfect parent. Because you keep trying to pick up more than you can handle, you keep dropping things back into the puddle. You think I'm not hearing and answering your prayers. Not so. Remember that I love you more than you love your daughter—and we both know how much that is! I am still Lord of your life, and I will *never* forget you. I want you to trust me as your daughter trusted you. So quit trying to pick up all the pieces and fix it by yourself. Do what you can, then stand and wait. When I come—and you know I will—I want you to look into my eyes, as Ann looked into yours, and say, 'I knew it. . . . I knew you'd come.'"

Attempting to use God's wisdom instead of my own, I gave up trying to figure everything out or make things perfect and worked with what I had: myself, my God, and my three precious gifts. I did what I could to hold our family together and let God fill in the spaces.

Did I remember this lesson every day? Of course not. Did I make mistakes? Let me count the ways! But today my children are all adults who love the Lord and are living purposeful, responsible lives. And I am more grateful than words can express.

I do not write or speak about single parenting because I am a professional. I write because I'm a survivor. I have authority only because I have walked in the shoes of the divorced single parent; I've been down the roads they travel. I have cried the same tears, pounded the same fists, pleaded with the same God, stored up some of the same rage and bitterness, agonized if it would ever end or be worth the struggle. And I can honestly say that as difficult as it is to be a single parent, single parents can experience some joys that no one else will ever know.

I was a single parent for ten years. Halfway through my wilderness experience, I was drawn to a place that has a very loving ministry for single adults—Single Point Ministries of Ward Presbyterian Church in Livonia, Michigan. After serving as a volunteer for three years, I had the awesome privilege of joining their staff, where I now serve as the business manager. My journey was changed dramatically for the better when I found a church that understood my needs and my situation and helped me survive and grow.

Lee Ezell, a nationally known author and speaker, came to our church a few years ago. One thing she said that has stuck with me is, "The worst thing that ever happens to you can be the best thing that ever happens to you. It all depends on what you do with what happens to you." In the first few weeks and months (perhaps even a few years) of being a divorced single parent, that statement may sound ludicrous. And yet, she made a believer out of me.

When I think of my Lord Jesus, I realize that Lee Ezell's statement also applies to him. He was rejected by family, friends, and church leaders. He was wrongly accused and tried unfairly. He was stripped, mocked, and tortured. There was even a moment when he asked why God had forsaken him. He gave up the ghost and died. And yet, three days later the tomb opened, and he was risen. He was alive—and he lives still. The worst thing that had happened to him became the best thing that ever happened, not only for him, but also for us (see Heb. 12:1–2).

It will probably take more than three days for divorced single parents to move to believing that the worst thing has become their best experience. Yet the same power that brought Jesus out of the tomb is available to us today—bringing healing, hope, strength, comfort, and love. When we let God be the engineer of our train, our journeys will take us places we never dreamed.

Barbara E. George is the business manager for Single Point Ministries of Ward Presbyterian Church of Livonia, Michigan. She is also a popular and humorous speaker at single adult and women's retreats, conferences, and seminars.

4

Coping as a Widowed Parent

RICHARD MATTESON

In researching this chapter, I was privileged to interview several widowed single parents. When they were widowed, some had college-age children, others had teens or elementary-age children, and one was three months pregnant. Through these sessions I began to understand the many differences between a widowed and a divorced single parent. I was able to see the hurt they face and the care or lack of care they received, and I gained some very important insights for every church that is eager to know how to minister better to the bereaved.

I want to thank Tom, Marilyn, Darlene, Phyllis, Lloydell, Dottie, and Don for being honest with me even though it sometimes hurt. At times we cried together during the interviews. My heart goes out to those who have lost a partner, and I hope because of the time I shared with these special people, I will be able to more effectively minister to the widowed.

The Uniqueness of a Widowed Single Parent

The death of a spouse is viewed differently from divorce or long-term separation, although both involve grieving. However, the widowed don't have to deal with rejection from a spouse, nor do they have to share the children with an ex-spouse. The casket and burial service provides a time of closure for the widowed spouse, whereas the divorce decree brings little closure because the ex-spouse may remain involved with the children, or there may be ongoing discussions concerning child or financial support issues. However, the widowed don't get a break from their children because there is no ex-spouse with whom to share parenting responsibilities.

The financial area may also be different for the widowed than for other single parents. Often life insurance leaves the survivor well taken care of, whereas in divorce financial resources are split among the parties. Of course, even if financial resources themselves are not a problem, the surviving spouse still has the pressure of making good decisions with death benefit monies—making them last till the end of life or having to maintain a full-time job to keep the family financially secure.

A further difference between widowed and divorced singles is in the issue of remarriage. Most churches have no theological problems with remarriage of a widow or widower, while there are still some theological issues for divorced persons. Death or divorce, however, do not determine the attitudes of the children to remarriage. In both cases the children may respond negatively or positively to the new marriage. They may see a stepparent as a threat to their loyalty to the other parent, living or dead.

Children of divorce may still remain close to the noncustodial parent. But if a parent dies, the child suffers a tremendous loss. At the same time, the widowed parent has lost a spouse who played many positive roles, such as lover, provider, mechanic, friend, companion, cook, husband, or wife.

Issues Faced by the Widowed

The most common problem dealt with by the widowed parents interviewed was trying to handle their own grief as well as continue to be attentive to their children's grief. All of them felt they had been too engrossed in their own grief and wished they had been able to spend more time helping their children cope with the grieving process. However, the widowed parent must take time to process his or her own grief as well as attend to the needs of the children.

Some found that in becoming widowed they were left with many jobs around the house that the other spouse used to do. They had been left with no service manual or previous experience to do home care, car care, roofing, painting, cooking, sewing, or making financial and parenting decisions. A number of widows expressed concern that they were taken advantage of by some business people because they were alone.

In cases when the wife or husband was not properly insured, the cost of the funeral and burial became a challenge. None of those interviewed felt they were properly prepared, nor were they aided sufficiently, especially under the tremendous emotional strain of the moment. Hospitals often sent bills that were not substantiated. Several felt they needed assistance from friends, family, and the church but didn't want to become dependent on others. In other words, they knew they had to be the ones to make the decisions, but they wanted good counsel.

There was, for the most part, no support group with whom the recently widowed could share their feelings, and the church usually did not sustain ongoing support. Church members were good about being present immediately after the traumatic event and during the funeral service, but the attention soon waned. There was little help provided with jobs around the house, few remembered to contact the bereaved family after the first couple of weeks, and dealing with the financial and emotional issues of the survivor and the children were not addressed. Surprisingly, people seemed to forget about the family in grief within a month or less. Although this sounds like an unbelievably short time period, it was true for all but one of those interviewed. In that one case, the pastor himself had been widowed, and so he had trained the church to do a better job of responding.

Research data also verified that the widowed will have a completely new set of friends within five years of the death of a spouse and will probably change churches within one year of the trauma.[1]

This is partly because they feel out of place in their previous relationships and partly because their original group of friends stop inviting them to functions. It goes beyond their friends and even extends into family relationships, especially the in-laws. Except for the parents of the deceased, most in-laws never come around after the funeral. Many of the children lose contact with the extended family members of their deceased parent. This is hard for the surviving spouse but even harder for the children. Only one of the people interviewed kept her children in frequent contact with the grandparents-in-law, and that was only because she made the effort.

In cases where sickness was the cause of death, it was difficult for the surviving spouse to have watched the partner deteriorate physically. Becoming the strong spouse was especially difficult for the women who were widowed, but they said it could be accomplished with a positive attitude, proper encouragement to the surviving spouse by the dying spouse, and a strong faith in God. Remembering that the Almighty is a part of the whole event and is present in subsequent circumstances helps one get through the tragedy.

The challenge of full-time employment created new tensions for some of the widows I interviewed. Now work became essential rather than supplemental, emphasizing the responsibility aspect of the loss. One widow had a recurring dream in which she saw herself carrying her spouse on her back, which to her meant that she was now totally responsible for the family. Another widow was forced to choose between full-time work, which would require placing the young children in day care, or part-time work and being home for them.

The widowed parents who had a strong faith in God's control over all things no matter what the circumstances had few spiritual questions. For them the question was not "Why?" but "Why not?" As one man said, "Why not us? It could have happened to anyone—including us. Why would we be free from tragedy or trauma as a family? Did God ever promise this? No." But for those with a weaker faith, being widowed meant a rejection of and isolation from God and the very real feeling that their prayers were just hitting the ceiling and bouncing back. For all, the real question of "Where is the church?" was predominant.

For those widowed in their thirties, another struggle was how much of their lives they had left to live. Viewing it as a lump sum of forty years was too overwhelming, so they had to think of getting through one day at a time to keep the future in perspective. For some that led to feelings of just going through the motions each day and sometimes feeling sorry for themselves.

Special Ways Churches Can Show Love for Survivors

The Word of God gives instruction concerning the care of widows. Several passages speak of the needs of widows and their families, their role in the church, and the church's responsibility to them. The stories of Naomi in the Book of Ruth and the widow of Zarephath with whom Elijah stayed (see 1 Kings 17:7–24) show God's care for widows. Specific instructions concerning widows are given in 1 Corinthians 7:8–9 and 1 Timothy 5:1–16, and James 1:27 says caring for widows and orphans is true religion. Throughout Scripture God is identified as the defender of the widow (see Deut. 10:18; Ps. 68:5; 146:9; Prov. 15:25; Jer. 49:11). There are several other challenges for us in Scripture: Job 29:13 says to make a "widow's heart sing." In Job 31:16–18 we read not to let the eyes of a widow grow weary but to guide them. And Exodus 22:22 admonishes, "Do not take advantage of a widow or an orphan." (See also Lev. 22:13; Deut. 24:19–21; Job 24:1–3, 21; Isa. 10:1–2; Mal. 3:5; Acts 6:1.)

Outside of these scriptural admonitions, the church can reach out to the widowed in many tangible ways. The key is for the church to initiate the support and to be there for the long term.

Support Groups and Counseling

The most obvious way the church can help is to form support groups for the widowed, making sure to include both men and women. (Although for some sessions it may be good to separate the sexes to encourage honesty about feelings, it is usually helpful to have them meet together.) Since there are not often a large number of widowed persons in the same church, there may be a need for several churches to cooperate in forming such a support group.

Some churches have Stephen Ministers, who are laypeople trained to listen and walk through crises with individuals. They are given specific training in how to help a grieving person. A grieving person will always benefit from the company of a caring individual, trained or untrained, who really listens.

Some churches encourage widowed family members to receive professional assistance in facing their loss and developing coping skills. Larger churches may have a counseling program as part of their ministry. Others may provide referrals and credit vouchers at a recognized Christian counseling center.

Children's Needs

In ministering to the widowed, we must not forget the needs of their children. Never assume the children don't need to talk with someone; it's important for the church to initiate contact. The church should not be so focused on the couples and nuclear families in the congregation that widowed single parents and their children are left out. Providing companionship with adult men and women through a Big Brother, Big Sister program is a way to provide Christian role models for children who have lost a parent.

It is also helpful to have a grief recovery workshop for children or to refer the family to a competent, Christian, child psychologist. The Dougy Center in Portland, Oregon, is a place that has successfully aided many grief-stricken children. It has established sixty-two similar centers throughout the United States, Canada, Australia, and Japan. They can be contacted at (503) 775-5683 for the location of the closest center to you or for information on how a center in your area can be developed.

In the natural flow of ministry, another important way we can minister to the children is to make their Sunday school teachers aware of potential problems the children may experience related to grief and ask them to keep the pastoral staff as well as the parent informed. Some important insights for teachers include:

Grieving children may find it hard to focus in the classroom.

Using time-outs to discipline these children is counterproductive because typically they are withdrawn and tend to isolate themselves from the other children.

It is okay to allow a grieving child to be withdrawn sometimes.

Death is an abstract concept to a child ten years old and younger, so talking about their feelings helps children deal with this major loss.

Spend time at the child's home to talk with them before asking them to share their feelings about the death in class.

Tangible Assistance

There are many tangible ways individuals in the church can help a widow or widower.

Bringing in food for the widowed is a wonderful display of love. Sometimes you may want to stay and eat with them. However, be aware of whether the family is up to having guests, especially if there are young children who need the parent's attention. Or having them for dinner in your home is a good option. In the privacy of a home (as compared to a public restaurant) they can talk about how they are feeling and express their real emotions or even cry.

Remember to send sympathy cards even months later to let the widowed know you care and know they still hurt. Let the survivor know if someone has visited the grave site, and remember and comment on significant events or dates in the lives of the deceased (birthdays, holidays, favorite jokes). It is important for the widowed to know that others also remember.

Those interviewed expressed deep appreciation for individuals who checked in with them periodically and helped them at first with disposing of the former spouse's clothing or later with the big, yearly household chores such as cleaning the gutters, washing windows, tree trimming, or painting. Unfortunately, most of the widows who did receive help had to initiate the request, because church members did not offer assistance. Some of the widowed who didn't like to be always asking for help simply stopped asking and were forgotten.

The church leadership should also pay particular attention to the financial situation of the recently widowed. Some would benefit greatly from financial advice from a qualified person. Others will need direct financial assistance from a deacons' or widows' fund. Those who are in need often do not volunteer information about their needs, so church leaders should take the initiative in this area.

Personal Needs

We must never assume as a church that the bereaved person's family will be there for him or her, and the family should never assume the church will be there for the widowed person. In one instance a widow was not contacted by her pastor until seven months after the funeral. It is safest never to assume contact has been made in any way and initiate contact ourselves.

The widowed need comfort, support, and encouragement. But it doesn't take a professional to provide these three things. We don't have to have profound things to say or make witty comments, but we must be sensitive. Sometimes it is best to not say much at all and just listen because in our ignorance we sometimes say hurtful things. One widower was asked, "Are you over it now?" His response was, "No, I'm just learning to adjust." Another person said to a widow, "I know you're going to get married again, and this time you can be picky." Her response was, "I was picky the first time." Another friend attempted to comfort a widow by commenting, "Well, you've still got your children." The widow responded, "Yes, I do. But I loved and lost my husband."

We also should remember not to share stories of people we have lost to death. The grieving person does not need to have death reemphasized.

As time goes by, we should avoid the "Hi, how are you?" questions. Most survivors will say they are doing well. Although this may be true, there is still a need for help, so we should never assume the surviving spouse no longer needs assistance.

One area in which the church could help the widowed is in establishing new friendships. This can be accomplished by creating opportunities where they can be involved with a variety of adults (both married and single) in different settings. But be careful to acknowledge the distinctions between types of experiences of single parents. Many widowed persons resent the assumption by some people that divorce and death are the same. Many of the widows felt that if they had small children it was automatically assumed they were divorced. They wished they could be given the opportunity to tell their stories so others would better understand their situation. Most widows don't like to be called single mothers but prefer to be called mothers whose husbands have died. They want the difference to be understood and declared.

Prayer is another important way to help the widowed and their children. However, the phrase "I'm praying for you" is often perceived as meaningless by the widowed. A better option is to actually pray for the widowed with them. The widowed I interviewed felt the church needs to be very careful about giving the impression that it will always be there for members, because most people do not fulfill this commitment.

A very important factor is that the widowed still need the church and pastor even after the first year anniversary of the death. People don't get over a death quickly and in some ways will never stop grieving. The pain may be more intense in the first three years, but a part of the pain never goes away. The widowed need to talk about the deceased spouses and remember important dates or events in their lives. This is one way of acknowledging that they were real, actual people who lived on this earth and had an important influence on the lives of people. The benefits of talking about the deceased spouse greatly outweigh the negative aspects according to those interviewed.

Insights to Help Us Minister Better

It is important that the surviving adult be given permission to grieve in whatever way is appropriate for him or her. There is no right or wrong way to grieve, but processing through the trauma is essential. Widowed parents also need to be assured that it is okay for their children not only to see them cry but also to comfort them when they cry and to cry with them. Crying in front of other people is also acceptable and can be therapeutic.

Most people try not to talk about the deceased person or say anything that would remind the spouse of that dead partner, but, in fact, it is good for the surviving spouse to think of the deceased spouse in the following years even if they have remarried. The children should also be encouraged to remember the parent who died. Both the spouse and children can miss the one who is deceased even while developing new relationships. As children grow up they will want to know more about the lost parent, so keeping alive the memories is important. Creating a scrapbook of pictures, written thoughts, and drawings is very helpful for children so they can review it and not be afraid of forgetting the person.

The widow or widower will also have to cope with the loss of intimacy. As one woman knew that her husband's death was imminent, she dealt with not having sex then and in the future by praying that God would take away her sexual desires. Later if she felt a need or desire for sex, she prayed again. Each time God took away her desire.

After a spouse's death, some survivors don't date at all, feeling that this would be cheating on their former spouse. However, many will eventually begin dating. It is wise to encourage the widowed not to begin dating too soon because they need to be sure they are fairly well healed before starting a new relationship. Providing a father or mother for the children is not a good reason for quickly remarrying.

Involving the widowed with others who have lost a spouse to death can help them see they will not always feel as bad as they do at first. The survivors interviewed thought that if they could just get through the first year, with its wedding anniversary, birthday, holidays, and anniversary of the death of the spouse, they would know what to expect in following years. Of course the reality was that after the first year they wondered,

"Will it be like this the rest of my life?" or, "I've got a lot of life left to live like this!" But the pain does become less intense as the years pass. Life has more possibilities and opportunities to experience.

There were three things that helped to encourage the survivors I interviewed:

1. They knew God had to be a part of their ongoing life or it was really going to be bleak and could have a disastrous end.
2. They knew they had to have a positive attitude about life and its new adventures.
3. They sensed they could be used by God in their new circumstances just as much as before.

Designing a Support Group for Grieving Spouses

The purpose of a support group is encouragement more than anything else. It should be informal, possibly a lunch setting, in order to provide an atmosphere where each could feel free to talk about their feelings. A discreet setting, rather than a crowded restaurant, usually offers a comfort level for the participants to express intimate details never before revealed. This will also be an opportunity to seek answers to questions concerning current issues they are facing such as:

how to deal with sexual desires and the loss of a sexual partner,
reentering the workplace,
going from part-time to full-time work,
just being able to sleep at night,
how to help the children.

Honesty is essential in a support group, and participants should be encouraged to express their feelings. Some find it beneficial to share their dreams, which may express hidden fears or anxieties. A key in the support group is for each person to make a determination that they can get through this even though sometimes it may be a day-to-day struggle.

Effects of Death on the Children

Children do go through grief; we must not ignore this. They handle it in a variety of ways, but most important to note is that children play out or act out their grief through their large muscles. One parent was unaware until much later that one of her boys was getting into fights at school. He was angry at the death of his parent and was acting it out on his classmates.

In dealing with a child who is acting out, it is important to understand the true reasons for the pain. One widow was surprised to find that her middle school son was getting into fights. However, further investigation revealed that his classmates would make the sound of a train as he passed by, cruelly reminding him of his father's death at a train crossing.

Children often fear they will forget the parent who died. It is good for them to hear stories about their lost mom or dad and continue to remember and love him or her. Children need to be told that God knows what happened and is in control. Remind them of God's goodness and continued presence with them.

Explain death to young children in concrete terms, such as "death means Dad's heart stopped beating." One parent said that "Grandma expired," to which a child retorted, "Can't we just get her renewed?"

Sometimes older children become the surviving parent's parent. If the parent is not coping with the death of the spouse, he or she may turn to the children for support, comfort, and care. This puts an undue burden on the children.

Widowed parents need to continue to parent their children and not encourage role reversal. One way to do this is to keep the house rules and discipline the same as it was when both parents were alive. Children need the structure and comfort of boundaries.

The life of a widow(er) is different than that of a divorced or never married parent. Their circumstances are unique. They face challenges, problems, and issues that can be similar to other single parents, but more support is often given by the church to the divorced parent. Too often the widowed are forgotten. Be sure to educate your church to the needs of the widowed and the opportunities to be of service to them. The Bible instructs us to do this, and experience shows us the need.

Rev. Richard Matteson is the pastor to single adults at Village Baptist Church in Beaverton, Oregon. He oversees three communities of singles: college adults, young adults, and single adults. He also leads a divorce recovery ministry offered twice each year. A trained Stephen Ministry leader, he holds M.A. and M.Div. degrees from Liberty University. Richard has been a singles pastor for over ten years and also ministered previously as a student pastor, camp director, associate professor, and itinerant speaker. He has been active in the Network of Single Adult Leaders since 1991 and in 1997 was elected to the board of directors.

5

Solo Parenting as a Married Person

KATHLEEN GANSTER

There is a unique group of people who function and live as single parents even though they are married. These solo parents are in a type of limbo exclusive to those in similar situations. How can married people be solo parents? This occurs when one spouse is gone from the home for an extended period of time due to serving in the military, working away from home, having a job that requires extensive traveling, or being incarcerated. The parent left to take care of the children is alone but not unmarried. They are *married single parents*.

More often than not the married single parent is a mother because women are still the primary caregivers in our society. Also, men are still more likely than women to serve in the military, travel extensively for work, or be incarcerated.

The married single parent limbo exists because these parents don't really fit into the typical single parent categories (never married, divorced, or widowed), and they may not be included in your single parent ministry programs because they are not unmarried. Yet married single parents experience many of the same circumstances and challenges as unmarried single parents, as well as some problems unique to their situations. Although they are definitely shouldering the major burden of raising their children alone, married single parents are not viewed with the same compassion and caring concern as unmarried single parents.

When my children were young, my husband was overseas for fifty weeks of the year for a period of two and a half years. I used to get frustrated when people would comment, "But you aren't a single parent." I wondered what I was. As leaders of single adult ministries, be sensitive to the needs of the married single parents in your church and structure your single parent outreach programs to include these parents who also need respite, understanding, assistance, and support.

Daily Decisions and Problems

While the married single parent theoretically has someone with whom to share decisions, in reality the day-to-day decisions are usually made by the parent who is taking care of the children. Often decisions are needed on the spot, and not every decision is worthy of a long-distance telephone call (if the spouse even can be reached). Deciding which decisions to handle alone and which are important enough to contact the absent spouse can be a challenge in itself. Maybe what seems important to one spouse isn't to the other. Time zone differences can also be a major roadblock in communication between parents. When a child comes home from school and needs an immediate decision for something, calling Dad in a time zone where it is the middle of the night for him is not usually a desirable option.

Handling problems poses the same challenges. A discipline problem is best handled immediately. Leaving issues unresolved for days or even hours can make the resolution or method of handling a problem ineffective. Placing a child on restriction two weeks after bringing home a bad report card will probably reduce the cause and effect correlation. Again, deciding what to handle on one's own and when to contact the absent spouse can cause stress.

There also isn't anyone available with whom to discuss problems at the end of the day or even just to share with about the day's events. In raising children, these talks can be helpful in making decisions and reducing the stress of parenting.

Financial Stress

Financial stress is not limited to unmarried single parents. Married single parents may also struggle to make ends meet. Often there is the expense for two households (the company may not pick up all of the expenses of one spouse). Long-distance telephone bills are a costly but important investment in relationships. And if the spouse taking care of the children works outside of the home, he or she faces the same problems as unmarried parents in finding and paying for child care, transportation, and other related costs.

If the spouse is incarcerated, the only income is that of the parent taking care of the children. And there are often extra costs incurred with visiting the spouse in prison, depending on the distance from the home.

When emergencies arise, there can be a delay in getting funds from the absent spouse, especially if he or she is out of the country. Fortunately, with today's technology, that isn't as big a problem as it would have been in the past, but it is still an issue to confront and resolve. Just tracking down a spouse on another continent and in another time zone can be difficult.

Chores and Maintenance of the Home

The physical, daily chores of raising a family and taking care of a household may fall solely on the married single parent's shoulders. I remember listening to the complaints of other women in my Bible study group about their husbands going out of town for a few days. When one woman said, "I wonder who he thinks is going to take out the garbage next week?" I wanted to respond, "Who do you think takes it out at my house *every* week?"

Unmarried single parents know the other parent is no longer in the home and there will be only the children and themselves to do all of the chores. So they develop a new strategy for dividing up the chores. But married single parents may not come to accept this reality for themselves because they know that the absence of the other parent is not necessarily one hundred percent of the time or will not last forever. This can result in resentment: "Where is he/she when I need help?"

Just as unmarried parents become exhausted by the sheer physical requirements of raising children and maintaining a house, so can married single parents. Exhaustion becomes a fact of life.

Marital Stress

This problem is certainly unique to this category of single parents. Marriage is hard enough when the spouses live together, working at their marriage. When separated by continents or prison bars, a couple may have difficulty keeping the loving relationship alive. I have a friend who once said, "Absence makes the heart grow fainter." Unfortunately, that can be the case with married single parents.

The responsibilities for the home-based parent can seem overwhelming, and resentment toward the absent spouse may build up and turn into bitterness. There may be times when trading places sounds tempting, as the custodial parent fantasizes about the glamour of traveling to the places the absent spouse goes. And the absent spouse sometimes thinks the grass looks greener on the other side and would love to be home. Donna's husband traveled overseas for six-week time periods. When he told her, "While I travel all over the world, killing myself to make a decent living, you get to sit at home with the kids all day," Donna was hurt and frustrated. It was humiliating to her and damaging to their relationship.

For a marriage already in danger, the absence of a spouse can destroy whatever hope is left. Long-distance commuting or incarceration may make marriage counseling impossible and may make it easier for one spouse to withdraw from the marriage.

One way the church can minister to married single parents is to come alongside them and show love, support, and encouragement.

Allowing them to talk about their frustrations in a safe, nonjudgmental environment can help prevent the buildup of resentment.

Reentry

Just as the astronauts needed time to reenter the atmosphere, returning absentee parents, spouses, and children need reentry time. Unfortunately, there are no decompression chambers in which anyone can hide. Getting used to being together after a long separation can be difficult. In many cases, just as the adjustments are made, it is time for the traveling parent to leave again, which starts the withdrawal process all over again. Some people wonder why even bother becoming reacquainted for the short visit home.

"I feel more like a visitor than a member of the family," one father commented. Since his office was 150 miles away and his family didn't want to move, he left home early every Monday morning and returned late each Friday evening. "The rest of the family have their plans, and I just tag along or do things by myself. I don't like this feeling. It's no way to live." But he hasn't yet found a way to work closer to home.

The children may have difficulty adjusting to the parent who is gone for long periods of time. Initially they may be shy with the returning parent. The parent, in turn, may go overboard trying to win back the affection of the children.

Keeping in Touch

Reentry can be made a bit easier if the absent parent has remained real to the children and vice versa. An absent parent is hard for children to think of as real after a while. My oldest child (the only one old enough to write) got tired of writing to her father, who wasn't much of a letter writer himself. My baby was so young he didn't even know his father when my husband moved overseas.

On top of all of the other responsibilities of single parenting, the married single parent needs to help the children and the absent parent stay in touch with each other. Pictures and letters or E-mail need to be exchanged as frequently as possible. Phone calls are great even though they are costly; consider them an investment in relationships.

Lack of Support

Perhaps the greatest burden is the fact that married single parents may be even more isolated than the unmarried single parents because other people are not as apt to offer them emotional, financial, spiritual, or physical support. It isn't as if others are trying to be cruel or ignore them; it is just that married single parents are not thought of as single parents at all.

Also, married single parents aren't as likely to seek out support services or organizations because they are different from the majority of those who use these services. In my own case, it took two years of going it alone before I finally took advantage of a support group for single parents at a local church. I found that just talking with other single parents in the same situation made life so much easier to deal with on my own.

Military Absences

Military absences may often be for extended periods of time and at locations far away. The spouse serving in the military may be stationed in a dangerous and remote area, making contact impossible or sporadic at best. This can cause stress on both partners. Fortunately, the government sometimes provides support for the families of those sent on location. But the role of the church in supporting one another needs to extend to married single parents in these situations.

Margaret was thrilled when her husband was stationed in their hometown of Alamogordo, New Mexico, at Holloman Air Force Base. But then her husband received orders to go overseas. If Margaret and their children accompanied her husband, the tour would be for three years. If they stayed at home, the tour would be reduced to one year. After weighing all of the factors, the couple decided to opt for the one-year tour of duty, even though they would be separated.

For a while Margaret was fine. But as time wore on, she spent more and more time at work, leaving her two young children almost constantly with her mother. She existed almost solely on coffee and snacks. Finally, her boss intervened, threatening to put her on medical leave unless she stopped working so many hours and started taking care of herself. It was the wake-up call she needed. She got herself into counseling, spent less time at work, and took care of herself and her children.

When asked if she would make the same decision if she had it to do over, Margaret said she would. "I missed Doug terribly, much more than I had thought I would. I didn't realize how much I depended on him, especially since I have always prided myself on my independence. But I would not uproot the family to live in the country where he was assigned."

Incarceration

Reverend Eugene Williams, pastor of Lifeway Baptist Church in Beaver Falls, Pennsylvania, works with inmates and their families through Prison Fellowship in the greater Pittsburgh area. He said, "Churches are not prepared to minister to those families who have loved ones incarcerated. Prison Fellowship works with churches and ministers to sensitize them to dealing with these families." Williams further explained that most services that exist are geared for the inmates themselves, not for the spouses and families they leave "on the outside."[1]

Reverend Bob Stevenson, prison chaplain at Westmoreland County Jail and director of Word of Life Ministry in Greensburg, Pennsylvania, also works with prisoners and their families. He explained, "It is very difficult for the spouse who is left to take care of the children. In about 85 to 95 percent of the cases it is the mother. When a spouse is incarcerated, it almost can be like a death in the family. The spouse left behind is much like a widow with all of the responsibilities, concerns, and losses with which to cope." Stevenson's ministry assists these spouses to understand what is happening to the imprisoned spouses and how to deal biblically with the fact of the incarceration. The ministry also offers financial support and advice. "The church needs to understand that this situation can be a disaster. If the husband was the only working spouse, and he goes to prison, the family often loses everything and ends up on public assistance," Stevenson said. He believes that with the right intervention and support services the marriage failure rate in these situations can be reduced. "I know people who are remaining faithful and married to inmates doing life sentences. The only way they can do it is through faith. It is very, very tough," said Stevenson.[2]

There are support groups and services for these spouses that help them through the difficult times. One such organization is called the Coalition of Prison Evangelists (C.O.P.E.), which is a national network that provides information and assistance for those working with prisoners and their families. Another resource is Prison Fellowship, also a national organization with representatives in virtually every state. Check your local telephone book for listings for C.O.P.E. and Prison Fellowship near you, or check out their web sites. C.O.P.E. is at http://www.ipm.org/net/cope and Prison Fellowship is at http://pfm.org. You may contact C.O.P.E. at P.O. Box 7404, Charlotte, NC 28241; (803) 548-2670; E-mail: 103436,2240@compuserve.com/ and Prison Fellowship at P.O. Box 17500, Washington, DC 20041-0500; (703) 478-0100; E-mail: bgil@pfm.org.

Work-Related Absences

Parents whose spouses travel extensively due to a job may hear a lot of criticism from friends and family members. People would often ask me, "Why doesn't your husband get another job?" or "Doesn't he miss you and the children?"

Because we do not know all of the issues that led to a decision that separated a family temporarily, we need to be sensitive rather than critical. Deciding to accept a job or an assignment that will separate spouses for a time is not an easy decision. It takes a lot of thought and deliberation on the advantages and disadvantages. Usually, there are no other positions available or there are reasons the entire family cannot or should not accompany the spouse who must leave. The other spouse may have a job in the hometown that it would be unwise to leave. Children may need to stay in their own schools rather than be bounced around. Some family members may have medical problems that require being near the family physician.

Reaching Out to Married Single Parents

Some churches are negligent in ministering to unmarried single parents, but many more ignore the married single parents. This may be because this group of people has not been targeted in the past by either the single adult ministry or the family ministry programs of the church. It may take a change in perception and an intentional effort for the body of Christ to begin to reach out to married single parents.

Just realizing they exist and recognizing what they are going through is a big step. I remember when a friend of mine said, "I don't know how you raise those three children by yourself!" That comment made me feel so good because I knew someone had noticed what I was going through and cared.

Inviting married single parents to participate in single parent family events is a great way to reach out to them. Include them on your mailing lists and offer counseling, practical assistance, and participation in support groups.

If your church is located in a community where there are a lot of married single parents (such as near a military base or prison), you might consider developing a special support group just for these parents. The support and assistance you provide can make a big difference in the lives of the married single parents and their children in your church and community.

Kathleen Ganster is the mother of Eliza, Kenton, and Cole and was a married single parent for two and a half years. Ganster has a B.A. in sociology and an M.A. in educational management and development. She writes for the Pittsburgh Post-Gazette *and is a freelance writer and educational consultant from her home in Gibsonia, Pennsylvania.*

6

Relating to a Former Spouse

DEBRA ROWE

*I*t never fails to amaze me when watching the television program *Cops* how many of the calls to the police are due to a domestic violence situation. I watch the verbal and often physical confrontations between the spouses or ex-spouses, the police officers trying to bring some order to the situation, and the little children standing by observing their parents' argument in tears. Dysfunctional relationships, divorce, and discord do not make a pretty picture, and all too often the relationships between former spouses are not always cooperative or civil.

The breakup of a marriage is almost always traumatic; there's no other word for it. And the ripple effect goes out in all directions as family members and friends stand on the sidelines in despair. Seldom have I seen a divorce situation end without some rancor or acrimony.

Some former spouses are able to work through or rise above the negative feelings and develop positive relationships as coparents of the children. These people we applaud and use as role models. But often one or both former spouses allow the disagreements that led to the dissolution of the marriage to continue and increase after the divorce. This creates an adversarial relationship, which makes coparenting difficult if not impossible.

How do we as leaders of single adult ministries counsel and assist these single parents?

Watch for the Negative Behaviors and Attitudes

It is important to recognize the potential issues that may create problems between former spouses. Sometimes both parents are at fault, intentionally or unintentionally doing and saying things that indicate a lack of cooperation and trigger an adversarial reaction in the other parent. Examples of such behaviors include:

keeping alive the personal emotional wounds and holding onto bitterness and anger toward the other parent;

criticizing the other parent frequently to the children;

causing any discussions with the other parent or decision-making attempts to degenerate into a time for arguing and name-calling;

allowing outside employment demands to interfere with the rearing of the children;

neglecting the children when making new friendships and dating;

abusing the children in any way (emotionally, psychologically, spiritually, or physically);

using the children as weapons against each other, a means of manipulation, go-betweens in custody battles, or witnesses in possible litigation;

asking the children to spy on the other parent during visits.

The Custodial Parent

There are several things the custodial parent may do that express negative feelings toward the other parent. These behaviors may reflect a response to negative behaviors from the other parent or may trigger conflict with the other parent. Some of these behaviors may be intentionally aggravating; others are reactive. All are disruptive and give the other parent the opportunity or the excuse to respond with equally destructive behaviors and attitudes. Examples of these behaviors on the part of a custodial parent include:

responding to receiving little or no assistance from the other parent by refusing to cooperate or coparent;

making frequent derogatory remarks to the children and to friends about the other parent's unwillingness to pay child support on a timely basis and the consequent financial difficulties;

not dressing the children properly for the activities planned during visits with the noncustodial parent even when these are known in advance;

not having the children ready for visits, canceling or denying visits without cause;

refusing to let the children come to the telephone to talk with the noncustodial parent;

giving in to the temptation of turning over too many responsibilities to the children (i.e., caring for younger siblings, cooking, cleaning, and other chores inappropriate for their age).

Sometimes the custodial single parent begins with a positive attitude toward the other parent and genuinely attempts to be cooperative as parents. If all he or she experiences is frustration, hurt, disappointment, or resentment from the other parent, the custodial parent may begin responding with negative behaviors of his or her own. One example of this would be withholding visitation access to the children because of a failure to pay child support. This and similar behaviors often punish the children and anger the noncustodial parent, who then does something else to retaliate, and the war is on.

The Noncustodial Parent

The parent who does not get to spend each day with the children often misses them very much. As one man said, "I wanted a divorce from my wife, not my children!" There is often a sense of guilt at not being there for the children every day. And there is often anger and a feeling of helplessness because there is a lessening of influence upon the children and the decision-making process for the daily issues.

The noncustodial parent may be the one who wants to have a cooperative relationship with the former spouse and finds little positive response. Or the noncustodial parent may initiate the adversarial relationship with intentionally destructive behaviors or exhibit anger toward the custodial parent.

It is not easy being either a custodial or a noncustodial single parent. It is particularly difficult being the one who is trying to build a cooperative relationship with someone who does not seem to want one. It is hard to maintain a positive attitude when the other person seems deliberately to do hurtful or irritating things. There are no easy answers for leaders of single adult ministries to give that will create perfect harmony between these coparents.

Once the negative cycle has begun, it tends to escalate into a spiral of increasing size. From involving the two former parents, it grows to include the children. Then other family members are drawn into the disagreements. Next, the dispute grows and includes friends, and finally, as the conflict enlarges, the involvement may include neighbors, the community, the church, and even the police and the courts.

Recognize the Different Family Circumstances

The single parents with whom you minister may be involved in any number of scenarios that brought them to the point where you have become aware of their problems getting along with the other parents. Problems have been known to develop between former spouses even when at the time the divorce was considered friendly by both partners.

The spouse who was most hurt emotionally by the divorce tends to be the one who creates or precipitates the adversarial issues. In my case, I did not want a divorce. So I fought back with vengeance and got even by moving away to another state and taking our children with me. I knew this would cause my ex-spouse the greatest hurt. But this revenge was also a severe detriment to both my children and me as years went by.

Some of the major disputes between ex-spouses involve financial issues and differences in personal and moral values. Payment of child support on a timely basis would eliminate a significant number of quarrels, but there is little you can do as a leader to ensure that this is done, regardless of which parent you are counseling. How each of the parents spends money is often an issue of contention. One young ex-husband told his ex-wife that he didn't have to pay her child support because he knew her family wouldn't let her starve. So he only paid when he felt like doing so, which wasn't often.

When one has personal or moral values that are different than the other parent's, conflict is inevitable. As leaders it is important that we assist single parents in sorting out matters of personal preference from those issues that could cause harm to the children. When the differences involve abuse, pornography, drug use, or drunkenness, there are steps that can be taken to ensure supervised visits or limited visits. When the other parent has a live-in lover, this can be upsetting to the Christian parent who wants the children to live by God's standards of moral purity, but in the absence of sexual activity in front of the children, the courts will do little to change custody or limit visitation because of this. The concerned parent will have to plan how to teach God's standards to the children and pray that the Holy Spirit will keep their hearts and minds pure. When the differences involve personal preference (such as wearing matching clothes, length of hair, eating between meals, eating products with sugar in them, or staying up late), parents must be taught that all they can do is enforce their values when the children are with them and pray for the children to make good choices as they grow up.

Give Good Counsel

Leaders should be prepared to give good counsel to those single parents who want to resolve adversarial relationships with former spouses. Here are some examples of things to share with single parents in these situations:

Don't use the children as spies, means of manipulation, or message carriers for negative issues. This is cruel to them and only causes greater friction and disharmony. Above all, the children's best interests need to be foremost in both parents' minds. Manipulative game playing can only hurt the innocent children.

If legal arrangements have been made and broken, use the proper channels to correct the situation. Seldom can the ex-spouses sit down and discuss things rationally and come to an agreeable solution on legal matters, particularly when an adversarial situation exists between them. In particular, any changes in the original legal documents should be made through the court system where they were filed and handled properly by an attorney.

Use a mediator if both parties can agree to do so. A pastor, Christian counselor, or church elder might be considered to act in a mediation role.

Do not criticize, belittle, or talk negatively about ex-spouses, especially in front of the children. This is often the hardest guideline to follow. Our human sinful nature and the need for avenging oneself too often supersede what's best for the ex-spouse and the children. Verbal bashing and accusatory ridicule in front of the children might feel good at the moment, but it only hurts the children in the long run and can cause irreparable scars, which they'll carry into adulthood as well as into their future relationships.

Frequently remind the children that the divorce is not their fault. Children need to be encouraged to talk about their feelings, especially in the months following the family breakup, and one issue common among children is their belief that they caused the divorce by their behaviors, attitudes, or shortcomings. It is extremely important to assure children that even if there is an adversarial relationship between their parents, the children will never be abandoned. Both parents need to keep their promises to the children, even if their adversarial stance prevents them from keeping their word to each other.

Let go of the bitterness and learn to forgive. As difficult as it is, forgiveness can be the greatest healer, especially in an adversarial situation. Involvement in a twelve-step recovery program or support group can often aid in understanding the extreme importance of forgiveness. In my case, as the adversary in my divorce situation, I spent many long, lonely, and often drunken nights planning revenge upon my ex-husband. How could I make him hurt as much as he'd hurt me? The anger and bitterness ate into me night after night, year after year, as my spirit and very being began to decay. Only after I became a Christian and was able to forgive him for leaving the marriage could I get on with my life. Now I often remind myself of Hebrews 12:15, "See to it that no one misses the grace of God and that no bitter root grows up to cause trouble and defile many."

Single parents need to accept whatever responsibility they may have had in the marriage breakup. Reflecting upon personal shortcomings might help in healing as they look forward to future, healthier relationships.

"Accept the things you cannot change" and "One day at a time" are wise counsel from the twelve-step recovery program. Single parents certainly cannot change their ex-spouses; they can only change or have responsibility for their own attitudes. Help them see that it is not what happens to them but how they deal with what happens that really matters. Recognition that life is not always going to be fair can help. The greatest hope, undoubtedly and ultimately, is knowing that they have a Creator God who will stick by them and offer hope forever.

Remember that professional Christian counseling or therapy might be advisable in the initial stages of divorce. Part of this counseling should focus on the specific tools for dealing with the adversarial ex-spouse.

Recommend any workshops, seminars, or reading materials dealing with building a positive self-image that would be helpful for the single parent. (See the list of resources at the back of this book.) Dealing with the blows of possible rejection, looking for real love in all the right places, and building one's self-worth through Christ can help the single parent reenter single life with a healthy attitude and perspective.

Encourage your single parents by reminding them of God's comfort. Paul tells us, "Praise be to the God and Father of our Lord Jesus Christ, the Father of compassion and the God of all comfort, who comforts us in all our troubles, so that we can comfort those in any trouble with the comfort we ourselves have received from God" (2 Cor. 1:3–4).

These verses speak loudly to me as I look back on my life and recall a most vivid memory that took place shortly after I became a Christian. I'd been divorced and a single parent for twelve years and had harbored bitterness and anger against my ex-spouse all that time as I wallowed in self-pity, only hurting myself and my children. When I asked Christ into my life, my greatest desire was to help others in similar situations. I knew I would never be fully available to him until I experienced my ex-spouse's forgiveness for my antagonism and anger toward him for all those years. After much prayer, the Lord provided that opportunity as my ex-spouse and I were able to exchange words of forgiveness and, as a result, I could let go of the heavy load of hate and bitterness that had weighed me down for so many years.

Lewis B. Smedes reminds us of that concept in his book, *Forgive and Forget:* "Hate eventually needs healing. Passive or aggressive, hate is a malignancy; it is dangerous—deadly, if allowed to run its course. Nothing good comes from a hate that has a person in its sights; and it surely hurts the hater more than it hurts the hated."[1] Solomon makes the same observation, "Better a meal of vegetables where there is love than a fattened calf with hatred" (Prov. 15:17).

There is no shortcut to getting through a single parent's hard times, yet Scripture does offer single parents a foundation on which they can build. There are no magic cure-alls but Scripture certainly provides comfort and concepts to reflect upon for those who seek stability. Some of my favorites that are relevant to single parent relationships are: Deuteronomy 31:6; Proverbs 3:5–6; Isaiah 41:10; 49:13; Matthew 6:25–34; Ephesians 4:31–32; 1 Peter 5:7; and Revelation 3:20. All of these verses, and many others, point single parents to God's unfailing love and constant presence in their lives.

Last Thoughts

As leaders of single adult ministries, we often work with single parents who continue to harbor hatred and bitterness against their ex-spouses, resulting in an adversarial climate. We must emphasize to them that surely they are on a road to self-destruction and, more importantly, they are going against the very teachings of Christ. As the adversarial single parent prays for God to soften his or her heart, God's transforming power can and will turn it into a heart of love, and lives can change from depression and despair into lives of hope filled with God's grace.

Shortly after I had experienced my ex-spouse's forgiveness and, through God's grace and power, had released the resentment and bitterness, the Lord was then able to use me as a missionary in Australia. I was allowed to serve him there through the Christian-based Fresh Start divorce recovery workshops, helping others understand that an existing adversarial relationship with an ex-spouse can only hurt them and their children. From firsthand experience, I was able to point these single parents to the living God, who can release the hurt, the anger, and the resulting spiritual cancer. Jesus is the only answer for the many struggles created by divorce and the accompanying challenges of single parenting.

As a singles leader, the greatest service you can provide to single parents, especially those in adversarial environments, may be that of being a good listener. More than advice or spiritual wisdom, just being available and willing to listen is often the most godly thing we can do for a single parent. I'll never forget my next-door neighbor when I was going through my divorce and facing the fear of parenting three children alone. Often she would leave what she was doing and just sit with me and listen. To this day, twenty-two years later, it brings tears to my eyes as I fondly recall her acts of love. She has often said to me, "I really didn't do anything." My response is, "But you came and listened, and I'll always be grateful for your allowing Christ's love to flow through you." We, as singles leaders, can learn from that example and extend our love to the single parents within our ministries. What a privilege!

Debra Rowe has been a single adult ministry leader for several years in Australia and the United States. She has served as director of single adult ministry at North Coast Presbyterian Church in Encinitas, California, at First United Methodist Church of Houston, Texas, Solana Beach Presbyterian Church in Solana Beach, California, and LaJolla Presbyterian Church in LaJolla, California. She has served on the national board of the Network of Single Adult Leaders and hosted NSL regional forums.

7

Teaching Christian Values

BOBBIE REED

"It is great to see Lori so interested in spiritual things," Mark commented to a friend about his fourteen-year-old daughter. "She started a Bible study with her friends after school and plans on being a missionary with the Wycliffe Bible Translators. I'm so proud of her!"

It is a good feeling for parents to see their children adopting Christian values that the parents have attempted to share. However, when it comes to teaching our children Christian values, the results are not always predictable. Some children respond by adopting many of the beliefs of the parents; other children respond by rebelling against the parents' values.

The moments when I've felt the most successful as a parent were when my sons voluntarily acted on values that I held dear. Conversely, the moments when I've felt the most unsuccessful were those when my sons chose to act on values with which I strongly disagreed. Many parents can identify similar experiences in their own lives. Those of us with a value system based on our faith feel a strong desire and obligation to pass on those values to our children.

However, values cannot be imposed on children. They can only be communicated and taught, modeled and explained, discussed and, finally, voluntarily adopted by the children. Each of us chooses which values we will hold and act upon. Therefore, the best option of single parents who wish to pass on values to their children is to communicate those values in a way that makes sense to the children and causes the children to understand the significance of those values.

What Are Values?

One definition of a value is that it is a belief that after careful consideration has been selected from alternate choices and is acted upon repeatedly and consistently over a period of time. Frequently values are given one-word labels such as *honesty, kindness, loyalty,* or *dependability.* But those are a form of verbal shorthand that don't fully explain the belief. One person's mental picture of *honesty* might not be the same as another's. One person might think failing to speak up and tell all one knows is dishonesty while another would say that dishonesty is voicing something that is untrue. Therefore, when communicating values to children, single parents will want to not only label their values but thoroughly explain them as well.

Everyone has values, even a young child. Our values help us evaluate and choose between alternatives and decide how to behave in an appropriate manner in a given situation. A three-year-old usually knows when to stop short of being actually punished with a spanking or being sent to the bedroom for a time-out. The value involved is avoiding the pain of the punishment. Later behavior choices are based on character trait values such as keeping one's word or being a loyal friend. As children develop and explore different values options, at first they may hold conflicting values, which result in inconsistent behavior choices and confusion. Part of growing up involves sorting through the conflicts and confusion and making new choices that eliminate the major clashes in values. Because they do not start life knowing how to function in a society, build healthy, reciprocal relationships, and be spiritually mature, children must learn all of these things as they grow up.

You may find that some of the adults in your ministry still hold conflicting values and act in inconsistent ways because they have not completed developing a strong and clearly defined set of Christian values. One function of ministry is to assist the adults in the area of defining their values and understanding the scriptural basis for them.

Of course, even with a set of clearly identified values, there will be conflicts from time to time. If one knows that a good friend is doing something illegal at work, one option is to keep quiet (loyalty), another is to report the offense (honesty), and a third is first to confront the person and encourage him or her to confess and to stop doing wrong things (friendship). Single parents cannot eliminate such conflicts from the lives of their children any more than they can eliminate them from their own lives. But single parents can assist their children in understanding the values so the children can develop a code of conduct based on those values they cherish and make better choices in difficult situations.

How Single Parents Can Teach Values

Most single parents truly want to pass on their values and consider it part of our Christian heritage and our God-given responsibility. God's expectation was that parents would communicate values to their children. We read Jehovah's instructions to the Israelites to commemorate the Passover every year after the exodus from Egypt so the children could be told the story and realize its significance (see Exod. 12:26). In several passages in the Old Testament parents were told to share with the children the stories of what God had done. In Deuteronomy 6:7–9 Moses reminded the Israelites that they were to teach their children diligently when they conversed together, when they sat at home, when they went out together, when they went to bed, and when they got up. They were to write God's words on the doorposts and gates of their houses. In the New Testament we read of Timothy, who is a good example of a young believer whose mother and grandmother were given credit for his having developed a strong, genuine faith (see 2 Tim. 1:5).

The most important value single parents can communicate and teach their children is faith in God. The other values follow in importance. Many parents claim Proverbs 22:6, "Train a child in the way he should go, and when he is old he will not turn from it." A close reading of that verse gives a clue to the process of teaching children values. It doesn't say "tell" children how to behave; it says "train" children in right ways.

Training is based on supervised practice. Parents naturally know that they have to train children in various skills (e.g., driving a car, doing laundry, baking, sewing, using power tools); just telling children how to do these things doesn't help them develop the necessary skills. But often parents fail to realize they must also train children to live by certain values in order for the children to develop skills in those areas. Training includes information given in small amounts (not lectures), explanation of what the goal is for a situation, description of the choice and behavior options, practice, review, evaluation, correcting, practice, review, evaluation, more information, and so on. Training is an ongoing process with many steps and lots of practice.

Because children receive many conflicting and confusing messages about values (from friends, movies, television, books, teachers, pastors, kids at school, and adults with different values), single parents have a lot of work to do when assisting their children to sift through the messages and make good choices. The following ten suggestions can help single parents teach their children Christian values.

1. *Identify their own values.* Before single parents can communicate values to their children, they must decide which values they want to emphasize and focus on in a priority sequence. You may be surprised how many adults cannot quickly list their most important values and give clear, concise descriptions of the core belief for each one. They may never have taken the time to identify, define, and prioritize their own personal values. As the par-

ents define their own values (which could be facilitated during a weekend retreat or an evening seminar), encourage them to identify and note the biblical basis for as many of these values as possible. Remind them to ask the Holy Spirit's guidance when developing their lists and considering whether they, themselves, live by the identified values (see Ps. 139:23–24).

2. *Tell the children the values the parent holds.* When the single parents have clearly and concisely defined their values and beliefs, they are in a position to communicate those values to the children. Suggest that single parents use word pictures, analogies, stories, and real-life illustrations when telling the children about values to increase the level of understanding. If parents invite the children to state the beliefs back to them, the parents can tell if the children understood what was being shared.

3. *Explain their values.* Telling children the values is the first step because it provides a foundation on which to build, but telling is not enough. Children need to understand the *why* as well as the *what* of values. Therefore, single parents will want to discuss how choosing a good value (e.g., honesty) pleases God, makes a person feel good, and causes other people to respond positively. It is also effective to describe how choosing a wrong value (e.g., dishonesty) displeases God, makes a person feel guilty, and causes other people to respond negatively. An important part of explaining values is sharing what the Bible says about each one.

4. *Explore their values.* Children learn best when parents use a variety of teaching methods that allow children to interact with value choices. They can choose from many methods such as drama, skits, role plays, art projects, drawings, discussions, debates, Scripture searches, and television show reviews.[1]

The important thing about exploring values is to have the children consider the possible consequences of making different choices in a given situation. So it is more effective to invite the children to discuss several options a character might have and what would be the consequences of each of the choices rather than just asking children to identify the option that would be pleasing to God. As parents guide such discussions, they can ask, "Would this option please God? Why or why not?" "Would this choice be right?" "Would this choice demonstrate kindness (or honesty, or loyalty, or another value)?"

5. *Model their values.* Our choices and commitment to values determine and shape the persons we are becoming. Single parents will want their children to observe them as living models of the values they teach. Children are exposed to models of many different values (some good and some bad), and they will eventually choose values for themselves. Parents who genuinely want to teach Christian values must give evidence of these values in their own lives. Parents whose walk does not match the talk have little chance of influencing the children with words. Actions still speak louder than words (see James 2:14–20).

6. *Use Bible stories to teach values.* There are two benefits to teaching values with Bible stories. First, children learn about the values and how they apply in a real-life situation. Second, the children's knowledge and understanding of God's Word is increased. As Bible characters come alive and experience choices and feelings with which children can identify, Scripture becomes more relevant to the children.

7. *Apply values to everyday experiences.* A significant key to passing on values is to help children see how they apply to everyday situations in their own lives. This is the essence of Deuteronomy 6:7–9. Each day there are teachable moments. It is important for parents to discuss the events of the day and the different choices made (by both children and adults). Comparing other choices that could have been made and determining why they were rejected is a terrific way to help children begin integrating values into their thinking and decision-making processes. Reviewing and discussing stories, television programs, movies, and anecdotes are other methods of applying values to everyday situations.

8. *Reinforce values with games.* Single parents can find a wealth of resources, including games, that reinforce values by going to a Christian bookstore. Learning values need not be all serious. Single parents and their children can have fun with talking about and demonstrating positive values.

9. *Reward the children when they choose good values.* Parents are often quick to notice, criticize, and correct children when

they make wrong choices but are seldom as fast to notice, compliment, and reward children for good choices. Advise single parents to become "good decision detectives," alert and ready to reward and celebrate good choices.

10. *Pray for the children.* When all is said and done, the parents can only do their best and then leave the children in the hands of the Lord. Praying daily that the Holy Spirit will work in their children's lives is an important step for single parents. Then consistently taking the above steps will increase the probability that children will have sufficient knowledge and understanding to make right choices.

How Children Choose Values

Phyllis taught her daughter, Annie, that stealing was wrong, and Annie didn't steal. She never took a candy bar from the convenience store, never stole money from her parents, never kept a library book instead of returning it. She didn't steal because she wanted to obey her mom.

Annie obeyed what she had been taught until she was thirteen. Then she and a friend were shopping at the mall, and the two of them decided to shoplift a couple of scarves. They were caught leaving the store by the store detective and taken to the manager's office.

Because the parents could not be reached for a couple of hours, Annie and her friend had to sit quietly in the office under the watchful eye of the detective and manager. Annie hated it. As Annie sat there, she thought about her decision to steal the scarf. She didn't like feeling so guilty, and she didn't like what the manager said about having her arrested if it happened again. She decided she didn't want to be a thief and she would never steal again. She didn't.

Until Annie made that decision for herself, she was only being obedient to her mother's values. After the decision, Annie had chosen a value for herself.

The steps for how children adopt a value for themselves are as follows:

Step 1: Understanding the value. Children cannot accept or adopt a value they don't understand and cannot define or relate to real life. They may hear the words and may be able to repeat them back to their parents, but until they can explain how the value is acted upon in an everyday situation, they cannot make that value their own. Understanding a value is an ongoing process. Even adults find they learn more about their own values as they encounter different situations that involve choices.

Step 2: Interacting with the values. The more children are stimulated to use their imaginations to think about possibilities and choices and to think through logical sequences of events depending upon which choices are made, the more they will become used to knowing that there are always choices in any situation. They can choose to go along with the crowd and do the wrong thing, or they can decide to do right (see 1 Cor. 10:13).

Parents can get clues to where their children are in the valuing process by inviting the children to share their feelings about choices they made and the reasons they made those choices. Listening without criticizing communicates to children that it is safe to be honest. Parents can ask, "What if you have a similar situation next week; what might you do differently?" And, "What might you do next time to make it easier to make a different decision?"

Step 3: Choosing to adopt a value. Some children have difficulty making even the smallest decisions; thus it is very hard for them to make decisions about values by which they will live. But until the children actually make such choices, they are merely living by someone else's values, not by values they have made their own. Therefore, wise parents find ways to encourage children to make decisions about values.

When fourteen-year-old Ken announced he wanted to become a clown when he graduated from high school, his mother encouraged him to research the job market, the average salary a clown can expect to make, the risks involved in being a clown, as well as the rewards. She contacted a professional clown to set up an interview with her son so Ken could ask his questions.

When Ken had all of the information, he discussed what he had discovered with his mom. During the discussion, his mom commented that being a clown did sound like fun and asked if Ken had considered other options for a career. She also suggested that Ken might want to go to a community college for two years and get his A.A. degree while pursuing a career as a clown on a part-time basis. That way he could have some college education to fall back on if he decided later in life that being a clown didn't pay enough for the lifestyle he wanted.

Ken thought his mom's suggestion was a good idea, and so he enrolled in the community college. After graduating with an A.A. degree, Ken worked as a clown for a year, decided he wasn't making enough money, and went back to college to finish his B.A. degree. But the key factor was that Ken did the research and made the decision. His mom only provided the input and ideas that led to a positive decision.

When single parents encourage their children to make good choices, they can expect that they are also preventing them from making the corresponding bad choices because often right and wrong choices are diametrically opposed. Jesus said that we cannot serve two masters; we must choose one or the other (Matt. 6:19–24).

Step 4: Demonstrating values by behavior. As children repeatedly and consistently act upon their beliefs, their value systems become integral parts of their lives.

When twelve-year-old Tom received his allowance, he usually headed for the video game arcade with a friend. Often he would share a few quarters with his friend, who didn't get an allowance but came along just to be with Tom. Tom also shared his after-school treats with that same friend. Tom had decided that being a friend meant sharing, and the more he practiced sharing, the more that became a part of who he was.

James 1:22–25 tells us that we are to be doers of the Word of God and not just hearers. That is how people know we are living by God's principles. The same is true of our values. If we are living by our values, our behavior demonstrates them through our actions.

Obstacles and Setbacks

Single parents will often encounter obstacles and setbacks when teaching values to their children. The children may see conflicting values presented, modeled, and taught by others, which causes them to question what the parents are attempting to communicate. Peers may tug children in the opposite direction from that which the parents desire. Even other family members, including the other parent, may live by an opposing value system. And the parents themselves may pose stumbling blocks by their own failures, because none of us is perfect. However, consistently following the above suggestions can help the single parents in your ministry be more successful in their attempts to pass on positive and Christian values to their children.

Bobbie Reed was a single parent for ten years, has been an author, consultant, and speaker in the field of single adult and single parent ministries since 1974, has authored thirty-three books, and is assistant director of the Network of Single Adult Leaders. She holds a Ph.D. in social psychology and a D.Min. with an emphasis in single adult ministry.

8

Raising Teenagers

JEENIE GORDON

Sixteen-year-old Tim had long hair that was shiny, clean, and always well brushed. Tim's mom hated his long hair.

"You look awful; I'm ashamed to be seen with you. Get a haircut," she complained frequently.

One day after school, mother and son were shopping in the supermarket. Walking toward the checkout stand, Tim flipped his head backward to get the hair out of his eyes. Since his hair fell in his face a lot, this was a rather frequent motion.

His mom exploded, "Do you know how stupid you look, always flipping your head back that way? This is how it looks." She then flipped her own head backward dramatically, then turned in horror to watch her wig sliding across the tiled floor. Before leaving home she had hurriedly put on the wig because her hair was dirty. Now the limp, greasy strands were stuck to the contours of her skull. Embarrassed, she picked up the wig and slapped it back on her head. Tim just grinned.

It took a while but even Tim's mom had to admit later that the situation was funny. Conflicts between single parents and their teenagers often do create humorous moments, at least in retrospect. However, many of the conflicts single parents have with teenagers seem to tear apart the family. Some conflicts are irritating; others are heartbreaking.

The best way you can help single parents with teenagers in your ministry is to give them practical, workable ways to minimize and resolve conflicts. Here are some ideas.

Conflicts over Chores

It's important for adolescents to understand that everyone in the family has to be responsible for certain jobs in the home. The method of assigning the chores will differ from family to family. Cooperation is often more likely if teenagers are allowed to choose from a list which chores they will do. Rotating chores helps as does doing chores together. Failure to complete one's chores must result in adverse consequences that make sense to the teenagers. (For example, if you bring the car back with an empty gas tank, then next time you pay for gas *before* you get the keys.)

Kathy Mills suggests that adolescents may "clean for dollars."[1] Each nonroutine job (washing windows, trimming trees, etc.) earns a set dollar amount, and complete instructions for exactly what must be done and how are written on index cards. Each job has a time limit, and when the job is begun a kitchen timer is set. When the timer goes off, wages are paid *if* the job is completed according to instructions. This gives teens earning power, teaches them how to do tasks the way their parents want them done, and reduces dawdling.

Conflicts over Clothes

Barbie, one of the teens I know, looks the part; she constantly sports new outfits. One day I asked, "How do you get all those clothes?"

"Well, I just ask Mom," she giggled. "Whatever I want, it's okay with her. She gives me the credit card, and I go to the mall."[2]

Barbie's mother may have the best of intentions, but she is teaching Barbie to expect instant gratification, even if it means charging to the limit. Kids (and some adults) have a strong desire, based on peer pressure, to wear expensive designer labels. None of us wants to look weird or out of step, and teens, in particular, need to feel they look their best.

Single parents can give teenagers a reasonable monthly clothing allowance and specify which items of clothing the teen must be responsible for purchasing from the allowance. Certain expensive items (such as winter coats, boots, school shoes, graduation suits and dresses, etc.) are normally above and beyond the monthly clothing allowance and can be paid for out of the family budget. As long as the single parent refuses to rescue a teen who foolishly spends all of the clothing allowance for one item and has nothing left over for other items he or she may need, the teen probably will learn to look for sales, shop at discount stores, and make wise choices. If not, the teen will have to go without some of the things he or she wants.

Sometimes teens want a more expensive item than the parent is prepared to purchase. If a single parent has agreed to buy the teenager two pairs of shoes per year, then usually a certain amount has been budgeted for each pair. So if the teen insists that a more expensive pair of shoes is needed, the parent can negotiate and contribute the budgeted amount for one pair of shoes to the purchase, and the teenager pays the balance.

Adolescents can also work for additional money for clothes. They may do extra chores for their parents or neighbors, or they may get a part-time job, take on a paper route, or baby-sit.[3]

Sometimes the conflicts over clothes involve not the cost of the clothing but the appropriateness of what the teenagers want to wear. Although most parents want their children to look attractive, be coordinated, and wear clean and unwrinkled clothing, teenagers sometimes want to wear what everyone else is wearing. I recommend that single parents not argue over personal preferences and only make an issue if the clothing is clearly indecent.

Conflicts over a Car

Most teenagers want their own cars, but many single parents cannot afford to buy cars for their children. Even if a single parent can easily afford to buy a car for a son or daughter, I recommend that the teen be required to pay part of the cost out of wages earned by working. If teenagers have worked and saved for several months in order to buy a car, they are more likely to value their cars and take good care of them. Also teenagers should have to contribute to the expenses for insurance, tune-ups, lube and oil changes, and gasoline.

Teenagers who do not have their own cars spend a lot of time asking to drive their parents' cars. Before the teen earns a driver's license, single parents will want to sit down and discuss the guidelines for using the family vehicle. There needs to be a clear understanding that failure to follow the guidelines will result in immediate suspension of driving privileges. If single parents are firm when enforcing the consequences, the teenagers tend to learn to follow the family rules so they won't be without a car when they need it most.

Conflicts over Telephone Usage

Kids and telephones have been virtually inseparable since the days they jiggled the receiver up and down to signal an operator to dial a number. Phone conversations are important to teens—especially girls. These can be healthy ways to develop relationships with friends, as long as talking on the telephone is not out of control. Teenagers are not usually very good at self-restriction, so parents need to set the limits.

Single parents need to consider telephone usage as a privilege and specify when teens will be allowed to call or receive calls from their friends (e.g., after dinner, following completion of homework, or when chores are completed satisfactorily). Parents can set a limit on the number of telephone calls per day, the length of time spent on the telephone per day, or the length of any one telephone conversation. The single parent can decide who will answer the telephone when it rings. And teenagers should usually pay for any long-distance calls they make to friends.

Some single parents install a separate telephone line for teenagers in their own bedrooms. Personally, I don't recommend this because monitoring calls becomes almost impossible.[4]

Conflicts over Friends

Single parents do not always agree with their teenagers' choices of friends. Changes in language used, attitude toward parents and house rules, and other behaviors signal that teenagers are copying what they see in new friends. Parents can certainly forbid a teenager to spend time with friends the parent considers inappropriate, but the truth is that telling a teenager not to associate with a particular friend is often ineffective in stopping the friendship. Obedient teenagers may comply, but rebellious teenagers can find ways to spend time with whomever they choose, and parents do not always find out about it.

Single parents can be encouraged to get to know their teens' friends and to make their own home a place where the teenagers congregate. This helps them chaperon and monitor what goes on when the adolescents are together. Keeping the teens involved in an active and Christ-centered youth ministry, praying for the teens and their friends, and having frank discussions with teenagers about the impact friends are having on their lives are additional ways to influence the types of friends teens have.

Conflicts over School

Attending high school, completing homework, earning good grades, and graduating are areas in which teenagers and single parents often have conflicts. There is a fine tension between letting the teenager take responsibility for his or her choices and letting the teenager fail or get so far behind that it is impossible to catch up. Single parents will have to discover just where they will draw the lines of personal involvement and set rules that will assist the teenager in establishing self-discipline and succeeding.

Conflicts over Music

The two issues single parents struggle with in the area of music are Christian convictions and personal preference. If the type of music the teenager prefers is simply not the personal preference of the single parent, then courtesy and cooperation are the solutions. Single parents may agree not to play classical music in the family room when the children are home, and the teenagers agree not to play Christian rock music when the parent is home. Or a certain time each day is given to the parent and the teenagers to each play their own preferred music.

However, if the issue is one of Christian conviction, then the single parent should explain to the teenager the reasons certain musicians or types of music are not allowed in the house. Consequences for having or playing forbidden music should be set and enforced. (Recordings can be confiscated and destroyed, cassette disc players taken away for ninety days, etc.)

Conflicts over Church Attendance

During teenage years it is not uncommon for children to rebel against going to church with their parents. Some single parents have expressed concern that if teenagers are forced to attend church, they will turn away from the church when they are on their own. However, if teenagers are allowed to not attend church, they will believe that church cannot be all that important to their parents and may turn away from the church anyway. Since sharing our faith with our children is one of our most important charges, I recommend that church attendance not be optional in single parent homes.

Of course, I also recommend that single parents investigate the youth program of their church to ensure that it is well organized, attractive to young people, and lively and that it offers a variety of activities. If not, then the single parent may decide to volunteer to help with the youth program, consider a different church, or talk with the pastor about improving the youth program.

Conflicts over Alcohol and Drugs

Watching someone throw up makes me nauseous—really sick. I thought I wasn't going to make it when fifteen-year-old Dan vomited a fifth of vodka into the wastepaper basket in the coach's office. Trying to keep my eyes away from the sickening scene, I looked closely at Dan. Alcohol had already taken its toll on this young man. I listened to him sob out the story of the pain of his parents' divorce. Liquor was the destructive way he had chosen to cope with the problems in his life.[5]

Many teenagers turn to alcohol for relief from their problems. Others choose marijuana, inhalants, cocaine, crack, and other hard drugs. Parents who expect adolescents to refrain from experimenting with drugs must first set a good example by avoiding all addictive substances themselves. It is wise to be alert for behavior changes that may signal the beginning of substance abuse. When there has been experimentation or drug use, parents can require weekly eye checks with pupilometers and periodic urinalysis.

There are several other things single parents can do to prevent involvement or to intervene on a timely basis. When parents really listen nonjudgmentally to their teens, there is a greater chance for a strong relationship to develop. Parents need to physically touch their teenagers frequently with hugs, arms around the shoulders, kisses on the foreheads, and pats on the back. And praying daily that the Holy Spirit will put a protective shield around their teens is possibly the most important preventative.

Conflicts over Sex

As a high school counselor of over eight thousand teenagers for nearly twenty years, I have learned that adolescents generally have a very different sexual belief system than do their parents. Single parents can begin long before their children become teenagers to teach godly standards for chastity and moral purity. Delaying formal dating until the midteens is a good idea because in most cases the earlier dating begins, the earlier sexual involvement occurs.[6] Frank discussions about AIDS, sexually transmitted diseases, pregnancy, safe sex, abstinence, and virginity should be held between parents and teenagers. Parents can restrict the types of movies and television programs teens are allowed to watch and what books they can read in order to reduce the exposure to sexually stimulating input. Appropriate house rules about who is and is not allowed in bedrooms or who may be alone in the house together help teenagers avoid needless temptations, as do restrictions on what types of dating activities are allowed.

Conflicts over Freedom

Teenagers tell their parents, "Give me more freedom, and I'll show you I can be responsible." Parents tell their teenagers, "Show me you can be responsible, and I will give you more freedom." The conflict is ageless.

Single parents will want to set clear guidelines for teenagers that define just what their freedoms are and where the restrictions begin. Violations of those restrictions should limit the related freedoms until the teenager has demonstrated trustworthiness sufficient to be given another chance. This includes honoring curfews, letting parents know where they are, doing what they say they will do, following through on responsibilities and commitments, and being careful with the family car.

Conflicts over Self-Esteem

Many teenagers have a low self-esteem, partly because they tend to compare themselves unfavorably with their peers. Also, when the conflicts increase between themselves and their parents, they may begin to feel they have lost acceptability in the parents' eyes. Often parents contribute to a low self-esteem by using derogatory labels *(stupid, crazy, dumb, silly)* or all-inclusive words *(always, never)* and by blaming the teens for all of the family problems.

Single parents can assist teens with developing positive self-esteem by affirming positive traits, accomplishments, successes, ideas, and grades. They can encourage teens to try new things without the expectation that every venture be a success. Parents can be encouragers by spending time with the adolescents, asking for ideas and opinions, listening attentively, and including them in family decision making.

Conflicts Over

There comes a day when the daily conflicts are over. The teenager has grown up into a young man or woman for whom the parent is no longer responsible. Parents may not agree—probably won't agree—with every decision their children make, but there is no longer any need to turn these disagreements into conflicts.

Remember Tim? His hair is still long, and he is now an exemplary man, husband, and father as well as a published musician in the Christian market. His mother still doesn't like his long hair, but she is proud of her son.

Single parents can take heart. This too shall pass, and with God's help they can survive.

Jeenie Gordon, M.S., M.A, is a single parent who has been a high school counselor for nearly twenty years and a therapist for fourteen years. She is now a national speaker and the author of There's Hope after Divorce *(Grand Rapids: Revell, 1996),* If My Parents Are Getting Divorced, Why Am I The One Who Hurts? *(Grand Rapids: Zondervan, 1993), and* Turbulent Teens of Panicking Parents *(Grand Rapids: Revell, 1997).*

9

Becoming Whole

LYNN SHIMKUS

Is there such a thing as being a wholesome and happy single parent? I think so. I'd like to believe there are many of us out there.

I am a very blessed single parent of two teenagers. Although things are not always easy, both of my teens are doing very well. Drug and alcohol free, they are also good students.

The old belief that children who come from "broken homes" are at a greater disadvantage emotionally than children from two-parent homes seems to be diminishing. I have observed that no matter where children are brought up, whether it be in a one-parent home, with both biological parents in the home, or with one biological and one stepparent, some children will have emotional problems and others won't.

I am very fortunate that I became a born-again Christian just prior to becoming a single parent. I thank God tremendously that things happened in that order for me. Yet it has been a challenge for me not to feel guilty for having wasted all those years before I became a Christian—all the valuable teaching and guiding that could have been taking place in my children's formative years. Now the challenge has been to step out boldly in faith to try to break the already learned attitudes and behaviors of not just myself but also my children.

Guidelines for Changing Negative Behaviors

Changing old behaviors and attitudes is a big challenge for someone who wants to change, but trying to convince your children to want to change their behaviors and attitudes is an enormous challenge. When children are already at the junior high level, initiating change in their lives takes a lot of prayer on our part and God's divine intervention. I wouldn't claim that things are perfect in our home by any stretch of the imagination, but I've learned a few things along the way that have become mottoes and guidelines to live by in my life. I think these guidelines lead to wholesomeness and happiness. These are the guidelines I share with the single parents who come to our single adult ministry; they may be helpful to you in your ministry.

A person who never makes a mistake probably isn't doing anything. This is one of my favorite quotations. I have multiple copies of it on neon yellow paper that I pass out to anyone (including my children) who seems to need a reminder. This phrase enables me to jump out in faith to try new and different things—to take risks. So what if I make mistakes or fail? If I have prayerfully considered taking a specific step in my life and I feel this might be something God wants me to try, then I ask God to give me the courage, strength, and faith to do so and then *jump.*

Taking risks can be very difficult for someone, such as myself, who suffers from anxiety (panic) attacks. I tend to *what if* something to death. I ask myself, "What if I embarrass myself?" "What if I fail?" or, "What if this isn't really something God wants me to do?" But I have learned that it is okay if I embarrass myself from time to time; it keeps me humble. It is all right if I don't always succeed; I usually learn more from my mistakes than I do from my successes. And I have learned that if God doesn't want me to do something, I'll know soon enough. I try to watch for doors that God appears to be opening to me, then work up all my faith and courage and go through them.

"Do not worry about anything, but in everything by prayer and supplication with thanksgiving let your requests be made known to God" (Phil. 4:6 NRSV). One of the most difficult things a person can do is to trust God completely, but we can get through anything if we put the Lord first in our lives. By nature we humans feel a need to control our lives all by ourselves, rejecting help from anyone, even God. As a single parent there were times when I've worried about: being alone, money, how to handle situations with my children, with friends, with coworkers . . . the list goes on forever.

When I realize that I am worrying too much, I immediately turn to God and ask for help. Before long I find myself counting my many blessings and sometimes finding solutions I hadn't thought of before. Many times a Christian friend or relative will call when least expected and offer advice and support. Or, if a solution doesn't come to mind, I am able to find peace and let the issues go for a while. I honestly believe Matthew 6:31–34 (NRSV).

> Therefore do not worry, saying "What will we eat?" or "What will we drink?" or "What will we wear?" For it is the Gentiles who strive for all these things; and indeed your heavenly Father knows that you need all these things. But strive first for the kingdom of God and his righteousness, and all these things will be given to you as well. So do not worry about tomorrow, for tomorrow will bring worries of its own. Today's trouble is enough for today.

Worrying does no one any good; it just causes health problems and shortens one's life. It is much healthier for people when they are feeling overwhelmed to ask God to take the problem from them, at least for a while, until they can better cope with it.

I also believe that God really does care about me and will not give me more problems or temptations than I can handle. Paul wrote,

> No testing has overtaken you that is not common to everyone. God is faithful, and he will not let you be tested beyond your strength, but with the testing he will also provide the way out so that you may be able to endure it.
>
> 1 Corinthians 10:13 NRSV

You're never too old to go back to school. Single parents can substitute "change my career" or "ask my children, friends, or former spouse for forgiveness" for "go back to school"—or fill in the blank another way. I recently had a discussion with my pastor about mature versus immature Christians. I asked him if there were such a thing as a mature Christian. *Mature* denotes completed growth, with nothing left on which to work. I believe Jesus was the only truly mature person—the rest of us are ripening on the vine. I consider myself to be constantly growing spiritually as well as emotionally and intellectually, and I hope I continue to grow for the rest of my earthly life. If anyone considers himself or herself to be totally mature, others instead will notice stunted growth.

This growing person cannot declare that my life is totally under control or that I am perfectly wholesome or always happy. But I know if I live by my mottoes, stay in prayer, read the Scripture and love the Lord, the Almighty will keep me on track for the most part because I'm much better off when God is walking my life with me. It especially helps single parents to know they can lean on Jesus.

You're never alone. The familiar poem entitled "Footprints" says it best. Just when everything in life seems to fall apart and become impossible, we may wonder if God has stopped caring and has forsaken us. The poem reminds us that when we, with our earthly perspectives, only see one set of footprints, this doesn't mean we are walking alone. Instead, it is during those times that God cradles us closely and carries us through the experiences. We must learn to feel the everlasting arms of the Almighty under us (Deut. 33:27).

Knowing that when I feel I can't possibly go on Jesus is there with me, carrying me if necessary, until I can get back on my feet, has helped me through many rough times.

Thank God for everything. At a really low point in my life a very wise woman suggested I thank God for even the bad things that were happening. At the time I did not fully understand why I should thank God for the bad, but I tried it anyway. I have discovered that, unfortunately, most emotional and spiritual growth comes out of suffering and pain. If everything were wonderful all the time, how much would any of us grow? Would we push ourselves beyond our comfort zones? Probably few of us would.

Another friend suggested that when I'm feeling low or depressed, I think of six good things that happened during the day, no matter how trivial they might have seemed at the time (for example, the sight of a pretty bird, a hug from a child or a friend, a beautiful sunset). Then I should thank God for those gifts. This easy activity helps one appreciate the little things in life and realize that life is not all bad.

Eight Steps to Becoming Whole and Happy

Besides the guidelines discussed above, I have eight steps I follow to be as healthy a single adult and parent as I can be. I repeatedly share these with other single parents, and they will be helpful for the single adults in your ministry.

1. *It is absolutely important to take time for yourself.* In this hectic world we all need to find the time to play, rest, and have fellowship. Suggest to single parents in your ministry that they list ten things they enjoy doing and make sure they find the time to do these now and then, even if they have to force themselves. They will be glad they did.

Tell your single parents to be sure to spend time with their children—playing with them, walking with them, talking with them, praying with them, and reading Scripture with them. Although it is becoming more and more difficult to get my teens to spend a lot of time with me, I keep trying. Even if my son comes in at 11:30 P.M. and wants to talk, I make an effort to wake myself up and hear what he has to say. If I wait until the time is better for me, he may not want to talk, so I take it when I can get it. We have had many late-night discussions, causing us both to lose precious hours of sleep, but I am very thankful that we talked about those important issues when we did.

2. *Discipline your children when necessary.* I am a mother who would much rather be my children's friend than their disciplinarian. Yet there are times—many times—when I've had to take a strong stand with my children. The hardest part is trying to

remain calm in the midst of a discussion that is quickly getting out of control. As tempers rise, I have found it extremely important to tell my children that we need to take some time to calm down. Then after spending some time alone in prayer, sometimes taking walks, we will get back together and try to work through the issue at hand.

3. *Always pray.* Single parents need to find some quiet time each day to spend with God in prayer (see 1 Thess. 5:17). This is absolutely essential if they want to remain sane and strong. I believe God gives me the energy I need every day to keep going. Children also must be encouraged to pray. When my children were younger, I prayed with them every night at bedtime. Even now that they are older, I remind them to say their prayers before going to sleep.

4. *Read Scripture every day.* This is the most important advice for single parents. I admit that I miss a day here and there, but I'm working on that. It is so important to be in God's Word. There have been times when I have been so tired I could barely read the page, but when I did, something fantastic was there for me. I have tried reading the little devotional *Upper Room* with the children, but again, as they got older it became tougher to get them rounded up to do this as a family. So I gave each child a personal subscription to the *Upper Room* and have asked that it be kept near their beds. Even if they don't choose to read it every day, there may be a time when they will pick it up and find comfort in it. God's Word is always helpful in our daily lives (see Ps. 119:105).

5. *Worship regularly.* It is important to spend time with other Christians in worship as well as in leisure activities. The church has become my family. My biological family is spread all over the country, but in times of trouble, my church family has been there for me. Making friends at church, getting involved in a committee or singles program, or teaching Sunday school are ways of storing up treasures in heaven, which will last for eternity. And our hearts are where our treasures are according to Matthew 6:20–21. When we put our hearts, time, and money into the church, we are often amazed at the return on our investment.

6. *Learn to forgive your former spouse, the children, and especially yourself.* God forgives us daily for our sins, and sets a perfect example for us (see 1 John 1:9). We need to follow that example and forgive as often as necessary. God's healing grace gives us comfort in life.

Refusing to forgive keeps us forever tied to a past hurt, memory, or experience. We never grow beyond the pain in that area of our lives. Forgiveness is the only way to "unhook" ourselves and to become free to move on. Too often people think of forgiveness as benefiting mostly the person one forgives. In reality, forgiveness benefits most the one who forgives. God is responsible for settling the accounts, and each of us will someday give account of our behaviors and attitudes while on earth. God is the ultimate judge and is responsible for "punishing" wrongdoers. Our job is to forgive failures and move on to become conformed to the image of Jesus Christ. David Augsburger's book *Caring Enough to Forgive* (Ventura: Regal Books, 1981) is an excellent resource for this subject.

7. *Become part of an accountability group to help keep you on track.* I'm part of a covenant group. Several trusted friends have covenanted to meet together every other Saturday morning and share where we are spiritually, how our important relationships are going, how things are at work, at home, and with friends, neighbors, and acquaintances. Each person gets about ten minutes to share. We also allow time to give each other feedback. Not all groups like to allow for the feedback, but we have chosen to do so. As single women, we feel we can use the advice, support, and encouragement we get from each other (see Heb. 10:25).

8. *Balance, balance, balance.* Probably the most difficult rule of thumb is to maintain balance in one's life. It is so easy to get caught up in a relationship and put the children on the back burner or to put in tons of hours at work either to earn more income or perhaps to escape problems at home or loneliness. But we absolutely must keep that delicate balance between God, ourselves, our children, potential committed relationships, and our jobs. We need to do our best at each of these things, and as a single parent it can become very overwhelming and stressful. If we

put God first, however, everything will fall into place (see Col. 1:18–19).

Maintaining balance becomes a significant issue when single parents get involved in dating relationships. Dating was hard in high school and college, but dating as a single parent is very complicated.

Yet the initial infatuation stages of a new relationship are euphoric. It is so easy and natural when one is falling in love to want to spend most of the available time together. But often the children feel neglected, hurt, and confused. The feedback one receives from the children can be upsetting:

"He's not my daddy."
"She can't tell me what to do."
"I don't like him/her."
"You love him/her more than you love me."

Children must be reassured that they are loved and that no one will take their place in their parent's heart. Many children will understand—although they may still choose to give the parent a hard time. The single parent needs to explain to the children that parents need a special adult friend in their lives with whom to talk, to give and receive support, and to help them through the ups and downs of life. When parents spend as much time as they can with the children without letting them consume every available minute, the parents need not feel guilty spending time developing a new romantic relationship.

One of the stresses of dating is that the expenses of the activity, the food consumed, and the child care fees can threaten a single parent's budget. Going Dutch or taking turns paying for dates alleviates the financial anxiety. Or even better, find inexpensive and creative ideas for dates. Walking in the park, renting a paddleboat or canoe, and taking a drive are lots of fun. Community or college theater productions usually cost much less than Broadway musicals, and are often almost as good.

Some single parents may want to wait a while before taking the children along on their dates, but if the relationship develops into a serious one, it is a good idea to include the kids from time to time. Any potential spouse needs to be able to relate with the children, or there will be many headaches and heartaches in the future.

Advise single parents who do find that special someone to attend a Blended Family seminar. The cost is well worth it. When the man I was dating (and eventually married) and I began considering marriage several years ago, we attended just such a seminar. I realized I was not yet ready to get married and take on the responsibilities that would accompany the marriage (including raising his three children along with my own two). I had some major thinking and growing to do first. Encourage your single parents to take their time making that second commitment when there are children involved.

Living by all these guidelines has helped me tremendously as a single parent, and I have witnessed them working in other single parents' lives as well. Remember, as leaders we also must put God first in our lives and trust the Almighty with everything. This is the key to being a wholesome and happy adult whether single or married.

Lynn Shimkus knows firsthand the struggles and joys of being a single parent because she was a single mother of two teenage children, Bill and Kelly, whom she loves very much. She works at Friendship United Methodist Church in Bolingbrook, Illinois, as the director of the singles ministry, which she organized soon after her own divorce when she realized she wanted to meet other Christian men and women in a safe environment. Lynn has recently remarried.

10
Finding Joy

RICHARD GAIA

Kris finished with the third highest grade point average in her graduating class and was named a National Merit Scholarship semifinalist. She and her mother, Evelyn, knew that the awards program would be bittersweet. Kris would have her name called a dozen times for different awards, and the audience would cheer when it was announced she would receive a full scholarship to one of America's most prestigious universities. But her leaving home would mean that Kris's mother would be facing an empty home for the first time in eighteen years.

Ten years before, Kris's father left home for another lifestyle, throwing Kris and Evelyn into one another's emotional arms. Evelyn had immersed herself in Kris's world and enjoyed every minute of it. She had chaperoned the band trips and driven a group of Kris's friends to the math tournaments. "What will I do now?" Evelyn asked herself. She desired the best for Kris and knew she must sever the apron strings. At the same time, she inwardly cringed every time she thought of being alone.

Randall's story was different. His soon-to-be-fifteen son, Charles, was a challenge. Randall was forever attending parent-teacher conferences to discuss Charles's latest escapade.

Charles didn't seem to fit in anywhere other than on the basketball court. He was a terrific shooter and one of the fastest boys in the eighth grade, but he constantly struggled in the classroom. He failed to maintain the required grades to play on the school team, and so he retreated further into his shell.

Even though Charles sat through numerous Sunday school classes, he didn't absorb much. When offered his first experience with marijuana, he didn't hesitate. It wasn't long before apathy consumed Charles. He didn't enjoy life and made it miserable for everyone around him, especially his single parent father.

Evelyn had a model daughter, whereas Randall had to struggle some days just to like his son. Both parents were totally committed to their parenting responsibilities. Both felt there was no greater priority on earth than to be the best role model and instructor their children could have. Believe it or not, both received abundant benefits from their task. Evelyn's were obvious; Randall's were not. Yet Randall would be the first to tell you that raising Charles was not only the greatest challenge of his life but also his greatest privilege.

A positive attitude is everything when it comes to raising children as a single parent. Both Evelyn and Randall had terrific attitudes. Evelyn had an ideal daughter, while Randall knew every day was a potential disaster. Even so, Randall was not defeated as a single parent. He saw his parenting as a calling—a difficult yet privileged task. He loved his son and wanted the very best for him. Depending upon the situation, Randall was willing to be tender or tough. He had developed an attitude characterized as "the glass is half full" mentality.

What attitudes permeate the single parents in your ministry? Are they victims or victors? Do they consider the parenting task a calling from God? Many parents have gone through divorce and received a less than ideal financial settlement yet were elated just to have custody of the children. Others bemoan raising their children alone regardless of how fortunate their financial circumstances turned out to be.

GIGO in computerese stands for "garbage in/garbage out." This is particularly true for one's attitude and mental state. Philippians 4:8 says, "Finally, brothers, whatever is true, whatever is noble, whatever is right, whatever is pure, whatever is lovely, whatever is admirable—if anything is excellent or praiseworthy—think about such things." The mental input your single parents accept or give to their minds determines their attitudes. As you read the following pages, consider the joys of being a single parent so you can help those with whom you minister to develop and maintain positive attitudes.

The Joy of Personal Growth

The difficulty of single parenting provides a fertile field for personal growth. Adversity is opportunity. Charles Swindoll wrote, "We are all faced with a series of great opportunities brilliantly disguised as impossible situations."[1] Single parenting continually alternates between being joyous, challenging, rewarding, or overwhelming. Single parenting challenges range from coordinating conflicting schedules to facing gut-wrenching decisions in the middle of the night.

James 1:2–7 (NASB) speaks volumes to the single parent at this point.

> Consider it all joy, my brethren, when you encounter various trials, knowing that the testing of your faith produces endurance. And let endurance have its perfect result, that you may be perfect and complete, lacking in nothing. But if any of you lacks wisdom, let him ask of God, who gives to all men generously and without reproach, and it will be given to him. But let him ask in faith without any doubting, for the one who doubts is like the surf of the sea driven and tossed by the wind. For let not that man expect that he will receive anything from the Lord.

Encourage your single parents to rejoice when the challenges of parenting come their way. Such thinking does not come naturally and does not seem logical, but God is focused on the product being formed by the process. The Refiner's fire is necessary for the precious metal to become purified. Single parents who pray through their struggles and seek God's wisdom through Scripture or godly counsel undergo immeasurable growth. Single parents' faith is developed when they experience God answering their prayers, providing wisdom, and giving them strength.

Responding to a single parent questionnaire, Emilie wrote, "I know God's love envelops me, even in times of exhaustion and overload, and when I need to be alone and don't have the opportunity. God gives me strength as challenges occur, and I grow through times when I need to make difficult decisions regarding the children and their well-being. My Lord is always there."

Emilie has grown dramatically in the years since her divorce. Her trust in God's provision doesn't eliminate the difficulties, but it does allow her to face each day with the knowledge that she can do all things through Christ who strengthens her (Phil. 4:13). In John 15:4 (NASB) we read that we cannot do it alone: "Abide in Me, and I in you. As the branch cannot bear fruit of itself, unless it abides in the vine, so neither can you, unless you abide in Me."

Single parenting certainly allows for developing spiritual dependency on God. In a two-parent family it is easy for a partner to lean on a spouse rather than just on God. Deuteronomy 33:25 tells us God will give us sufficient strength for each day. No one has a better opportunity to experience this truth than the single parent.

The Joy of Relationships with the Children

Single parenting provides the opportunity for a stronger one-on-one relationship between single parents and their children. Connie related, "My three boys and I are very close. I think the relationship between married people sometimes infringes upon some of the time and attention the children might have received." One major reason children often don't want their single parent to remarry is their selfish, but understandable, desire not to allow another person to reduce their one-on-one time with the parent. They don't want to lose that closeness.

For the children, dealing with one parent is often easier than with two. Having only one parent making rules for behavior can be a good thing. The advantage in a single parent home is that there is only one set of rules or regulations at a time. Debra stated one of her joys in single parenting, "I've been able to exercise my own judgment and make the decisions affecting my daughter without strife or disagreement." When conflicts arise, children are forced to work through the issues with the single parent. Such conflict resolution can create a bond and closeness that is a blessing to both parent and child.

The Joy of Peace

The absence of day-to-day marital conflict in the home is another benefit of single parenting. Those couples who have stayed together for the children often provide a horrible example of marital intimacy and communication. Couples should be applauded for staying together for their children's sake, but only if they are willing to work on their relationship to build a functional and loving marriage. Studies indicate that family disharmony adversely affects the self-esteem of children. Conversely, the absence of conflict positively affects children. Confusion is lessened and children are less tense.

In *Love Must Be Tough,* Dr. James Dobson revealed the results of a sixth-grade creative writing exercise. The students were to complete a sentence beginning with the words *I wish.* The teacher expected the children to wish for trips, bicycles, or material things. She was shocked to see that two-thirds of the class's wishes were related to resolving relationship problems at home.[2]

Children become tired of anger, tension, and confusion, yet they usually feel helpless to do anything about it. Living with one parent may spare children the misery of seeing someone they love under constant attack. Paula, a teenage victim of divorce, said, "I'm glad my parents split up. Now I don't have to listen to them fighting every night."

The Joy of Teamwork

Single parents tend to involve the children in family negotiations and decision making. Consider how parents tend to make plans for summer vacations. In many two-parent families, the adults talk, share, and make decisions about when and where to go. The children may be uninvolved in those discussions. Wise parents get their children's input, but typically the parents make the decisions.

Single parents, however, may involve their children more in selecting vacation times, locations, and activities because they find it important to be certain their children are excited about the summer or holiday trip. Since there won't be another adult present to distract and to help discipline unhappy children, the single parent plans for positive experiences. If the children are miserable, the parent will be also.

Pam discussed the commitment she made to allow her son to compete in BMX bicycle racing. "I worked overtime during the week, and my son and I cleaned offices on the weekends to earn money to participate in this sport. Many times I wondered if I was out of my mind. We awakened at 5:00 A.M. to be at a 6:00 A.M. race. I would sit in ninety-five degree heat. Often we would drive back late at night, sometimes just in time to clean offices again. Crazy? No. I was reaping the wonderful blessing a child can bring in your life." Pam and her son worked together to accomplish goals. In two-parent families such a hectic schedule might create marital strife.

The Joy of Bonding

Unique bonding between parents and children can occur in a single parent family. Pam's time with her son developed an inseparable bond. One daughter of a single parent said, "Other kids see how close my mom and I are and wish they had the kind of relationship we have."

This special bonding might start out with, "We have to stick together," or, "No matter how bad things get, we will always have each other." But over time, the relationship develops depth. Single parents and their children often do things together that two-parent families normally don't do. A single mom might help her teenage son change the oil in the car. A single dad might take his ten-year-old daughter to the ballet if she aspires to become a ballerina.

Time together allows children and parents to see each other as people rather than just as family members. Debra declared, "Sami and I are able to discuss anything, and I believe she values my opinion. She is truly my pride and joy and my best buddy."

A caution is needed at this point. While it is wonderful for parents and children to relate to one another in friendship, parents must be parents first. One single father often said to his children, "While I would like to be your friend as well as your parent, if forced to make the choice, I will be your parent now so I can be your friend later."

You will want to help the single parents in your ministry remember to be careful not to become so enmeshed in their children's lives that they cannot parent. They must not become so attached to their children's friendship that they become threatened when the children leave for college or develop other close relationships with their peers. Each child needs the freedom to develop apart from parents. One of the greatest accomplishments for parents is training their children to live successfully independently.

The Joy of Learning

In a single parent family children get to experience a variety of roles and learning experiences. In two-parent families each parent does certain tasks, usually along gender lines. Dad mows the grass and washes the cars while Mom washes the clothes, cleans the house, and cooks the meals. In one-parent families the chores are shared between the children and the parents. In single parent homes all the tasks still exist, yet with only one parent to complete them. Children learn to help by doing a variety of jobs. The tasks are delegated based on abilities rather than normal gender mores.

Regardless of their gender, children in single parent homes seem to learn to cook earlier than children in two-parent homes. They may also learn to wash, dry, and fold their own clothes at a very young age. Usually these tasks are thrust upon a child by necessity. While children may not like the responsibility, and the single parent may feel guilty at times, children are learning to do things that will be beneficial to them as adults.

Children in single parent families are more likely to learn to maintain a home, which helps prepare them for adult living. Survival skills are also taught as children observe their single parents dealing with financial responsibilities, living on a budget, and saving for major purchases. Children with single parents are given the opportunity to develop greater self-discipline as they must do numerous things for themselves that might be done for them in two-parent families.

The Joy of Including Friends

Single parents often involve other adults in their family lives. Whether these other adults are siblings, coworkers, friends from church, parents, or significant others, each of these people have the potential of bringing great benefit to the children's lives.

One single mother, Peggy, felt that "roughing it" meant staying in a Motel 6. Yet her son, Brad, longed for the outdoors. He dreamed of camping out, fishing before dawn, and bow-hunting for deer. Fortunately, his counterpart existed in the church they attended. He was a young married man who had no children of his own, had gone to high school with Peggy, and had grown into a fine Christian. Peggy's friend was the person her son needed. That relationship provided incredible benefits for Brad, because the man spent time with Brad, taking him to sporting events, on camping trips, and fishing once a month.

The Joy of Coparenting

Sometimes the noncustodial parent provides a stable and healthy secondary residence. The secondary home can be a haven of relief for the children from the everyday stresses and grinds and a source of relief for the custodial parent. Every household

117

has conflict. Even Evelyn and "ideal" Kris have their angry moments. When the noncustodial parent provides positive time away, both parents and children are refreshed.

Again, attitude is everything. Rather than dreading the weekends when the children visit the other parent, single parents can begin viewing these times as personal retreats. They might spend time with friends, accomplish tasks difficult to achieve when the children are present, read a book, or sleep.

Single parents who are widows, never married, or have uncooperative ex-spouses can still find ways to develop positive time away from their children. Planned weekend retreats when children can spend time with the grandparents are great. Single parents might swap rest and relaxation time with each other. Or the children can participate in carefully investigated programs that include retreats or summer camps. The time apart improves the time together.

In many cases, there are noncustodial parents who spend more quality time with their children than parents from two-parent families. Sadly, statistics indicate that very few minutes of heart-to-heart communication take place between parents and children each week. Noncustodial parents often miss their children so much that they are awakened to the importance of their relationships. Therefore, when they are with the children, these parents enjoy being together and are less likely to take the children for granted.

The Joy of Teaching

Living in a single parent family can provide an environment in which children learn to cope with disappointment and rough times. Some children are fortunate enough to be protected from painful experiences by loving families. Yet this protection often fails to provide opportunities for young people to face difficulties, learn to work through adversity, and develop coping skills that can help them throughout their adult lives.

Children of divorce can learn firsthand that marital dissolution does not solve all the problems inherent in a dysfunctional marriage. Wise single parents will use everyday situations to teach positive life lessons concerning the need for commitment or the importance of resolving conflict. Children of divorce can learn to be discriminating in selecting a spouse. Single parents can speak from personal experience to their teenage children about the pain of rushing into relationships, overlooking major character defects, or hoping to change a person following marriage.

The Joy of Modeling

Single parents have the opportunity to establish a positive example of Christian dating. Children examine the behavior of their parents with a critical eye. They watch for inconsistencies, wanting to know just how much parents mean what they say. When godly single parents establish good boundaries in their own dating relationships, they model the Christian principles they want their children to emulate.

This principle is a sword that cuts both ways. The failure to set a good example often provides enough of an excuse to allow teens to justify their own unacceptable behavior. "So what if I stay overnight with my boyfriend," says seventeen-year-old Leigh. "Jim stays here overnight all the time." Even if Jim sleeps downstairs on the couch, Leigh has seen a weakly defined boundary that justifies doing what she wants to do.

The best-case scenario would be for Mom to be able to truthfully say to Leigh, "Jim and I have been dating for two years. He lives twenty-five miles away, but even when we were going to do something early in the morning and had people around as chaperons, Jim has never spent the night here, and I have never spent the night there. Follow our example."

The Joy of Impact

The knowledge that one is making a difference in this world as one sees the children grow up, mature, and become successful is a terrific thrill. Just as Hannah knew her life was significant because her son, Samuel, belonged to God and God would use him as a wise judge over Israel, so single parents can know the joy of having an impact on their children.

Emilie knew her hard work made a difference when her three children set up a lemonade stand on a sunny day to raise money to fund a birthday party for her. Emilie recounted, "It's moments like that when love shines through and the joy of being there for them speaks loud and clear."

Connie felt this intangible aspect on Mother's Day when for the first time she received three separate cards, one from each son. Her oldest son's card thanked her for not only being his mom but also being his role model. Recently that same son sat next to his mother as he received his Eagle Scout award—the highest achievement within Boy Scouts.

Pam, who cleaned offices for BMX racing money, saw her son get involved with the Fellowship of Christian Athletes and later the Navigators ministry. God has directed him into full-time Christian vocational ministry. Currently he is entering his second year in seminary.

These stories are marvelous, but the little everyday things are just as important. Remind your single parents to keep their eyes open for the nuggets of joy.

The Joy of It All

Single parenting is often difficult, but it appears the difficulties bring about much of the benefit. The children may never make the dean's list or win athletic accolades. More than likely they will be typical children—a joy at times, a headache at other times. But one doesn't have to have exemplary children to enjoy single parenting. The benefits extend to any parents who open their spiritual eyes to observe God's handiwork in their family's life. Attitude is everything.

Surround your single parents with people who can help them see the positive aspects of the task. Encourage single parents to network with and support each other. Provide inspiring books on single parenting in the church library. Over time the joys and benefits of single parenting can come more clearly into focus.

"I alone know the plans I have for you, plans to bring you prosperity and not disaster, plans to bring about the future you hope for" (Jer. 29:11 TEV). This message, originally spoken to the exiles of Israel, is a principle any child of God can embrace. Even in the midst of distress, God is there. There is a divine plan; it's a good plan. Single parents will reap significant benefits as they allow God to work out his plan through their family. And they will find the joy!

Rev. Richard Gaia has served on church staffs for over twenty years—the last ten years in the area of single adults. He has a Th.M. from Dallas Theological Seminary. Richard has experienced single parenting firsthand, having lived through an unwanted divorce and becoming the custodial parent of his two children. He is now married to Beverly, and the Gaia family resides in Hendersonville, Tennessee, where Richard serves on the staff of First Baptist Church.

Part 2

THE CHALLENGES
FOR CHILDREN
OF SINGLE PARENTS

11

Dealing with Multiple Changes

MARCIA JENKS AND DOUG ROHDE

When a parent dies or parents divorce, children experience multiple losses and changes in their lives. Reactions to these losses can vary between children, even in the same families. As leaders of single parent ministries, we can help single parents understand and assist their children in coping with the upheavals.

Children in newly created single parent families often face change in where they live and go to school, the frequency with which they see the noncustodial parent (in a divorce), the amount of time spent with the custodial or surviving parent, the number of responsibilities assigned in the home, and the financial resources available in the family. In addition to these changes, the children will be grieving the loss of the intact family.

This chapter will provide suggestions you can pass on to the single parents in your ministry. Encourage them to use these ideas to ease the stress of relocating to a new home and school, facilitate the visitation process, and minimize custody issues. Financial and grief issues, responsibilities for chores, and spending quality time with children are covered in other chapters in this book (see chapters 16, 17, 18, 22, and 23).

Relocation Issues

Most single parent families move at least once. Some moves are eagerly anticipated, such as when a new, more desirable home becomes affordable and available. Some moves are planned long in advance; others are sudden. Most moves are stressful even if all family members are in favor of relocating.

Moving has traditionally been a time to cull through one's belongings and throw away the unnecessary, the unusable, and the unwanted. However, single parents need to be sensitive to the emotional needs of the children when making *take/don't take* decisions. If one of the children resists throwing away a ragged teddy bear, perhaps the bear should go to the new home with the family.

Single parents can prepare children for the idea of a move by reading Bible stories about people who moved or left their homes and discussing what good things happened in the stories (e.g., Abraham, Noah, David, Mephibosheth, Paul on missionary journeys). Also, a trip to a bookstore or library might produce good children's books about moving, which could be read together. Praying with the children about the move, the new neighborhood, and new friends includes God in the process. The single parent may read Scriptures to the children that promise God will never leave them and discuss how God is the same in the old neighborhood as in the new.

Children are often apprehensive about unknown places, and a sudden relocation can result in fears and bewilderment. Moving to a new home, neighborhood, or city can be a challenge for the single parent and the children. The single parent can help make the move an adventure. If possible and appropriate, the children can be taken along to look at and help select the new home or apartment. They do not need to be involved in the entire search process but at least in the final selection between the best two or three options. If it is not possible for the children to be physically involved in the selection, then photographs of the best options can help familiarize the children with the choices.

Ways the single parent can make the new neighborhood attractive to the children include discovering the locations of the closest grocery stores, church, library, playground, schools, video rental store, video arcades, museums, mall, fun centers, sports stadium, tennis court, water slide, and so forth. The single parent can do this alone or with the children. The search could be planned as a treasure hunt for teenagers using maps and telephone books.

If the new home is within driving distance and there is time to do so before the move, the single parent can help make the new neighborhood more familiar by taking the children (and some of their friends) to the new neighborhood for some activities—going to the movies, having a picnic, shopping, eating at a pizzeria, or attending church.

The separation anxiety, which is natural for children when leaving friends and familiar surroundings, can be alleviated if the single parent lets the children know they will be returning to the old neighborhood for visits. The first visit should be planned within the first thirty days—even sooner if the children are between the ages of six and ten, because a month is a long time for children at those ages. If the move is to a place too far away to return that quickly, then a vacation back at the old neighborhood could be planned so the children know the ties will not be broken. Sometimes children can bring a friend along to help with the physical move. This is an adventure for the friend and comforting for the children who are moving. Or friends can be invited to come visit within the first thirty days (if close enough) or on a school vacation.

If the noncustodial parent has had frequent visits with the children in the old neighborhood, the parent with custody of the children will want to be sensitive to how the move will affect the children's relationship and visitation with the noncustodial parent. It can be helpful for the children if the other parent is invited to come see the new home or apartment. This allows the noncustodial parent to listen with understanding when the children talk about the new home, neighborhood, and school.

Budgeting for extra long-distance telephone calls to the other parent and friends back at the old hometown for the first couple of months after the move is another way single parents can help their children cope with a long-distance move. Having the children take pictures of their new rooms, school, friends, and neighborhood to send back to friends strengthens the sense that the new is being shared with the old.

It's a good idea for single parents who move to a new neighborhood to make a special effort to meet the neighbors as soon as possible—especially those who might have children of the same ages as their own. The new neighbors and their children can help the single parent family quickly learn about activities available in the new location. Single parents might even contact parents of children or teenagers in the same grades as their own children and arrange introductions, playtimes, or a joint activity so the children don't have to go to a school classroom where they do not know anyone. Hosting a fun neighborhood party is another way to meet new neighbors.

Once the move is completed, single parents will want to consciously build good memories for the children in the new location. Doing something together that the children have always wanted to do builds a positive memory. Starting a new family tradition (with great pomp and flair) can be great. Planning a family progressive dinner with different courses at different restaurants or eateries can result in fun memories. ("Do you remember the look on the waitress's face when we announced that all we wanted was a side dish of vegetables for each of us?") Families often take years to build a history of good memories. Building a number of great memories in a short period of time is one way to make the new more familiar and enjoyable. (This concept is also applicable to adjusting to living in a one-parent family. If single parents work to build new memories and traditions as quickly as possible, the adjustment to and acceptance of the new living arrangement is accelerated.)

When the move requires the children to switch schools, the single parent will want to go to the new school(s) before enrolling the children. If the children are in elementary school, the single parent can meet with the assigned teacher and explain the home situation. In this way the teacher will be better prepared to assimilate the children into the classroom because of knowing something about the family. If the child is in middle, junior, or high school, the single parent might meet with the school counselor to discuss the teenager's situation and to find out about the classes and extracurricular activities available for the students. The information gathered should then be shared with the children so some of the unknown is eliminated before the first day of class.

One of the most important factors in making moves less stressful for the children is the attitude of the single parent. If the single parent demonstrates a sense of adventure and excitement, the children can also respond positively. If the single parent exhibits a negative, complaining attitude and a sense of dread or regret, the children also tend to respond negatively.

Visitation Issues

In a divorce situation, visitation issues can be extremely challenging for the parents and confusing for the children. Or they can be worked out cooperatively by all concerned.

Before a divorce the children usually have access to both parents on a daily basis, but after a divorce, the contact with one parent is often significantly reduced. Adjustment for the children can be difficult and take time. Once again, the parents' attitudes toward each other and visitation challenges influence the children's adjustment.

Single parents must learn to put aside personal animosity toward one another and to coparent the children. Mandated court schedules must be followed, but whenever possible flexibility should be encouraged. Children need positive relationships with both parents if at all possible. Scripture tells children to honor both mother and father (see Matt. 15:4).

If children want to spend more time with the noncustodial parent, the parents can negotiate how this can be accomplished. If the children want less time or no contact at all with the noncustodial parent, the custodial parent faces a challenge. It is important that the custodial parent not see this as a personal victory or encourage the children by demeaning the other parent. Instead, the children's feelings and thoughts need to be explored and handled in a tactful, caring manner. There may be a need for discussions with a counselor, pastor, or other adult friend so the children can resolve negative feelings such as anger and bitterness. There may be a valid reason for the resistance, such as conflicts with other plans or activities. These can be worked through in most cases.

The two parents usually can make visitation a positive experience. Offer them these guidelines to help:

1. The children need to know the schedule—the departure and return times.
2. It is helpful for the children to know in advance what activities, if any, are planned so they can be prepared and dress appropriately.
3. The children need to have everything together for the visit before the scheduled departure time. When the noncustodial parent rings the doorbell is no time for a panicky search for lost shoes or a missing baseball glove.
4. Communication between the parents should be civil. Arguing in front of the children sets a negative tone for the visit and is inappropriate any time (see Rom. 12:18).
5. The children's return should be welcomed with the attitude that the children have had a nice visit, not as if they have been to the enemy's camp.
6. Children need to be allowed to talk about their visits with honesty and excitement. But children must not be used as spies or be interrogated by parents after their visits.
7. Children sometimes need a little time and emotional space to make the transition from one home to another when visits last more than a day or two.
8. Visitation schedules should not be changed unless there is an absolute need to do so. Commitments to the children need to be honored, and visits should be given priority.
9. Visits should not be withheld to manipulate or punish the other parent.

Custody Issues

Custody of the children is generally settled initially at the time of the divorce. One parent has full custody or there is some form of joint custody granted. However, subsequent to the initial ruling, further custody issues often surface. One or more of the children may want to go live with the noncustodial parent. The parent with custody may decide that the other parent is better equipped to handle one or more of the children. A change in the marital or financial status of one of the parents may suggest that a change in custody would be appropriate.

In most cases, custody issues are best resolved by single parents and their attorneys. But as leaders of single parent ministries, we can help single parents work through their feelings toward the other parent. Here are some points to share with single parents facing custody related decisions:

1. A desire to go live with the other parent is more often than not a result of curiosity about the other parent rather than a rejection of the custodial parent. Children often want to get to know the other parent better or see what it would be like living in a different home. A comparison can be made with children who have been adopted and who love their adoptive families yet still are curious and want to know the biological parents.
2. Children often idealize the other home. It is not unusual for children who do switch primary homes to later want to return to the original home. Sometimes it is helpful to arrange an extended visit at the other home rather than a total change of custody.
3. Children usually develop a very close and loving relationship with the parent in their primary home. If there is a change in living arrangements, that parent can consciously and deliberately work at continuing that relationship with telephone calls, visits, and letters. At the same time, the children have an opportunity to develop a closer and more lov-

131

ing relationship with the other parent. This can be a positive experience for both parents and the children.

Change Can Be Positive

Going from a two-parent home to a one-parent home does result in many changes, but not all of the changes need to be negative. There are many ways for single parents to help their children see their situation as fun and positive. Encourage the single parents in your ministry to look for the opportunities and use creativity to show the children the abundance of God's blessings to them.

Marcia Jenks directs the Single Parent Fellowship ministries at Willoughby Hills Evangelical Friends Church in Ohio. She and her husband, Ken, live with their six children in Mentor, Ohio.

Doug Rohde coteaches the Single Parent Fellowship Class at Willoughby Hills Evangelical Friends Church. He is the custodial parent of two teenagers and works full time in the department of pathology at the Cleveland Clinic Foundation.

12

Living in a One-Parent Family

CHERYL MACOY

Growing up in a one-parent family can be seen as a negative or positive experience. Actually, it is a combination of negative and positive experiences—at least it was for me.

I grew up in a single parent home. Do I feel cheated? No. Do I feel privileged? No. I do feel satisfied and know that God helped my mom raise me. God loves me, and I was shown that love by my family and church, and now I am serving my God. To me that sounds like a successful childhood.

As I work with single parents and their families, I can identify with many of their experiences, which is helpful to my ministry. One thing I frequently remind single parents is how much influence they have on how their children respond to growing up in a single parent family. If the parent believes it is the worst possible life, so will the children. If the parent believes the children have been cheated out of a good life and will be marred and scarred for life, guess what the kids will think. I know my mother's attitude toward our situation created a positive home environment for me.

Here are some of the hints I share with single parents to help them make living in a one-parent family a positive experience for their children.

Turn to Family Members for Support

I was born during my parents' sixth year of marriage. Tragically, my father had been diagnosed with cancer shortly after my parents learned I would be joining the family, and he died when I was six months old. My mother needed immediate financial support now that a baby was part of her life. Her uncle was a bachelor, and he offered to move in with us and help by sharing expenses. Because my mom and her uncle eventually purchased a larger home in the same community, I have only vague memories of that first house, but those memories are warm and consoling.

Until I was seven I was surrounded by family. My great-uncle was a surrogate father who not only helped Mom with housing concerns but also contributed to my discipline and training. We lived in the same town where my grandmother resided, which allowed for frequent visits and telephone contact. Some single parents relocate to places much farther away and the contact is disrupted. Our eventual relocation for Mom's employment still allowed for frequent contact with relatives since we were only a two-hour drive away from them. This also allowed me to maintain strong friendships with people in my hometown.

Some single parents don't have family near enough or willing to assist them. But families have a way of rallying around a member who truly needs help.

Improve Your Lifestyle

As I approached school age, Mom felt she needed to become more of a provider and not rely on her uncle or social security for all our financial needs. She was a high school graduate but had no further education, so she decided that earning a college degree was the next step she should take. When I started kindergarten, she started college.

For some single parents, returning to school to earn a degree or acquire a skill is the key that unlocks the doors for job opportunities. For others, taking the initiative to apply for promotions or better jobs results in improved income. Even if going to school takes years or if one applies for a dozen jobs without being hired, these efforts will help in the long run.

Spend Quality Time with Your Children

I remember spending my afternoons after kindergarten with a baby-sitter waiting for Mom to come take me home. My sitter was an older woman who loved to read stories to me, and I can recall sitting in her lap listening to every word she said. I enjoyed the baby-sitter and the activities she had for me, but I always looked forward to seeing Mom.

School and work schedules often keep parents away from the home environment for long stretches of time. My mom made major efforts to be with me as much as she could. I don't remember her dating anyone during this time, so she was usually home in the evenings. We would play games, watch television, do my homework, or just be together, perhaps each reading a book or doing a quiet individual activity. These evenings created lasting memories and made me feel loved.

I was fortunate that my mother did not need to work at a job while she was attending college, so we had our evenings together. This is not always the case. There are many, perhaps a majority of single parents, who work two jobs or attend school and hold down a job. This type of schedule greatly limits the family time available. I know that many of these parents desire to spend more time with their children, but circumstances have made that desire a dream instead of reality.

Single parents can work to ensure that their time with their children is spent developing strong bonds. My situation was made even more special because I was an only child in a single parent family. My mom and I grew very close. Our relationship was almost that of sisters, we shared so much together. If I would have had siblings, I'm sure Mom would have made the same efforts

135

to help them feel special, but as it was I benefited by being an only child. My mom made a lot of time schedule sacrifices to make sure she could be with me. She didn't miss any of my band or choir concerts, piano recitals, school plays, or other extracurricular activities from elementary through senior high school. I knew my mom was in the audience whenever I performed.

Mom spent time with my friends also. She was there to make lunch runs for our yearbook staff and pep club. My friends knew her as "Mom" because she took time to get to know them and help them on a personal level.

Single parents who have little time with their children need to become very creative in order to maximize the time they do have together. Leaving kitchen cleanup until younger children go to bed gives more evening time to spend together. And doing physically active or interactive things together means more to most children than simply watching a video.

Although household chores are often viewed negatively and can become another activity that robs family time, a little creativity can turn chores into a family activity. Single parents may have everyone help with each of the chores so that family members have fellowship while they work. Other single parents divide the chores among all family members and everyone does assigned chores during a set chore time. Many single parents have discovered that some chores can be totally neglected or done less thoroughly or less frequently. Any of these ideas create family oneness and free up more time to be together.

Make Moving a Positive Experience

My mom graduated from college at the end of my second grade school year. Her job hunting resulted in employment in a city seventy miles away from my hometown. I was at an age when the move seemed more like an adventure than a negative experience. If this move had occurred later in my life or if I had been an insecure child, perhaps it would have been more traumatic for me.

Uprooting the home environment can be a negative experience for single parent families, and the uprooting can take various forms. In many single parent families the initial uprooting takes place at the time of the death of one parent or a divorce if the custodial parent has to move to a different home. This change in the family situation can cause anxiety for the children as they look to their future. Their secure environment is shaken, creating fear and doubt. The initial trauma may be short-lived, but it may have long-term effects. The single parent needs to be alert to signs of negative reaction to such instances (i.e., behavior change, attitude change, physical change).

The home environment can also be uprooted physically throughout a child's life as the single parent relocates. In *The Nation's Families 1960–1990,* Masnick and Bane state that the average single parent home moves several times every couple of years.[1]

In my life from ages eight to seventeen we moved four times. Each time we moved I had to find new friends and adjust to new schools and homes. Mom was very sensitive to my needs, and so twice our moves were timed to coincide with my normal school changes (i.e., elementary to junior high). Other than our initial move to the city of Mom's employment, we always relocated within the same city.

Masnick and Bane's research found that, especially among single mothers, local moves were a common trend. The reasons given most often for these types of moves were reduction in available finances, changes in parental employment, convenience needs, or to escape from parents or a former spouse.[2] These relocations are understandable, but they can be detrimental to the home environment unless steps are taken to minimize the disruption. (See chapter 11 for further ways single parents can help make relocation easier on the children.)

Find Good Role Models for Your Children

Another negative consequence of living in a single parent family is the absence of one of the parental role models. If the mother is the parent raising the children, there is no male parental role being filled. The opposite, of course, is true when a man is raising the children. These missing role models can be supplied in many ways on a temporary basis by friends, dating partners, family members, teachers, or coaches, but the consistency of the role model is lost. I was fortunate because my great uncle was around our family quite often, and we spent our summers and holidays at his house. (See chapters 22 and 23 for further information on this important topic.)

Live within Your Income

Obviously one less income in a family results in less available money. Many single parents face living with less resources. What income they have now may not be as constant or reliable as previous income. Alimony and child support payments may not be paid regularly or on time. Having to pay alimony can deplete a single parent's income. Sometimes there are employment changes that impact a single parent family's resources.

Masnick and Bane also point out that even though income may fluctuate, expenses remain constant and even may escalate for the single parent. Housing and utilities, which were previously paid by two incomes (or at least a larger income in most cases), are now a challenge. The single parent finds that compromises must be made to cut the expenses. Usually the areas of expense that are adjusted include food, clothing, and recreation, and the family may move into more affordable, although less desirable, housing.

This financial compromise, which is a negative, can be made more positive by a creative parent. Recreation can be more home and family based, which will unite the family and allow additional parent/child bonding. Single parents need to remember that how they handle their money will influence the way their children will deal with money. So living on a budget, curbing impulse buying, and comparison shopping are a must.

Look for Teaching Opportunities

Among the positive aspects of the single parent home is the opportunity to teach children to become responsible. I learned early in life that some chores wouldn't be done if I didn't help.

My mom made sure I learned to be a good steward of my time and money. She stressed that my schoolwork was top priority and made sure my homework was completed.

I also learned financial responsibility through what my mother taught me and by her example. Mom instilled in me the importance of saving money and frugality with funds. When going on shopping trips together, Mom would share with me reasons why a certain item that we liked was not being purchased. Many of those conversations help me avoid unnecessary spending today.

Eliminate Destructive Conflict

During my childhood there was very little negative conflict since there was no other adult or siblings to contribute to the clashes. My growing-up years were not interrupted by parental fighting. I didn't have to take sides (except my own whenever I disagreed with Mom). My peaceful home environment shaped my concept of what a home should be. My picture is of a loving, warm family atmosphere. This is a definite and positive result of the single parent home my mother structured for me.

Many children of divorced parents experience a lot of conflict, and they may come to believe that such behavior is normal and expected. However, single parents can develop a primary home environment that is close to conflict-free and learn productive ways to resolve conflicts between children and with the children.

Instead of always arguing with a former spouse, single parents can choose to communicate with courtesy. Arguing resolves very little and definitely upsets the children. If a single parent needs to confront a former spouse, I suggest doing it in a neutral location with just the adults present or with a neutral third party to assist. It's important that children don't overhear or have to listen to one parent belittle, mock, or criticize the other.

Encourage Children to Develop Independence

I learned independence growing up in a one-parent home. Because my mother didn't have a man to help with household

139

and automobile maintenance, she changed electrical fuses, fixed door locks, did emergency plumbing repairs, and performed various other repair jobs. I watched her learn from mistakes and saw her use sources of guidance for accomplishing these tasks. Through her example I learned that a person can try new experiences. I saw that I didn't necessarily need to rely on another person to get me through life's emergencies.

Of course, Mom always asked Jesus for help and strength. She taught me to do that also. She has said many times that she would not have survived and overcome as much as she did without Christ.

My mom also showed me, however, that there are times when a professional or skilled individual is needed. She was willing to ask people for help at those times. That was a good lesson for me: Be independent, but know when to ask for or accept help.

Accept with Grace What You Cannot Change

Perhaps the greatest benefit I received from my family situation was the realization that being single is not wrong or bad. I'm sure my mom had some lonely times, but she never let me know about them. She had several good friends, both single and married adults. Many of her friends became friends of mine also. Mom was content (Phil. 4:11); what a valuable example.

I hear so many single adults today stating that they are unhappy being single. They are constantly seeking a potential mate and feel unfulfilled. This is not a worry for me. I realize that God is in control and is using me in the ministry. In a church world that seems preoccupied with marriage and family, it is good to be accepted in my singleness.

My mother was very involved in the church. I saw her involvement accepted, which solidified my positive feelings regarding singleness. I saw Mom deal with problems creatively and saw her survive and overcome. I am grateful for the example my mother gave me, and I know that whether I remain single or I find a mate God has provided for me, serving God is my goal. I am and will be content in any circumstance as long as God is with me and I follow the divine will.

Cheryl Macoy is the former district director of single adults for the Central Florida Nazarene District. She is involved in planning the Nazarene Single Adult Solocons. She also is Sunday school superintendent and the worship pianist in her church and serves on the district council of children's ministries. She is a graduate of Mid-America Nazarene University with a B.A. degree in church music and Christian education.

13

Having Special Needs

BRYAN GRANT

oday the church is being called on more than ever before to train up children in the way they should go (Prov. 22:6) due to the overwhelming increase in divorces and unwed mothers. In fact, only half of the adults in America are married, but single parents lead as the fastest growing defined population segment.[1] Richard Estrada reported that the number of children involved in a divorce annually exceeds one million.[2] Therefore, even though the divorce rate dropped slightly in recent years, the actual number of children of divorce steadily increased. Because of this, the church must be available to aid, assist, and support the spiritual and emotional requirements of both single parents and their children. Children of divorce have special needs.

They Need God

All children (and all adults) need God, but children of divorced or widowed parents have a special need for God, who fills in for the absent parent (see Job 29:12). In times of difficulty and crisis, many of us turn to God, and children are no exception. "I talk to God every day," nine-year-old Jenny told her Sunday school teacher. "I ask God to help me be strong and help Mommy. There's only the two of us since Daddy died."

The church is one place where children can learn about God and learn to know God on a personal basis. So single parents must be encouraged to ensure their children are in regular attendance not only in worship services but also in Sunday school and midweek programs. Doug Easterday says that parents can mistakenly go from asking the children which restaurant they want to visit to asking whether or not they want to attend church.[3] While it is appropriate to allow children choices about many things, such as where to eat, it is not appropriate to offer them a choice about attending church.

Many of us do not wish to visit a doctor, but to maintain a healthy body, a regular medical checkup is advisable and required by some insurance companies for preventive maintenance. In the same way, church attendance should not be a matter of choice but one of commitment to a necessity for spiritual health. As Christian parents bring their children to church, they are providing one more positive influence in their lives.

They Need Reassurance

Children who have gone through a trauma, such as the divorce of their parents or losing a parent through death, often experience self doubts and anxieties about being abandoned further. To some degree children of all ages seem to assume some responsibility for their parents' divorce. Young children may believe that failure to obey, get along with siblings, or do chores resulted in one parent leaving. Older children may suspect that their problems at school or in the neighborhood or the financial stress of providing for a family caused one of the parents to give up on the marriage. Adult children sometimes wonder if there was something they could have done to prevent the deterioration of their parents' relationship. Children need reassurance that they are not responsible for any decisions their parents make. And this reassurance must be given several times before a child can even begin to accept the truth.

The second thing children need reassurance about is that the remaining or custodial parent will not abandon them. Very young children may develop a strong attachment to and dependency on the parent with whom they spend most of their time. Without defining their fear of abandonment, they demonstrate their insecurity by clinging and refusing to allow the parent out of their sight. Older children often become determined to have their parent's full attention whenever they are together. They can make conversation with friends almost impossible for their parent. Single parents can recognize these fears and anxieties and give their children the needed reassurance.

The church can also help by providing stable relationships with the children. As children learn they can count on seeing and talking with certain adults and friends every Sunday at church, they can develop a sense of security. The circle of people the children see as dependable and reliable in their lives widens to include those members of the church who take time to cultivate friendships and relationships with them.

These relationships also help children cope with the loneliness that often occurs when one parent is no longer in the home. Loneliness is one of the results of the trauma of divorce, according to the single parents in Green Acres Baptist Church in Tyler, Texas. "My son is experiencing loneliness coupled with depression because of his father leaving us," one single mother said. Another stated, "My son continues to ask when Daddy is coming home."

Single parents appreciate when church members step in and fulfill some of the relational needs of the children. Caring for one another in this way is part of the purpose of the body of Christ.

They Need Healing

Children need a divorce or grief recovery ministry just as much as do adults. For too long we have simply patted children on the head, given them milk and cookies, and told them not to cry. We have expected them to grieve without acting out, to heal without help, and to understand without explanations.

Today there are resources for churches to use when developing a support group for grieving children. These programs help children identify their negative emotions, appropriately express their grief, and strengthen their faith in God. The divorce recovery ministry of your church is not complete if you ignore the children's grief.[4]

They Need Mentoring

Children of divorced families, especially females, have difficulty trusting other adults. More often than not this distrust is focused on males, perhaps because more children live with single mothers than with single fathers. For children to grow up with the ability and willingness to trust people, they need positive experiences during their formative years.

The church—married couples and single adults alike—can reach out to children with the intent to prove trustworthiness and to develop trust. Making and keeping commitments to children, choosing to spend time with children, and listening to and valuing the opinion of children are ways to restore their faith in others.

Just as Paul mentored young Timothy, the adults in your church can provide spiritual guidance and direction to the children in your single parent ministry. A model for mentoring is provided in chapter 22 of this book.

They Need Role Models

Children of divorced or widowed families may grow up without a clear idea of how two-parent families relate, work together, and resolve problems and conflicts. One way children can learn how men and women interact in a marriage is by associating with two-parent families. The church can facilitate this learning process by having a single parent family and a two-parent family adopt each other as described in chapter 23 of this book.

They Need Same-Sex Adult Relationships

Separate from the need for developing trust in adults, receiving spiritual guidance, or having role models is the need children have for same-sex adult relationships. These may or may not be provided by the same people who are filling their other needs. Single parents can assist one another in meeting this need of their children.

John has a daughter who at age fourteen is rapidly becoming a young woman. John is not a doctor nor knowledgeable in answering his daughter's questions on women and their physical and psychological maturing. Nancy has a thirteen-year-old boy who is embarrassed to ask her about the changes he is experiencing through puberty. John and Nancy are single adults, Christian friends in a local church, and experiencing similar needs for adults of the opposite sex in the lives of their children.

John and Nancy made friends with each other's children and became available to discuss difficult subjects with them. Periodically John and Nancy meet to discuss any concerns they feel the other should be aware of and ways of resolving the children's issues. John takes Nancy's son fishing, camping, canoeing, and to ball games. Nancy teaches John's daughter to cook and takes her shopping and to activities they both enjoy. In this way, Nancy and John have taken Galatians 6:2 to heart and are helping each other in a special way.

They Need Grandparents

Grandparents play a wonderful part in raising children, and children can develop a special relationship with Grandma and Grandpa. Grandparents can be more involved with loving and enjoying the children than with teaching and disciplining them, so they are usually remembered as adults with whom to have fun. Yet many children of divorced or widowed parents do not live near enough to their biological grandparents to enjoy these relationships. In such cases the church has another opportunity to minister to these children with surrogate grandparents.

Many churches are now including a special emphasis on the role of senior adults in the life of the church. One way senior members can be involved is to participate in a surrogate grand-parenting program. Senior adults, especially those who may be experiencing feelings of no longer being useful, usually welcome the challenge to love, inspire, and spur to greatness a young member of their church.

A surrogate grandparenting program is easy to organize. Interested seniors and children of single parent families are matched up. When the program is first initiated, a party could be held to introduce participants to one another and to break the ice. Monthly dinners, breakfasts, Sunday lunches, or parties will allow the participants to share some of the fun experiences they have enjoyed.

They Need Christian Values

The church can be an important source of learning Christian values and their scriptural bases. A common problem for children of divorced parents is the differing lifestyles of their parents.

Tony was ordered by the courts to stay with his mother on the weekends and his father during the week. His mother's lifestyle includes entertaining men overnight, heavy drinking, and vulgar language. She sets no curfew for Tony, leaves him to cook his own meals, and allows him to watch anything he wants to on television.

Tony's father, on the other hand, has become a Christian since the divorce and has adopted a totally different lifestyle. Rules are enforced, homework required, television monitored, and language policed. So Tony is now catapulted back and forth between two different worlds each week.

When parents have conflicting lifestyles, children become confused. They may question which parent is right. The church can participate in training children in the right ways (Prov. 22:6) by not only teaching what is right but also focusing on the scriptural basis for each of the values, morals, and ethics that are taught. In this way children see what God says about right and wrong and have a higher authority on whom to rely for guidance in their decision making. (There are a variety of resources for teaching biblical values available through your local Christian bookstore. Also see chapter 27, "Teaching Spiritual Disciplines.")

They Need Love

When parents divorce, children often wonder if they are still part of a family. They fear that if it is possible to stop loving one's spouse, it may be possible to stop loving one's children. The need to feel loved can cause some children to become compliant, afraid to risk alienating the remaining parent, or to become demanding of parental attention. The demands may be direct: "Please play with me" or "Please read to me." Or they may be indirect: interrupting, becoming disruptive at school, regressing to former childish behaviors, or disobeying.

It is the responsibility of the church of Jesus Christ to reach out and love all children, including the children of single parents. Love makes children feel welcome, whole, and included as a part of the community of faith. Love reaches past behaviors to the heart and gives a message of healing and hope. Love is part of the Christian message, for God is love and we are to love one another with godly love (1 John 4:7–10). One of the greatest gifts a church can give to children of single parents is love.

They Need Recognition

Children of divorced parents may experience a loss of self-esteem as they blame themselves for their parents' divorce and as they cope with multiple changes in their lives. Therefore, one way to minister to children is to provide appropriate recognition of their significance and of their contribution to the church community.

Ask children to be greeters for church services, hand out bulletins, participate in work days, accompany adults on visitation calls, or be involved in other ways. List their names in church bulletins along with those of adult contributors. Thank them from the pulpit. Find creative ways to recognize the children in your congregation.

Another way to give children recognition is to sponsor birthday parties. No child should have to go without a birthday party due to time restraints or lack of funds. As the single adult minister, you could compile a birthday list and plan a monthly birthday party for all of the children having birthdays in the month. Some church members could donate decorations, cakes, ice cream, and party favors. Others could participate as entertainers, games coordinators, and food servers. Present these parties to the church as opportunities for the body of Christ to serve one another and to minister to single parent families.

They Need Prayer

Children not only need the prayer support of the church, but they also need to understand the unique and awesome power of prayer. One way to facilitate this process is to print prayer request cards. Use your imagination to design the cards and include Scripture promises about prayer. Give the children the cards and encourage them to write their requests so that others can pray specifically for them. The blank cards can be kept in Sunday school classrooms, in worship center pew racks, or on tables in the church lobby. This easy accessibility encourages parents to take the cards home and get their children's prayer requests in writing. The prayer request cards may be handed to a teacher or church leader or be placed in the offering plates during worship services.

The prayer requests can be shared during a special night of prayer, in a church newsletter, or in small groups. During Sunday school, children could pray for each other's requests.

If the prayer request cards have a place for the children to write their addresses, those people praying for that request could send notes of encouragement to the child. Most children would be excited to receive a "prayer-gram" in the mail. These become reminders of God's never-ending love and concern as evidenced by the church.

They Need Christian Friends

Friends are critical in the lives of children. The wrong friends can start a child down the wrong road in life. The right friends can encourage a child to a godly lifestyle. Therefore, the youth group organization of your church plays a vital part in the lives of the children of single parent families, for it is there they can find the right kind of friends. Because young people desire to be accepted by their peers, single parents will want to provide Christian peers for their children. By associating with other Christians, children can develop strength of convictions, healthy relationships, accountability, and even lifelong confidants.

They Need Their Childhood

Ken Brumley aptly stated, "The church needs to reach out and help children who are being forced to accept adult responsibilities."[5] Sometimes divorce or the death of a parent robs children of their innocence and forces enormous decisions to be made long before their developing character is established. Children in single parent families sometimes seem to grow up too fast. Single parents may be tempted to place too much of the emotional burden on their children. They mustn't; children need to be children.

The tendency for single parents to allow their children to take the place of the missing spouse by letting sons become "the man of the house" and daughters to become "Mom's best friend" must be resisted. And church members must be careful not to reinforce this by making such comments as, "You be sure to take care of your mother and little sister, okay?"

They Need Fun

Children need to have fun. In the early days after a divorce or a death of a parent, the home may not provide a lot of opportunities for laughter and play. The stresses of rebuilding a lifestyle, moving, making adjustments, and grieving can rob not only the single parent but also the children of normal enjoyment.

The church can plan opportunities for fun for the children by making every holiday a celebration. For Easter, Christmas, St. Patrick's Day, Valentine's Day, Halloween, Labor Day, the Fourth of July, and any other holiday, use the church gym or a large classroom for a party. Enlist a clown, magician, or other entertainer. Advertise the party; provide refreshments; arrange for contests and games. Have several adults present to supervise, encourage participation by the shy children, and enter into the games with the children.

Due to financial strains placed upon the single parent's income, the cost of going out to eat, to the movies, to theme parks, and on family vacations may be prohibitive. Having a video night at church complete with popcorn and soft drinks (which can be sold for a nominal charge) is a cost-effective alternative. Parents can participate in the selection of the videos to be shown. With the right publicity, this can be an effective outreach for single parents and their children. Single parent friends and coworkers might come to a video night before they would come to a church service or single adult ministry.

Because so many videos are inappropriate for viewing by children, the church might form a committee to buy good children's video programs for the church library. If funds are insufficient for this, a list of approved videos could be presented to the church in a bulletin insert. Individual church members who wish to do so could purchase a tape and donate it to the library. These tapes can be used not only for the video night but also as a checkout library for home viewing by church families. (This process would apply to educational books and tapes as well as entertainment videos.)

Evaluate Your Ministry

In summary, church leaders who want to meet the needs of the children of single parents should:

1. Pray for God's guidance in reaching those children and their families.

151

2. Put themselves in the place of a single parent and ask: Does this church have an effective ministry for my children? Does this church make me and my children feel welcome? Are there people in the church willing to partner with me?
3. Identify people who care about meeting the needs of single parents and their children and enlist their help in implementing the programs outlined in this chapter.

Rev. Bryan Grant has an M.Div. from Southwestern Baptist Theological Seminary and is currently associate minister to single adults at Green Acres Baptist Church, Tyler, Texas. His ministry includes giving leadership training seminars and single parent workshops emphasizing divorce recovery.

14

Struggling for Control of Their Lives

TOM MC ENROE

*D*ivorce wreaks havoc on children. Most of the modern research is in agreement that the negative effects of divorce on children are long-lasting, often lingering into adulthood. Speaking of the long-term effects of divorce on children and adolescents, one ten-year study concluded, "We have in recent years become increasingly aware of the enduring effects of psychic trauma, and these effects may not be visible immediately in subsequent specific behaviors or symptoms, but may forever shatter the individual's guiding conception of the world as relatively safe and reliable."[1]

This same study also concluded that the older the child, the greater the effect, with older teenagers being the most vulnerable to long-lasting damage.[2] Other studies have shown that children of divorce have a higher incidence of overtly aggressive behavior and sexual behavior problems[3] as well as a higher risk of dropping out of school, being out of work, or if female, becoming pregnant as a teenager.[4] Greg Cynaumon, a former Los Angeles police officer and now an expert on single parent issues, confirms these conclusions in his own research and through his experience in law enforcement.[5] In addition, post-traumatic stress disorder (PTSD) may be a factor, which means the full effects of the divorce on the children may not be felt for months or even years.

How Children Try to Control

Given these facts, it is no surprise that children often react to divorce by trying to grab for some kind of control over the situation. Sometimes this is no more than a desperate attempt to fix what has gone wrong. More often it is simply a way to survive emotionally. Children may adopt codependent roles, pit parent against parent, spiral into antisocial and disruptive behavior, become overly responsible, attempt to reconcile the parents, try to sabotage any new relationship a parent may have, or try to matchmake for one of the parents.

At the core, all of these strategies are attempts to avoid the deep grief issues and helplessness that are at the heart of experiencing the divorce of one's parents. They are reactive strategies, which ultimately become blockades to true healing and recovery. The following fictitious composites of real stories will help illustrate typical ways children seek to regain control in a setting of divorce.

Case 1: Rachel and Julie

Janet is a forty-something single mom with two teenage daughters. Her divorce has just been finalized, and her daughters see their father on a sporadic basis. He has a new live-in girlfriend.

In her effort to control her situation, Rachel, the thirteen-year-old daughter, has taken it upon herself to report to her mother all of the inside information she can gather about her dad's new relationship, and she has been very careful to paint as negative a picture as possible. While visiting her father, Rachel subconsciously tries to sabotage her dad's new relationship. Janet has fallen into the habit of listening to Rachel's accounts of the new relationship and subconsciously rewards Rachel for her reconnaissance efforts.

On the other hand, Julie, Janet's seventeen-year-old daughter, has adopted a completely different controlling technique. She detests her father and spends as little time as possible with him. Instead, she has immersed herself in managing the house for her mother. She helps with laundry and cleaning and asserts herself in making family decisions. Her mother welcomes the help and often out of sheer exhaustion yields more and more responsibility to her daughter. Julie prides herself on her strength and increasingly takes care of her hurting mom.

Case 2: David and John

Mark and Wendy, an upwardly mobile young couple, had two sons, ages eight and twelve. The pressures of work and money and Mark being away on business eventually eroded their intimacy, and Wendy nurtured a secret affair with a coworker in her firm. Mark, often loud and abusive, learned of the situation and threatened Wendy and the kids. She filed for a restraining order, he moved out, and eventually they divorced. Wendy's affair also failed, as it became clear that the affair had been motivated not out of love for the coworker but by a need to escape Mark's abusive behavior. Because of Mark's threats, the children were restricted from visiting with their dad unless a neutral third party was present.

David, the twelve-year-old son, normally a passive, compliant boy, began to fight with schoolmates. His grades plummeted, and he started associating with gang types. Wendy was at a loss as to how to handle the situation and was actually afraid of David, so she sidestepped the problem, rationalizing that it was just a phase. Reality set in when the police picked up David for vandalizing a car. These behaviors were David's attempts to control his situation.

John, the younger son, exercised control by becoming withdrawn and clingy around Wendy. Wendy was attracted by his neediness, and she felt a sense of power in being there for John. Her fear of David and sense of powerlessness drove her ever more

155

toward John, who soaked up as much love as Mom could give. Mom felt valued and useful as John continued to cling to her.

Case 3: Sylvia and Alice

In our third scenario, all the parties are adults. Mary is a divorcee in her fifties with several grown children and grandchildren. She has been single twelve years after divorcing her alcoholic husband of twenty-five years. The marriage had been a nightmare from the beginning.

When Mary casually mentioned to Sylvia, one of her grown daughters, that she might be open to dating again, Sylvia told her sister Alice. Soon the two of them decided to take control and set up a date for Mary with Ron, a man Alice knew to be single and lonely.

After the very first date Ron began talking about long-term commitment. Mary had a lot of reservations, but Alice and Sylvia encouraged their mother to go for it. Mary caved in to their pressure and married Ron within a month. Very soon Mary found out Ron had a history of alcohol abuse and bouts of rage. Mary felt bewildered, yet because of her insecurity she decided, as she had in her first marriage, to make the best of it.

All three of these scenarios share a common issue: control. In the chaos of divorce, both young and adult children are thrown into situations that are for the most part out of their control. Since one of the most feared states in human experience is to be helpless, it is only natural to expect that children of divorce will, by whatever means, attempt to regain some kind of control over their situations, even if it is at the expense of their own healing or that of others.

How children strive for control varies greatly from family to family, and almost every case is complex in nature involving many variables. The above scenarios are given as examples of common ways children grope for power in a single parent setting. They are oversimplified in order to make the key issues clear. In reality, many other variables factor in, such as the family legacy of the parents, emotional and personality issues, and the level of spiritual maturity.

Resolving Issues of Control

Single parents in your ministry may be experiencing these types of problems with the children trying to take control or with giving up control to the children. As leaders of single parent ministries, we can assist single parents in understanding control issues and resolving them through acknowledging their powerlessness and helplessness, relying on God, and intervening in the family.

Acknowledge Their Powerlessness and Helplessness

Many children whose parents divorce feel powerless and helpless and that they are not in control of their lives. Being powerless in a situation of intense grief and pain is a terrible experience for anyone. Grasping for control is a natural reaction, both in single parents and in their children. Manipulating for control is one way children attempt to deny the reality of feeling powerless to prevent or fix a divorce.

Facing and accepting one's helplessness and powerlessness and allowing oneself to fully experience loss is the beginning of healing. This is a great paradox. Coming to face and accept the thing that is most feared leads to freedom, change, and new beginnings.

Rely on God

Biblically, in the most basic sense all humans are helpless before God. We cannot control God. We cannot make God love us or forgive us, and we cannot do anything that will obligate the Almighty to come to our assistance. Because of sin and ignorance, all of us fall short of God's standard and are in need of forgiveness and healing. We are completely at the mercy of God.

Jesus often spoke paradoxically, "Whoever finds his life will lose it, and whoever loses his life for my sake will find it" (Matt. 10:39). Or, "Unless a kernel of wheat falls to the ground and

157

dies, it remains only a single seed. But if it dies, it produces many seeds. The man who loves his life will lose it, while the man who hates his life in this world will keep it for eternal life" (John 12:24–25). The truth Jesus was alluding to is simply that new life comes only on the heels of the death of the old life.

Paul says, "When we were still powerless, Christ died for the ungodly" (Rom. 5:6). Because we are powerless before God, our only hope is that the Lord will share divine power with us and act on our behalf. This, of course, God has done in the person of Jesus and his work for us on the cross. Receiving God's forgiveness and new life begins when we face our own helplessness and powerlessness and trust in God.

Similarly, children of divorce must come to the place where their own powerlessness in the face of their loss is fully acknowledged. This necessarily entails ceasing attempts to manipulate things through control. By giving up and accepting the situation, new healing power becomes available through the grace of God. Paradoxically, the road to self-control and spiritual and emotional growth involves a releasing of control to God.

Parental Intervention

It has been said that a healthy single parent family begins with a healthy single parent. There is much truth to this. However, many single parents were not healthy in their own childhood years and in their marriages. When divorce occurs and they become single parents, often their own pain and unresolved issues make it difficult to cope with, let alone resolve, the issues facing the children.

On the positive side, children of single parents will still respond to the direction of their parents, and if a single parent takes steps toward healing, the children will tend to notice, learn, and benefit. What a child sees happening in his or her parent will set the tone for the direction the child goes. If single parents remain in denial and attempt to manipulate or avoid the pain, then they can expect the children to follow suit. If children see the parents face their own powerlessness and pain and begin to accept them, the children will have a harder time keeping up the walls of denial.

In short, the healing of children of divorce is a family affair, and as the adults in the family heal, so will the children. The following are some practical suggestions you may want to share with the single parents in your ministry to help them cope with control issues in their children.

1. *Single parents must come to terms with their own powerlessness over life's situations and relinquish control to God.* Few single parents are capable of being instruments of healing to their children without outside help. Fortunately, the Lord provides power and resources through his people. Church support groups, friends, pastors, and counselors are essential parts of any single parent's support network. When single parents seek support, they demonstrate to the children that it is okay to ask for help. Surrendering to God means accepting the divine provision and resources, which are often provided through others. Isolation is the surest route to disaster in single parenting.

2. *Single parents must recognize that power and control games are normal for children facing trauma and that it will take time for them to fully face their loss.* Help your single parents understand why children who lose a parent through death or divorce adopt the roles that they do and how they try to shield themselves from the full impact of their situations. Understanding can give a single parent confidence to lead the children firmly, yet patiently, to the core grief issues of loss and helplessness. This can lead to an eventually diminishing need in the children to adopt codependent roles or try unhealthy methods of control.

Again, single parents must model in their own lives the process they desire to see happen in their children. The healing process may take much time. Patience, acceptance, and willingness to allow the children to take small steps are musts for any single parent.

3. *Single parents must avoid at all costs becoming emotionally dependent on the children.* In the scenarios given earlier, a common thread weaving through each story was that the parents had in some way become emotionally dependent on their children. It is imperative that every single parent have a strong support system of friends and counselors, but this support system should not include the kids.

4. *Single parents cannot shield the children from the pain of their loss.* Single parents who see the children experience sadness and loss often have guilt feelings. So those single parents may try to shield their children from the pain that is a natural part of what they have experienced. They may overcompensate or try to make up for the situation with extra gifts or fun opportunities. It is very difficult for a single parent to witness the grief process in their children, especially when the cause of that grief was the actions of the parents. Yet the beginnings of healing come only after the deep pain and helplessness are experienced. Therefore, coming alongside their children in their pain is necessary, but trying to minimize, repress, or shield the children from their own grief is counterproductive.

5. *Single parents need to set firm boundaries that are lovingly maintained in their households.* Single parents who have the primary custody of the children should draw firm emotional and behavioral boundaries in their homes. When a single parent refuses to become emotionally dependent on the children, he or she has set a firm emotional boundary. When the parent refuses to try to meddle in the affairs of the ex-spouse, a concrete relational boundary has been set. When parents model their own recovery by seeking a support team and accepting God's grace in the midst of grief and helplessness, definite spiritual boundaries have been set, and the children have the opportunity to learn that ultimately only God can bring healing.

6. *Single parents need to strive for cooperation with the ex-spouse when possible in the healing of the children.* Often the circumstances of a divorce preclude effective communication between the divorced parents regarding the raising of their children. Where possible, however, parents should try to discuss the issues facing their children in a way that puts the needs of the children in clear focus. Sometimes this takes the help of counselors and third parties. When a divorce occurs, a marriage ends, but coparenting by both parties does not. Children do better when both of their parents are communicating responsibly regarding parenting.

7. *Single parents must allow for fun, spontaneity, and laughter to enter into the single parenting process.* Even in the grips of

a divorce, a young child should be permitted to be a kid. A teenager should be encouraged to be a teenager and nothing more.

Sometimes the deep emotional release of tears shared with others can lead to laughter and lightheartedness, especially if the tears were long overdue. Part of the joy of being free with one's painful emotions is that it opens the door to positive emotions as well. Finding the ability in the grace of God to laugh, joke, and be spontaneous in the midst of recovery can literally be a lifesaving skill.

Resolution Is Possible

God is an expert at bringing surprises of joy out of seemingly hopeless situations. A wrong theology or poor attitude can cause single parents to miss these surprises. God's grace is always made perfect in human weakness, and the single parent journey is no exception. Laughter can spring from a sea of tears.

Being helpless before God puts us in the best position to be helped. When single parents truly come to God in humility and helplessness and receive power and forgiveness, they are on their way to regaining the proper balance of control in the family.

Rev. Tom McEnroe is the pastor with single adults at Calvary Church in Los Gatos, California. Tom has been in the ministry for thirteen years and in single adult ministry for most of that time. He has an M.Div. from Fuller Theological Seminary and an M.Th. from University of Nottingham in England. Tom has served on the national board for the Network of Single Adult Leaders. Tom is married to Katherine, and they have two children.

Part 3

THE CHALLENGES
FOR MINISTRY
WITH SINGLE PARENTS
AND THEIR CHILDREN

15

Demonstrating Scriptural Christianity

BOBBIE REED

"Religion that God our Father accepts as pure and faultless is this: to look after orphans and widows in their distress and to keep oneself from being polluted by the world" (James 1:27). The Holy Spirit included in Scripture several instructions on the care of orphans and widows that God outlined for the Jews in the Old Testament. And we see that those same expectations continued into New Testament times when we read about the early church in the Epistles of Paul and James. Reaching out to help single parents and their children in their distress is but an extension of that mandate.

A Historical Background

When God told Adam and Eve to have children, the institution of the family was established. As we read the Old Testament, we see that the social order revolved around family relationships. People inherited through their families. Sons inherited land from their fathers, wives and children were cared for by their husbands

165

and fathers. Spoils of war were divided by families within the tribes of Israel.

There were some people, however, who did not fit the family social structure. So God made special provisions for these people, which included strangers (foreigners who had embraced Judaism), the poor, the oppressed, widows, orphans, and in some cases the Levites.[1]

Strangers did not belong to a tribe nor to a family within a tribe, so they would not automatically receive a share of captured goods. So God made special rules to provide for the strangers, who were to have the same legal rights as the Jews (see Exod. 12:49; Lev. 24:22; Num. 15:16, 29; Deut. 24:17). Dropped sheaves during harvest were to be left for the strangers, widows, and orphans (Deut. 24:19). Late ripening olives and grapes left on the vines or on the ground during harvest were to be left also for the strangers, widows, and orphans (Deut. 24:20–21). And these same three groups were to share in the third-year tithes and the freewill contributions made during the Feast of Weeks (Deut. 14:29; 16:11; 26:12–13). The food that grew during each seventh year was to be harvested by the strangers and the poor (Exod. 23:10–11; Lev. 25:6). And God also said the strangers were to be accepted and loved as if they were Jews and members of the family (Lev. 19:34; Deut. 10:19).

The poor and the oppressed also came under God's personal protection and provision regardless of the reasons for the poverty: misfortune, mismanagement, or failure to inherit. In various passages we read that the Almighty lifts up the poor and gives them an inheritance (1 Sam. 2:8), protects the rights of the poor (Job 36:6; Ps. 72:4), delivers the poor and oppressed (Job 36:15), and promises them an inheritance in the kingdom of God (Luke 6:20). The Jews were instructed to return to the poor all of their forfeited possessions during the Year of Jubilee (Lev. 25:28). And the Jews were admonished to be compassionate and to give to the poor (Deut. 15:7). The Levites were included in the distribution of the special tithe at the end of each third year (Deut. 14:28–29).

Yet God's unique provision for the widows and orphans went beyond that for the other special groups. Psalm 68:5–6 says the Almighty takes the place of the missing parent and the missing husband by protecting the widow and placing the lonely in families. The Lord was described as the executor of justice, righteous judge, helper, defender, and reliever as well as the listener and giver of mercy to the orphans and widows (Exod. 22:22–24; Deut. 10:17; Pss. 10:14, 18; 82:3; 146:9; Isa. 1:17; Jer. 49:11; Hos. 14:3).

Specific actions were prohibited when dealing with widows and orphans. A widow's garments were not to be taken for a pledge (Deut. 24:12–17). Widows and orphans were not to be oppressed, robbed, taken advantage of, or afflicted in any way (Exod. 22:22–24; Deut. 24:17). The fields of orphans were not to be entered into by force (Prov. 23:10).

The Israelites were promised that if they complied with these instructions for caring for these groups of people, they would have favor with God (Isa. 1:17–19; Jer. 6–7). They were also warned that those who did not follow these instructions would be cursed (Deut. 27:19; Job 31:16–23; Isa. 10:1–3).

Jewish tradition incorporated God's special treatment for the widows and orphans. The tradition specified that Jews were not to hurt a widow because she already had a broken spirit. Widows were to be spoken to gently, shown respect, and spared bodily or mental grief, and their property was to be protected more carefully than one's own.[2]

The early Greek Christians criticized the Hebrew Christians for not taking adequate care of their widows during the daily distribution of the alms and food (Acts 6:1). It is clear from this incident that the expectation of caring for those with special needs was carried over into the new Christian community. It was regarded as more than a Jewish tradition but as God's revealed will for caring for those in need.

Paul wrote to Timothy about caring for widows. The first responsibility was placed on the other family members, but a second responsibility for their care was given to the church (1 Tim. 5:3–16).

In the Old Testament the term *widow* was used to include not only the woman who had no husband because of the death of a spouse but also the woman who had been discarded, divorced, desolated, bereaved, or forsaken.[3]

In 2 Samuel we read that Absalom had sexual relations with the ten concubines King David left behind when he fled Jerusalem. When David returned, he put those women away and would not go in to them again. He fed them and took care of them, but he kept them shut up until they died (2 Sam. 15:16; 16:15, 20–23; 20:3). According to 2 Samuel 20:3, they lived the rest of their lives as widows.

Another example of the use of the term is in reference to Israel being the adulterous wife of Jehovah because of a lack of faithfulness to God (Jer. 31:32). Hosea wrote about how the adulterous wife (Israel) was put away from Jehovah (Hosea 2:1–23), and Isaiah prophesied about the subsequent restoration to Jehovah with the promise that although Israel was as a woman forsaken, she would no longer remember the reproach of her "widowhood" (Isa. 54:4–6). In this case, the adulterous "woman" who was "put away" from God was referred to as being in "widowhood."

Applying the term broadly, then, we could say that all formerly married women are widows because some lost a husband through death and some once had spouses, and then through divorce were "put away" or "took themselves away" and were left without a husband. Since many of the needs of the truly widowed and the "divorced widowed" are the same, I believe that God's provision for widows can be expanded to include all women on their own—perhaps even never married women who no longer live at home under the care and protection of their biological fathers.

Orphans

The Old Testament term *fatherless* and the New Testament term *orphans* refers to those who did not have the protection of a father or parent, those who were lonely, and those who were bereft of a teacher, guide, or guardian.[4] Jewish literature addresses the need to care for the genuine orphans (those whose parents had died or who had been abandoned by parents).[5] They were to be taken care of, taken in, and taught the law. So the term *orphans* can be applied to those children of divorced or widowed parents who do not have both parents to teach, raise, and love them.

Single Parents and Their Children

In biblical times the Jews were to care for those who stood outside the family unit (widows and orphans) and for those who were strangers, the poor, and the oppressed. God's special patronage would be administered by the community.

Single parents and their children fit these categories in many ways, and God's special patronage must be administered by the community of faith, the church.

Some single parents and their children are oppressed. Children are labeled as disruptive, discipline problems, and dysfunctional because they come from a "broken home." Never married parents carry the stigma of having conceived children out of wedlock. Instead of oppressing them, the church must begin supporting single parents and their children emotionally, physically, spiritually, socially, psychologically, and at times, financially.

Some single parents are poor. They may be working for minimum wages, unemployed, on welfare, paying off the former spouse's debts, trying to make ends meet on an inadequate income, depending on child support payments that never arrive or are consistently late, or paying more child support than they can afford. Some single parents are homeless. Some live in shelters with almost nothing to call their own. Those of us who have been blessed by God must recognize that what we have belongs to the Lord, and these resources are given so that we can redistribute them to those in need (Luke 6:30–38).

Some single parents are strangers. Not many single parents and their children live with large, extended families who will or can take care of them. In fact, many single parents do not even live in geographical proximity to other family members. There is usually no one from whom to expect a large inheritance or a job in the family business. They may be very much the lonely strangers, isolated and on their own. As the church reaches out to embrace and include these single parents, they become members of the local church family. No longer strangers, not just friends, they are family.

All single parents can be treated as widows in an expanded application of the term. These widows need the church. In some cases the needs are physical, just as when God gave the original instructions. Physical needs include shelter, food, clothing, transportation, assistance with difficult tasks, and money. Other needs involve the protection of rights and assistance with the legal system. Many single parents have additional needs such as emotional support, recovery assistance, regaining self-esteem, developing a social network, fellowship, and spiritual development. While still fulfilling its primary mission of evangelizing the lost, the church can be a catalyst for meeting some of these needs of the widows.

However, if we only reach out to women who were formerly married, we fail to meet the needs of the single fathers. In a very real sense these men have the same needs as single mothers. The men can be also treated as widows.

The emphasis on the special protection of widows in the Bible reflects the cultural situation of that time. In the ancient world, men were expected to care for themselves, and women were to be cared for. Because there was no husband to care for a widow, and because there might be no living father to care for them, God stepped in and provided for the widows. Today, while there may be some needs that are unique to women who were formerly married, most of the basic needs of the formerly married are not gender specific. Men have many of the same needs as women. Single dads need the church just as much as single moms do.

Children of single parents are at least partial orphans. Children who no longer have two parents at home have some of the same needs as genuine orphans. Too often one of the parents becomes an absent parent, with intermittent, negligible, or no contact with the children. Even if children have frequent contact with the noncustodial parent, there are adjustments they must make to their family relationships. The church can be of assistance by offering support, instruction, role models, and love.

The Opportunity

Developing a ministry with single adults and their families is one way the church can carry out God's special patronage to those people who might otherwise get lost and feel abandoned or like strangers because they are not part of a traditional two-parent family. When we minister with single parents and their families, the church becomes their new family and provides the care God mandated.

Bobbie Reed was a single parent for ten years, and she has been an author, consultant, and speaker in the field of single adult and single parent ministries since 1974. She has authored thirty-three books and is assistant director of the Network of Single Adult Leaders. She holds a Ph.D. in social psychology and a D.Min. with an emphasis in single adult ministry.

16

Healing the Wounded Heart

DICK INNES

I was on the second date with the first woman I had gone out with after a twenty-five-year failed marriage. My date, whom I shall call Lynda, brought up the subject of marriage. She was very attractive, and I was flattered and excited by her interest in me. However, as the ink had barely dried on my divorce papers, I was not interested in discussing marriage. In fact, I felt a sense of panic.

"Are you angry with me because I've been divorced three times?" Lynda asked.

"Angry? No. Frightened? Yes!" I answered.

"Well, they were all turkeys," she commented defensively.

"Then why did you marry them?" I couldn't help asking.

Lynda was offended, and that was the end of my "Post-Divorce Romance, Chapter One."

Soon afterward Lynda started dating an alcoholic, but that relationship didn't last long. She quickly married again, this time to an abusive partner. The marriage lasted two years.

Lynda never seemed to take time for healing between relationships, and consequently she may be destined for repeated failures.

Everyone Needs Healing

God designed us for relationships. We are to have a special, loving relationship with the Lord (Luke 10:27), we are to love one another (John 13:34–35), and when we marry, we are to become one with our spouse (Eph. 5:28–33). When any of our relationships break apart, both parties are wounded and need healing. Problems that contributed to the failure of the relationship need to be examined in an effort to avoid similar problems in future relationships. It's almost an unwritten law that what we don't resolve, we are destined to repeat. It is either resolution or repetition.

Some single adults, like Lynda, bounce in and out of relationships and from one relationship to another without reflecting on and learning from their experiences. Other single adults, crushed by a rejection experience, retreat from any involvement, refusing to trust anyone as a partner ever again. The fear of being vulnerable imprisons their hearts, preventing love from hurting or blessing them. Some of these people rebuild otherwise happy lives and are content with the choice to remain unattached, but others allow bitterness to take root and remain victims for the rest of their lives.

Children who have lost a parent to death or whose parents divorce also have a need for healing. They experience a lot of confusing and conflicting feelings as they try to sort through the issues, emotions, and realities of the changes in their lives.

Some of the single parents and children who come to your ministry already will have experienced healing and will be living wholesome and happy lives in their one-parent families. Others will need healing and may not be ready for it. Many will have come to your ministry for help.

There are different types of healing ministries you may want to incorporate into your single adult ministry from which your single parents may benefit. These include: divorce recovery, grief recovery, relationship seminars, and recovery programs for children.

Divorce Recovery

In the early 1970s church leaders began to recognize that there was a need for divorce recovery and grief recovery programs for single again adults. So leaders such as Dr. Bill Flanagan and Rev. Jim Smoke began workshops and seminars to meet this need. Today divorce recovery programs can be found in most cities in the country.

Divorce recovery programs are offered in various formats ranging from a single weekend to a series of weekly meetings. The advantage of the weekend format is that a single adult may find making a commitment to set aside a weekend easier than committing one night a week for several weeks. Therefore, the participants get the entire block of information you want to present because they will be at all of the sessions.

On the other hand, the weekly meeting format seems to have a more lasting impact. Because participants are given information in small blocks and have a week to reflect and take action on that information, they are more likely to put into effect what they are studying. Also, one does not heal from a loss in one weekend, so the weekend format does not allow you to walk the journey with those who are grieving. The weekly meeting program, on the other hand, allows you to develop an ongoing relationship with the participants, see measurable growth and healing, and be available to encourage, assist, and affirm. Through recovery programs, we live out Paul's admonition to rejoice with those who rejoice and weep with those who weep (Rom. 12:15).

Most of the successful divorce recovery programs have a similar pattern of presenting information to the entire group followed by small group discussions using prepared questions. In most cases a discussion facilitator is assigned to each small group to keep the discussion on track. Facilitators are usually persons who have been through a recent divorce recovery program themselves and find that going through the program again as a facilitator further aids in their own healing. (See the resource list at the back of this book for written materials and video programs that will be useful when planning a divorce recovery ministry.)

Grief Recovery

The grief cycle experienced by widows and widowers is similar to that of divorced persons, but there need to be separate ministry programs for assisting each group to heal from their losses. One reason is that part of the healing for divorced persons is to let go of the past, to stop looking back, and to move beyond talking about the former spouse. On the other hand, part of the healing for widowed persons is to look back, remember the good times, and talk about the former spouse. So often widowed persons complain that no one will talk with them about the one who died.

The format for grief recovery programs is usually similar to that described for divorce recovery ministries. However, Dr. Harold Ivan Smith has developed a unique seminar for dealing with the reality of death. His primary focus is on grieving the death of a friend, but entire families have gone through his seminars and found healing for the loss of a loved one. (For more information on this program, contact Dr. Smith at the address in the resource section of this book.)

Relationship Seminars

Separate from recovery ministries is the need for relationship seminars for single adults. These seminars can assist single adults in learning more about themselves, why they are attracted to certain types of personalities, and how they tend to respond in relationships. Lynda could have benefited from a seminar that might have challenged her to consider why she seemed to have a relational radar that honed in on men whose symbiotic needs meshed with her unresolved issues.

If you can help single adults understand what went wrong in previous relationships, you may prevent future relationships from being dysfunctional. Often the problems are a result of being attracted to someone for unhealthy reasons. We are sometimes attracted to others because they repeat a pattern that was familiar in our childhood.

For instance, the son who grew up taking care of his mother and sisters may be attracted to a woman who needs someone to take care of her. Some people are attracted to anyone who will have them because of an overwhelming need to have someone in their lives. Other people overcompensate for past failures, such as the woman who was once married to a very dependent man and is now attracted to extremely independent men. Understanding what is behind one's attraction for another is an important step in learning to develop healthy relationships.

Relationship seminars can include such topics as:

sexuality
handling conflict
confronting productively
communicating clearly
forgiving
letting go of the past
learning to risk
dating
commitment
personality/temperament types
relating to friends in Christian love

Some of the single adults in your ministry may not have grown up with biblical principles being taught in their homes. This may be the first opportunity they have to learn what God has to say about how they ought to relate one to another. Be sure that your relationship seminars are based on Scripture and provide the references for the participants so they can do further study on their own.

Recovery Programs for Children

Children need recovery programs just as much as adults do. The responsibility for grief and divorce recovery programs for children may be assigned to the children's ministry or the single adult ministry of the church, but someone must provide help for the children.

A good way to schedule these programs is to hold them at the same time as the divorce or grief recovery programs for their parents. The sessions need to be interactive and physically involve the children in role-playing, acting out stories, using puppets, and drawing as ways to express their feelings about their loss. Using Bible stories that have elements to which the children can relate helps personalize the Scriptures for them. Examples include: Samuel, who didn't get to live with his parents and only saw them once a year (1 Sam. 1–3), John Mark, the young man who caused two partners to separate (Acts 12:25–13:5; 15:36–40), and Joseph, who moved to a new city and new home and was separated from his father and brothers (Gen. 37, 39–47). In each of the stories the children can see how God made good things happen in spite of the negative circumstances.

It is not necessary to be a child educator, counselor, or therapist to effectively conduct a recovery program for children. Resources that will help you in designing these programs are listed in the back of this book.

Love Heals

All of us are sinners, and none of us had perfect parents or perfect love as we grew up. Every family is dysfunctional to some degree. Consequently, we all need healing. The healing of our relationship with God comes through maintaining a right relationship with Jesus Christ; the health of this relationship is evidenced in our level of spiritual maturity. The healing of our relationships with others comes from repairing damaged emotions; the health of these relationships is reflected in our emotional maturity. Both of these are essential if we are to have healthy and loving relationships with God, ourselves, and others. As we are damaged emotionally through damaging relationships, we are healed emotionally through healing relationships.

Love is the foundation for all healing. That is, we are healed from past relationships when we choose to love again with the *agape* love we learn from God. If we model our love for others on God's love for us, then we can develop wholesome, healthy relationships. Paul said that if we just lived the law of love, we would automatically fulfill all of the requirements of the law (Rom. 13:8–10).

For healthy living and wholesome relationships it is essential that we learn to live this kind of love. Jesus showed it to us, not only through his death on the cross, but also through others who are safe, loving, accepting, and affirming. James, the brother of our Lord, gave us a divine principle for healing when he said, "Confess your sins to each other and pray for each other so that you may be healed" (James 5:16).

If you are to help the single parents and their children to be healed from their pain and their past, you will need to love them through the process, both in word and in deed.

Dick Innes is the assistant director of the Crystal Cathedral Single Adult Ministry, assistant to the dean of the Robert Schuller Institute of Successful Communications, and founder and director of ACTS International, a nonprofit, multichurch organization that helps churches bridge the gap to their nonchurched community. His ministry also focuses on relationships, developing wholeness, and successful living as a single adult. He conducts seminars in the United States and Australia. He has authored two books: How to Mend a Broken Heart *(Grand Rapids: Revell, 1994) and* I Hate Witnessing *(Upland, Calif.: ACTS Communications, 1994). He also writes and distributes ACTS Encounter brochures on various topics.*

Encouraging Fun and Laughter

BETH SWENSON

A merry heart does good, like medicine, but a broken spirit dries the bones" (Prov. 17:22 NKJV). Often having fun together is a missing element in the lives of the people who come to our single parent ministry. I consider providing frivolity and frolic for both the parents and their children an important part of my ministry emphasis. When the children of the single parents beg to attend our events because they don't want to miss out on the excitement, I know we are meeting a very real social need. I have found that it is a short step from genuine laughter to real rejoicing (see Phil. 4:4).

In our single parent ministry, we provide a balanced approach. We have a weekly gathering to study spiritually relevant curriculum and support each other in prayer. But some of the best community builders we offer are our social events. These allow for safe, supervised interaction for both adults and children during which we build trust in one another. Boys without a positive Christian male role model have benefited from exposure to single parent fathers during these social events. Girls without a godly woman to influence their lives have been nurtured by our single parent mothers. Our ministry is completely orchestrated *by* single parents *for* single parents. In fact, I began the single parent ministry because I was a single parent myself.

Because we are aware that some of our single parents have alternating custody arrangements, we schedule events with this in mind. We vary weekends for events so those who only have their children every other weekend will be able to bring their children to at least half of the activities. However, we also welcome parents to come and enjoy the events on their own even if they don't have their children that weekend.

Spending time socializing together helps to open lines of communication, which enables single parents to realize they are not alone in their daily struggles. Paul told us to "rejoice with those who rejoice; mourn with those who mourn" (Rom. 12:15). We do that. Sometimes we laugh together; sometimes we cry together. But I also have found that having fun and laughing together can cheer up a mourning single parent.

I would like to share some of the ideas for fun activities that work well in our ministry. They fall into three categories: theme parties, weekend adventures, and social events.

Theme Parties

We host a potluck meal in our church for the single parents once a month with food and decorations based on a theme. The themes have been diverse and colorful, with wall decorations and centerpieces to provide atmosphere. Often we develop games and crafts that relate to the month's topic. Mood-setting background music plays while we are eating. Everyone brings food and wears costumes, hats, or clothing that fits in with the month's theme. We sometimes research the themes at the public library to get ideas for games, decorations, and costumes. If we locate a video the children will enjoy related to the theme, we show it after the meal. We often have a special speaker or devotional to give spiritual insight relating to the theme. Here are some examples of ideas we have used for our potluck parties:

Oriental. We provide chopsticks and fortune cookies, do origami paper-folding crafts, and make Chinese kites and lanterns.

Mexican. We break a piñata full of candy, celebrate with a Mexican hat dance, and hold limbo competitions.

50s rock 'n' roll. Bubblegum blowing contests, hula hoop competitions, and a sock hop dance (complete with swing dance lessons) set the mood for 50s fun.

Beach party. In the middle of winter we bring out our sunglasses, shorts, and sandals and play beach volleyball, make sand sculptures (in a sandbox), and have watermelon seed spitting contests.

Pirates. Secret clues are hidden all over the church for a treasure hunt, and we all design and wear unique sailor hats.

Hawaiian luau. We dress in Hawaiian prints, wear flower leis, and learn the hula dance.

Country western. We round up the cowboy apparel and practice lassoing chairs. We have a pretend rodeo and learn country line dance or square dance moves.

Snow daze. When the snow is abundant, we make snow sculptures, have snowball fights, and eat snow cones or make snow ice cream.

Thanksgiving. We make turkeys out of pinecones and construction paper and have a traditional Thanksgiving feast. A bowl of candy corn is passed around, and we each take a small handful. Each kernel is supposed to represent something for which we are thankful, and we share those things with each other as we eat the candy.

Christmas. The Christmas story is acted out, complete with costumes for each character. We create Christmas tree ornaments and make gingerbread houses out of graham crackers, frosting, and candy. Holding votive candles, we close the evening by singing carols.

Valentine's Day. After making cards for each other, we deliver them as singing telegrams. We bake heart-shaped cookies and decorate them with frosting.

Easter. We provide an egg hunt, make a cross necklace out of nails, and have a devotional about the meaning of Easter.

Independence Day. We wave flags in a parade of decorated bikes and wagons. Everyone is encouraged to wear red, white, or blue and sing a patriotic song as a family. We top off the evening by watching fireworks together.

I'm sure you can think of other themes to make the potlucks interesting. We've even pushed the edge with a few bizarre ideas, like "Roadkill Cafe" and "Swamp Thing." It is amazing what a little food coloring will do to change the presentation of food, and it's fun to watch people respond to brown punch laced with licorice worms. (The kids love it!)

After our potluck meal, we offer four play areas for the children. They can choose from a game room (with billiards, Ping-Pong, foosball, and other games), a gymnasium for assorted ball games, a room with comfortable furniture in which to view a video, and a craft table with new projects each month. We recruit volunteers or hire teenagers and adults to supervise the children in each play area when we have a speaker for the single parents. The topics range from inspirational to practical.

When the children go off to play, the single parents enjoy two childless hours to clean up from the potluck, listen to the speaker, interact with the subject the speaker presents, and spend time in prayer triangles, sharing their praises and requests with each other. This two-hour block of time is never long enough for the single parents, but it at least gives them some reprieve from the responsibility of caring for their children. This is one way we follow Paul's admonition to help share one another's burdens (Gal. 6:2).

Our potlucks become picnics once the weather is warm enough to be outside. After the picnic, we engage all ages in softball, kickball, soccer, volleyball, and touch football. Each July we have enjoyed water balloon volleyball, catching the balloon in a beach towel held by two people. We've created our own Olympic games with unusual relays and strange competitions, such as human wheelbarrow races and synchronized swimming with no water. Noncompetitive play is stressed, allowing even the youngest children to enjoy the sporting events.

Everyone wears clothes that can get wet and dirty when we have water pistol fights or water balloon fights, or when we go for hikes in the woods. A tug of war over a mud pit is a great motivator for teenage attendance at our picnics. The key to successful theme parties is to be creative and think of unusual, fun-filled activities that will appeal to children of all ages as well as to adults.

Weekend Adventures

We've found that when we spend longer periods of time together, casual friendships become much deeper, close Christian community begins to happen, and faith is strengthened as people hear and tell stories of God at work in their lives. A variety of activities have kept our single parent families occupied for a weekend or part of a weekend.

Summer camping. This allows those people new to camping to pursue the rigors of this activity in a group with others who are experienced campers. Sleeping in a tent, preparing food together as teams, fighting off the wildlife, and singing around the campfire at night have made camping a special experience for our group. We have survived storms that blew down trees in our campsite, bears digging through our garbage, and skunks trotting by our tents. It has been a joy to watch as both children and parents enjoy God's creation and develop their friendships over the course of a weekend.

We have gone backpacking and roughed it in wilderness areas, but only with the die-hard campers. Attendance is much higher for a camping trip when we choose a campground with modern conveniences, such as hot showers and clean, contemporary bathrooms. We've discovered one campground that offers hayrides, swimming, boating, roller-skating, crafts, and movies. In this setting we don't have to plan our own activities each day. During our unique outdoor Sunday worship services, the children and adults act out parables or familiar Bible stories. This has been a delight for everyone to watch and is interactive, which keeps the children involved with the service.

Winter retreats. In Minnesota winters can be long and cold, so we celebrate the snow and ice. Speakers for the adults and activity directors for the children help structure the weekend. We take advantage of the many available winter sports, such as cross-country skiing, snowshoeing, ice fishing, snowmobiling, ice-skating, and building snow sculptures. Last year we even had dogsled rides and played snow football.

At night, playing board games around the blazing fire and munching on popcorn has given us a cozy environment to nurture friendships while on retreats. Dreaming up silly games for the adults to play after they have put their children to bed has resulted in hours of laughter. We haven't had problems on retreats with getting our kids to bed on time, but the adults who choose to stay up all night and talk are a little bleary-eyed in the mornings. Those long talks at midnight are when we open our hearts to each other and when friends become family.

Spring weekend outing. Each spring we steal away to a hotel with great indoor activities. We've discovered a place within an hour's drive that has basketball and volleyball courts, Ping-Pong tables, billiards, swimming pools, saunas, hot tubs, exercise rooms, and party rooms. Families share the hotel rooms so they can split the expenses and also get better acquainted. Part of the fun has been finding ways to bring food to share for the weekend and prepare it within the confines of a hotel room. Finding a quiet place to hold a worship service has been a challenge, but we have managed to experience spiritual enrichment for the adults as well as the kids. Other hotel guests have joined our worship services sometimes when they heard us singing praise songs.

A week at family camp. This is our favorite activity each summer. For some of our families, this is the only vacation they can afford, and they have appreciated the opportunity to enjoy a safe, economical vacation. We have found corporations to help us underwrite the cost of up to half of the expense of camp for those families who need to be subsidized. Church bake sales have helped to match those corporate dollars.

No other time has been as valuable in forming our ministry into a caring, loving community as the week at family camp. Our church camp affords us the opportunity of gathering the single parents together for teaching each morning in addition to the nightly church service. Between the two sessions each day, we enjoy the rich programming resources provided by the camp: archery, rifle shooting, arts and crafts, nature walks, swimming, boating, and waterskiing. To keep costs low and encourage friendships, we put eight to ten people in a dormitory with bunk beds. Evenings are topped off under the stars with s'mores, singing, and praying around a campfire. Nothing revives one's spirit like a week at church camp with fellow Christians.

Social Events

Each month our single parent ministry schedules a social event away from the church property. We carpool to the activity and cover half of the cost for anyone who needs financial assistance. Several events have become annual favorites.

Fall hayride. We have horse-drawn hayracks and ride through the crunchy, autumn leaves. We return to a bonfire to roast hot dogs and marshmallows and drink hot apple cider. The outing is complete only when we have been pelted with hay, have rolled in the leaves, and smell like horses.

State park hike. This hike gives us a breathtaking view of a river and cliffs. Afterwards we enjoy a ball game, then unpack our brown-bag suppers and wait for the deer to come out at dusk. All of this fun for the cost of a car's entrance fee to the state park. It's a real value for our money.

Snow sledding. In the winter we careen down the hills, stacked high on sleds. Whether the day requires dressing for subzero weather or contending with melted snow that puddles at the bottom of the hill, our motto is, "Never cancel an event because of inclement weather." Luckily, we always have a warm house nearby and finish the day by baking cookies and drinking hot chocolate to warm the hands, toes, and hearts.

Dive-in movies. This event helps the winters seem shorter. When the outside temperature is freezing, we enjoy swimming at an indoor community pool that shows a movie while we swim. We bring snacks to share and enjoy good conversation while we bask in the hot tub. Have you ever floated on a raft while watching a Disney movie? Try it, you'll like it.

Talent show. This is a delightful way for parents and children to perform silly skits as well as showcase genuine talent.

Costume party. While we don't allow scary costumes or celebrate Halloween, we do make use of the abundance of costumes during the fall, with prizes for a variety of unusual categories. The memories from both the talent shows and costume parties have people talking all year long because they are so much fun.

Backyard swimming pool party. We combine swimming with an ice cream social every summer. It is called our "Triple Dip" event because everyone is invited to take a dip in the pool, share a favorite dip for chips or vegetables, and eat a dip of ice cream. Bingo and board games are available for the nonswimmers.

Boating, fishing, and waterskiing. Single parents with homes on a lake have given us the opportunity to teach our children some of the joys of living in Minnesota—the land of ten thousand lakes.

Canoeing and rafting. Canoeing down a calm river and rafting the white-water rapids of a turbulent river have been thrilling activities to enjoy with some of the older children. We attempt to program events that appeal to our single fathers, not just the mothers.

Bowling, roller-skating, roller-blading, minigolfing, or going to historical places, zoos, plays, sporting events, and concerts. All these activities seem to be more fun when there is a group involved. We have the advantage of living in a large metropolitan area with many resources, and we find the events that we attend together are always more interesting and community building than those we choose to attend by ourselves.

There are risks associated with many of these activities; therefore we can only sanction some of them as official church events because of insurance restrictions. Amazingly, in five years we have only had a few scrapes and bee stings—situations handled quickly and effectively by the accompanying medical personnel among our single parent group and with the first-aid kits we carry. Activities in community facilities require the parent to assume responsibility for some risk, but the benefits of providing exciting social events have far outweighed the risks. Through it all, God has been faithful to protect us from injury and negative incidents.

We have found it is essential to draw clear boundaries for the interaction between men and women so there isn't pressure to date or participate in activities that make one uncomfortable. We're careful to provide safe transportation when carpooling and supervised accommodations when staying overnight. Because we offer healthy Christian community between men and women, we sense single parents are less likely to rush into unhealthy dating relationships just because they are lonely. While several marriages and many fulfilling dating relationships have resulted from our single parent ministry, we make it clear that matchmaking is not the purpose of our group's interaction.

To summarize our activities, I would say we specialize in good, wholesome fun. We program for a wide range of ages and interests. The children are always included, or we provide free child care if we offer something only for the adults. Even though we attempt to make all our events affordable, we also cover half of the cost for those who require financial assistance. We try to create a balanced yearly slate of events for single parents and their children that provides them with entertainment and a sense of community.

We believe our ministry offers solid spiritual growth in our weekly small group meetings as well as social enrichment through our fun, bimonthly events. Together, these are forming us into a godly family. I hope these ideas will assist you in creating innovative and exciting activities for your single parent ministry. Having an enjoyable time together on the weekend is a quick way to chase away the single parent blues we may acquire during the week.

Beth Swenson is on staff as the single parents' director at Church of the Open Door in Crystal, Minnesota. She developed this ministry seven years ago when she discovered after her husband's death that the loneliest place for her was at church. Beth is currently attending Bethel Seminary in St. Paul, Minnesota.

18

Providing Financial Assistance

TERRY MANN

My secretary's voice came over the telephone: "Terry, call for you on line three. It's Sarah Anderson. Do you want to take it?"

"Sure," I responded.

Sarah was a single parent whose children were grown, but she was still very aware of the struggles single parents go through. Consequently, she always had her eyes open for people who needed help from the church.

As we chatted, Sarah told me about Nancy, a single parent who had had some unexpected emergencies and was in extreme need of financial assistance.

Calls such as this are not uncommon in church settings. If we cannot help our own, who will help them? The church should be one source of encouragement, strength, support, and financial assistance for single parents who are trying to do the best that they can.

Guidelines

Any church that is willing to offer assistance to single parents should begin by setting up clear guidelines and instructions for people applying for assistance. The guidelines should state when and how financial assistance will be granted. Nothing is more frustrating than unclear or lack of directions. Although as a pastor I feel the frustration is more marked on my side of the desk, it is no doubt just as frustrating for the person sitting across from me.

There are only so many hours in a day, and to give up some of that time to seek assistance for a person in need only to hit roadblocks is a nightmare. It is embarrassing for me to try to explain to someone what I can or cannot do when I myself am not sure. It is also a waste of precious time—time that the single parent may not have. In many cases the parents with financial needs will not come for assistance until they have exhausted all other resources, which means they quite possibly are in serious financial straits, where time may be of the essence. For instance, in requests for money to pay utility bills, the parent may have already received a shut-off notice.

When a person is sitting in the pastor's office seeking assistance, that is no time to be developing guidelines or making policy. The church and the single parent are served much better when these things have been thought through prior to a crisis. If your church has a care committee or benevolence committee, be sure you know their rules for helping people financially. If you discover the procedures inadequate or nonexistent, suggest that this be remedied as quickly as possible.

Issues the guidelines should address include but are not limited to:

amount of gifts
frequency of aid
differentiation between members and nonmembers
aid directed to a third party

At Memorial Park we have guidelines in place that clearly set annual limits on the amount of assistance that can be given to any individual in a calendar year. In addition, there are differences in amounts depending on whether the person is a member of the church or a nonmember. We also have a method to give immediate short-term emergency aid while evaluating a situation for possible additional assistance.

There are numerous books and guidelines available in local Christian bookstores and through various publishers that can give needed assistance in setting up a financial assistance program. There is no need to reinvent the wheel. Avail yourself of such materials and put the labors of someone else to work for you.

When giving monetary assistance, remember to consider and protect the self-respect of the single parents. Many people have difficulty asking for or accepting assistance. At the very least, let the recipient know you will keep to an absolute minimum the number of people who will be aware of the assistance. This confidentiality can be a real boost for their self-esteem, which may already be very low.

Another way to protect the self-esteem of people who need assistance but do not accept help easily or are embarrassed by their need is to consider the money a loan with several options for repayment. If the monetary need arose because of unforeseen, emergency expenditures (e.g., car repairs or medical bills), the single parent may be able to repay the loan over a period of time. He or she agrees to pay a set amount from each paycheck (make it very affordable and within his or her budget). This could apply to cash advances, scholarships, or canned food from the church pantry.

If the single parent simply cannot spare even five to ten dollars from a paycheck on a regular basis to repay the money, then perhaps he or she could use the income tax refund or annual bonus on his or her job to begin repayment of the loan. Or single parents could repay financial assistance by doing volunteer work for the church for an agreed number of hours. This time could be spent doing clerical work, gardening, landscaping, painting, washing windows, sewing or mending clothing for the church clothes closet, coordinating a canned food drive, or doing chores for elderly church members. Even though single parents are often tired and overworked by their own responsibilities, they will usually welcome a chance to earn financial assistance rather than have to accept charity.

Types of Assistance

There are many ways to provide financial resources for single parents. The type of assistance you provide will depend on the individuals, the church's resources, and the needs. You might offer the following types of help to meet the diverse needs.

Direct Monetary Gifts

The most obvious type of assistance is a cash gift. There are several things that should be considered when giving money. First, how trustworthy is the person? There are some single parents to whom we wish to give aid, but we doubt their ability to adequately handle the money. I have found that a good option is to make the check payable to the creditor.

Before authorizing any cash gift, I always ask several key questions:

Has the person requested help in the past? If so, how recent was the last request? If very little time has elapsed since the last request, is the problem one of money management, impulse spending, or a failure to budget properly?

Is giving money going to assist the problem or only postpone actually dealing with it?

Is it possible to meet the need without giving the money directly to the person involved?

If the situation is serious, can we give cash and have some strings attached to it, such as financial counseling?

How will my decision affect the children involved?

For example, it may be necessary to turn down a request for funds if the single parent seems to be making asking for help a habit and instead needs to face the issue of a change of lifestyle. Any time a decision is made that the parent needs to wait or be turned down for a monetary gift, for whatever reason, other steps must be taken to ensure the children are cared for adequately.

If the church has set clear guidelines for providing financial assistance, the decisions are easier to make, although each case still requires personal evaluation.

Other Types of Monetary Assistance

There may be times when a single parent has an immediate need that you can meet in other ways than giving cash directly to the person. Sometimes the problem is an empty gas tank and the person has no other money for gas or bus fare to get to work until Friday's paycheck. You might work out an arrangement with a local gas station (possibly one owned or managed by a church member) to accept signed vouchers from you to fill a person's tank with gas. The gas station would then invoice you and attach the sales receipt and the signed voucher.

Many churches keep a food pantry with nonperishable canned and boxed foods. When there is an emergency need for groceries, you might be able to meet the need from the pantry instead of having to give the person cash. At the least, the amount of money you might give could be reduced to what would be needed for milk, bread, fruit, vegetables, and meat.

Providing assistance with a clothes closet, a place to stay in an emergency, help with moving, and other practical issues are discussed in chapter 19 of this book.

Financial Counseling

Some single parents may have an immediate monetary need but also a much deeper need for counseling or training in managing money, setting up budgets, balancing a checkbook, or other related skills. I often counsel with newly single mothers who had little or no say in the handling of money during their marriages. Their basic need is education and training. I believe it is part of my ministry to provide this training.

Our church has a couple of elders with a great deal of wisdom on financial matters who are willing to sit down with single mothers (or fathers) and help them develop a workable budget. Several single parents have benefited from these sessions. Even when there were tough decisions to make, the single parents were willing to be accountable and pleased to have someone to call on for answers to questions. Given time and direction, anyone can improve his or her skills in this area.

If no one in your church is willing or able to provide money management training, obtain some of the wonderful video and audio resources available through your local Christian bookstore to train these parents or pay their registration for a local seminar on the subject. Creativity may be your biggest asset here.

Referral to Community Services

Every community has outreach programs that offer assistance to those in need. They offer everything from food and utility assistance to counseling and referrals services. The staff or volunteers in these organizations quite often are trained individuals with an excellent track record of helping hurting people. In many cases, they can help single parents better than we can, since providing assistance is their primary job.

I have heard some people emphatically state that Christians should not take advantage of public assistance. However, many churches actually contribute to community organizations and agencies. I'm not sure if the objections voiced are biblically supported convictions or are simply personal opinions or personal pride. I know many of the individuals at these community service organizations in my area by name and can give a referral that will get single parents assistance faster than they could get by going into the office on their own. Do not rule out this option, since in some cases it may be your best one.

Child Care

Some means of assistance are so obvious that they slip right under our noses. One of the best I have found is to provide child care free of charge (or for a nominal fee) at many activities sponsored for the single parents in our church. I include child care expenses in my single adult ministry budget.

It is still a good idea to leave some of the responsibility on the single parents for the care of their child. I accomplish that by simply requiring advance reservations for child care. The time frame for advance notification of a child care need may be as long as a week or as short as a few hours, depending upon the event. There have been times where only one or two single parents needed child care. In such cases I have had them get a sitter on their own and reimburse them from my petty cash.

Scholarships

Whenever possible, I like to provide scholarships for single parents for retreats and major events. There are at least three ways to fund this. The most obvious is to budget a certain dollar amount for scholarships, making it a first-come-first-served basis (upon approval, of course) until the funds are used up.

A second option is to ask people in the ministry or the church at large to give especially for this purpose. In the past I have done this with tremendous success. In one church where I served I had designated gifts given by single adults with extra resources to help single parents afford retreats. There were times when I had several hundred dollars for scholarships for a specific retreat. Some single adults would totally underwrite the expenses of a particular single parent the Lord had placed upon their hearts. Don't deprive these people of the joy of giving by not making this option available.

A third option is to budget each retreat with scholarships figured in. Figure the cost of the retreat, and then add a certain dollar figure to the total cost before dividing up the cost for each participant. I have never had anyone complain about my doing this as long as I carefully and prayerfully administered the scholarships.

You may even have a single parent who has a difficult time making ends meet but who can do some work to earn the scholarship. At two of the churches in which I have served there was a single mother who was a travel agent. In each case it was easy for us to use the single mom's services to plan some retreats and have her waive part of her commission to pay for her registration without costing the company a cent of its profit.

Cautions

Anytime you provide financial assistance there is an opportunity for abuse of the church's generosity. It is well worth it to consider the possible difficulties ahead of time rather than be taken by surprise when it happens. In ministry we strive to be caring and to see the best in others. Yet, no matter how carefully you set up guidelines and police these programs, you are going to be taken advantage of at times. Simply being aware of potential abuses may not eliminate them, but it could prepare you for coping with them.

First, expect that someone will attempt to take advantage of financial assistance. It is much easier to cope if you expect it to happen at some point in time. You do not feel any less used, but the anger and frustration may be lessened.

Second, be as gracious as you can when the church's generosity is abused. Nothing is gained by responding in a non-Christlike fashion. That only makes you look bad, gives the church a bad name, and leaves you feeling worse to have acted improperly. This does not mean that you are weak. It means you attempt to control your emotions and not let them control you.

A third recommendation for action in abuse is to let the offending party know in no uncertain terms that you are aware of what has happened and will not be as gullible the next time. As pastors we always want to see repentance. Be aware that people know this, and if they would deliberately abuse a church's offer of assistance, they could feign repentance with ease. If the offender is truly repentant, he or she will not mind doing what is necessary to earn back your (and the church's) trust.

Finally, learn from the experience. There comes a time when you must evaluate what has happened, cut your losses, and make the necessary changes to prevent a recurrence. This does not mean that you overreact. Don't cancel all financial assistance. We have all heard of the parent who is frustrated by one of the children constantly touching a brother or sister to get attention. In a moment of exasperation the parent yells: "Okay, no one touches anyone else in this house ever again!" Do not make the same mistake if the church is victimized by someone abusing the system.

How Fast Do You Respond?

Everyone is aware that it is possible to move too slowly when providing aid to a single parent. The issue of the utility company mentioned earlier is one example. However, it is also possible to offer assistance too quickly. There are times when people need to spend more time wrestling with their problems to see if they can resolve these themselves. If we bail them out too quickly, they may not have learned all the Lord has for them to learn in their situations. I am not talking about letting children suffer, but sometimes adults need a touch of reality before they will make significant changes, especially if the changes are character issues.

Unfortunately, there is no set rule here. Each case is distinct and must be evaluated on its own merits. Carefully consider the needs of the parent and the children and the urgency of the situation. After doing all of that, seek the Lord for guidance in offering assistance.

How Much Do You Help?

The danger of giving too little to meet the need is evident to everyone, but the danger of giving too much also exists. It can be just as much of a disservice to the recipient to be given too much assistance as not to be given enough. It simply may take longer for the results to show.

As Christians, we should always seek to meet the needs of other people. We must realize, however, that we have limited resources and cannot help everyone. While on earth, Jesus did not meet all the needs he encountered. For every hungry person he fed, thousands of hungry people in other areas received no food. For every disease he healed, multitudes received no healing and many died from the disease. We must be aware of our limitations, do what we can, and be satisfied with that. We should thank the Lord for using us in the places he chooses.

I come out of a background of legalism. That being the case, I have made the conscious decision that if I am going to err, it is going to be on the side of grace. I will extend grace, even when I think it is undeserved, because that is what the Lord does for me. Who am I to have a higher standard than the Lord? This means I sometimes need someone to keep me in check in areas relating to meeting financial need. My point is that each of us should always be aware of our biases in deciding how much to give to single parents in need.

Ask yourself if you can truly justify the amount of your gift to a single parent. Is it too much? Is it too little? Where will it go? How will it be used? This alone can make you be sure you are attempting to really meet a need and not just trying to get someone out of your office.

Professional versus Lay Pastors

The full-time pastor has a much different job when it comes to meeting needs of people than does the volunteer or lay pastor. I did not say it was easier or harder; I simply said it was different. Having served in both capacities, I can truly say that both have their advantages and disadvantages.

Full-time pastors usually understand the process of obtaining approvals, checks, or cash because they are on staff. Their credibility is usually high, and their status makes it easier to get things done. Part of this is due to the fact that they are at the church more and can give time to meet an emergency, simply because this is their job. Their assistance is especially helpful when a situation is crucial.

There is a disadvantage to being a full-time pastor, however. Some people may feel you do not have a full understanding of their situation. This may keep them from fully trusting you or make them less apt to reveal certain information. The lay pastor may be at an advantage with persons who have that view.

There are two ideas that apply to everyone. The first is to be creative. Look for innovative ways to offer assistance; you will surprise yourself. Second, be selective. You cannot help everyone with every need. Extend grace to yourself and your church if some needs simply cannot be met.

Rev. Terry Mann is the executive pastor and pastor with single adults at the Memorial Park Presbyterian Church in Allison Park, Pennsylvania. He has a D.Min. from Northern Theological Seminary with an emphasis in single adult ministry. He has been involved in single adult ministry since 1984. Terry and Kay, his wife of twenty-two years, have three children ages fourteen, sixteen, and eighteen. A former Baptist, Terry served for eighteen years in Chattanooga, Tennessee, before moving to the Pittsburgh area.

19

Offering Practical Assistance

JOHN WESTFALL

When I became the minister with single adults at University Presbyterian Church in Seattle, I knew we needed a special ministry for single parents. So I planned one. Selecting a weeknight I thought would be good, I scheduled one of the rooms at the church, arranged for refreshments, announced the new ministry, and showed up prepared to run a support group.

The program was a flop. The single parents in our church didn't seem interested in the support group or the family socials I planned. Finally, after several weeks I gave up. No one seemed to mind that the single parent ministry had been canceled. I was puzzled. I knew that programs such as I had designed for our church were successful in other churches, but for some reason this format didn't appeal to single parents in our church.

As I came to know several of the single parents in our ministry, my heart went out to them. They were brave, courageous, and overworked. Although tired, they did their best to spend time with their children and ensure that the children attended youth group activities and participated in church. Many of the single parents had to live on inadequate resources. So I decided one way I could minister to single parents was to offer practical assistance.

I approached different church members who owned or managed businesses and asked if they would give free services or goods to single parents. I made up gift certificates for those services or goods to distribute to single parents when there were needs. A dentist gave free dental exams and X rays. An auto shop manager gave free oil changes. The single parents truly appreciated these certificates, and I was overjoyed to see how church members began to look for ways to reach out to single parents.

The Possibilities Are Unlimited

There are lots of ways to offer practical assistance to single parents. In fact, you may want to create a new position on your leadership team for coordinating this ministry. Here are some ideas for helping single parents:

Gift certificates. At least four times a year make up blank gift certificates as bulletin inserts for the worship service. Certificates would read,

This certificate is redeemable for _____

Provided by

name _____ address _____ telephone _____

You could also include a list of suggestions for church members, such as hauling a load to the dump, trimming hedges or trees, baby-sitting, painting, changing the oil in a car, mending, lending a pickup truck, or giving a haircut.

Urge each church member to think of something he or she could do for a single parent family and to complete at least one certificate. Provide extra certificates and invite church members to take them to their employers to see if they would be willing to contribute to the ministry. (For example, a restaurant manager might give "kids under twelve eat free" certificates.) When making the announcement about the certificates, have a single parent give a brief testimony about what it meant to him or her

OFFERING PRACTICAL ASSISTANCE

201

to receive practical help. You might even have someone who was blessed by giving a certificate share a story, for it is often more blessed to give than to receive (Acts 20:35).

Moving assistance. Develop a list of people in the church or single adult ministry who have trucks they would be willing to either lend or drive when single parents need to move or haul large items. The longer the list, the less frequently any one person will be called upon to assist. This is a practical way to "bear one another's burdens" (Gal. 6:2 NKJV).

Linens. Contact hotel managers in your area and explain your ministry with single parents. Ask if they would be willing to donate their used sheets, pillowcases, and towels to the ministry. (Hint: The more expensive the hotel, the better condition the discards will be.)

Clothes closet. Set up a clothes closet for donations from church members and single parents. Invite single parents to shop for free clothing. Because children usually outgrow clothes before they are worn out, this can be an effective way for single parents to avoid some expenditures. A variation of this would be to have a swap meet in the church parking lot a few times a year. Church members would bring clean, mended clothing, which would be displayed on tables or racks. Single parents would be invited to come and take what they need. Any leftover clothing could be stored until the next swap meet.

Furniture. Develop a system by which church members can advertise when they have furniture they are willing to donate to a single parent family. This might be a bulletin board, a newsletter, or a bulletin insert. There could be a deadline set in the advertisement for when the item must be picked up so people don't have to store unwanted furniture too long.

Toys. Barbara Dycus at Calvary Assembly Church in Winter Park, Florida, developed a "Recycled Christmas" program for single parents. Each year in early December church members and single parents are invited to gather up toys their children no longer use but which are still in good working order. These are brought to the fellowship hall and displayed on tables. Single parents are invited to come and take a toy for each of their children as a

Christmas present. This has been a favorite activity and has been very successful.

Work days. Set up a work day each month and invite single adults and other church members to sign up to work. Then have single parents make their needs known (moving, painting, tree trimming, major yard work, etc.) and schedule the tasks for the different work days. You can either announce what project will be tackled on the next work day or let it be a surprise. (If you choose to surprise workers, make an exception in the case of painting so people will know to wear old clothes.) If the project will take all day, suggest that people bring a sack lunch or a potluck dish to share. The single parent being helped can provide iced tea, lemonade, coffee, or juice.

Sewing clothes. One of the ways the women's ministry could assist single parents is in sewing clothes for the children. The fabric and patterns could be purchased by the group or by the single parent. This might also be something individual women in the church would like to do, even if they do not attend a daytime women's ministry meeting.

Remember Tabitha (Acts 9:36–42)? Sewing was her single parent ministry. She sewed for the widows in the early church. Hers was a wonderful gift that was very much appreciated by those who received help from her.

Birthday parties. Plan a monthly birthday party for all the single parent children with birthdays in that month. Church members can provide cakes, candies, decorations, and games. There might even be church members who are clowns (or who have secretly wanted to be clowns) or magicians or who have a pony for pony rides who would be willing to assist with the parties on occasion.

Tutoring. The pastor at the First Baptist Church of Brawley, California, set up an after-school tutoring program where children come to do their homework before their parents get home from work. The homework is supervised by senior adult volunteers. When homework is completed, the children are free to play Ping-Pong, basketball, or table games until time to go home. Single parents report that this program frees up evening time that would normally be spent coaxing tired children to do homework. Parents can then use the extra time for family activities.

Housing. There are occasions when single parents need a place to stay on an emergency basis. This might be provided by a family who has a mother-in-law's cottage on their property, a spare bedroom, or an apartment over the garage. This type of need might arise if a single parent has been evicted and has not yet found a place to live or if a single parent has come into town for a week or a weekend to visit his or her children and needs a place to stay. The agreement would be made that the arrangement is for a specified, short period of time.

More permanent housing assistance might be provided by a single parent family being willing to share living arrangements in a house with another single parent family. Both families would share the expenses and the chores.

Fun. Not all of the practical assistance has to come from the church at large; single parents can help one another. The single parents in one church plan an informal picnic every Sunday after church during the summer. Families bring a change of clothes, sports equipment, and something to eat (sack lunch or a potluck dish). After church everyone meets at the local park and spends a restful afternoon. Some of the single parents participate in the sports activities; others quietly read a book while the children play. Often the parents just talk with one another; sometimes one will take a nap under the trees. All of the adults share the supervision of the children, and everyone has fun.

Baby-sitting. Encourage single parents to baby-sit for one another or alternate weekends taking each other's children to provide respite. Invite other church members to assist with child care during conferences, seminars, or weekend retreats so single parents can afford to attend.

Meals. Suggest that single parents who live close to each other share their evening meals, alternating who does the cooking. Or some churches have community meals one night during the week for a nominal charge, which many single parents find a welcome break from cooking. Other single adult ministries provide a simple lunch (such as lasagna or spaghetti) for a reasonable charge after church on Sundays.

Prayer. Set up a prayer chain for single parents to use when they have special needs. Invite church members to become prayer partners with individual single parents. Pray daily for the single parents in your ministry, asking that God meet their needs and that you will know how best to provide practical assistance for them.

Ask your single parents how you can assist them in practical ways. You don't have to think of everything yourself. Let them help design your ministry so it is meaningful to them.

Grow the Ministry When the Time Is Right

About a year after I discontinued the single parent support group at University Presbyterian Church, a couple of single parents challenged me, "Don't you care about single parents? You have a ministry for all other types of single adults, but nothing for us single parents!"

Smiling to myself, I responded, "Well, what type of ministry would you want?"

They began to describe a program that included a support group, family socials, and sharing of resources, which was virtually identical to the ministry I had attempted. I listened quietly. Then I asked, "Do you think there would be other single parents who would be interested in such a ministry?" They were positive there would be. I suggested they ask around and see how many people they could recruit to participate in a single parent ministry.

Within a couple of weeks they had obtained a list of several parents, suggested a night of the week when they could meet, and were well on their way to developing a program. I let them finalize the plans and run the ministry. It was very successful.

The difference between what I tried to do and what they did was their perception of the need and their ownership of the ministry. Be willing to listen to the single parents in your church when planning to minister with them.

Rev. John Westfall, D.Min., was in single adult ministry for several years before becoming senior pastor at Walnut Creek Pres-

byterian Church in Walnut Creek, California. He coauthored
Building Strong People *(Grand Rapids: Baker, 1997) and authored*
Coloring Outside the Lines: Discipleship for the Undisciplined
(New York: HarperCollins, 1991) and Enough Is Enough: Grace
for the Restless Heart *(San Francisco: Harper Collins, 1993). He
is a member of the Network of Single Adult Leaders and has
served on the national board of directors for the organization.*

20

Organizing Support Groups

KEL TRUNGIAN

ome over to our house tonight. My wife will prepare dinner, and we will talk," I told Amy, a visitor to our church, who had called to say she had something important to talk over with me.

Amy replied, "That sounds good, but I'll have my kids with me. Is that OK?"

"Sure. About six o'clock?" I asked.

"Six will be fine," she agreed.

When I called my wife to let her know we'd be having guests for dinner, she assured me there would be no problem. We were having stew. Promptly at six, the doorbell rang, and there standing at the door was Amy and her children. It was Amy's appearance that shocked me. She stood neatly dressed in her work uniform. The logo of the tool company was brightly displayed over her left pocket and her name over her right.

I thought, *Here is a mom on her own trying to scratch out a living in the predominantly male-dominated world of scrapers, hammers, drills, crescent wrenches, and table saws. How on earth does she do it? It must be extremely difficult to work in that environment.*

That night I learned that Amy had been through a difficult divorce and was still hurting deeply. She had come to our church in the hope of finding support for her situation.

"Does your church have anything for single moms?" she asked.

Embarrassed, I apologetically said, "Our church is not presently structured to meet the unique needs of single moms."

Amy started to feel flustered—not from what I said; it was her children. They were running around the house, pulling on their mom, and taking no heed of her requests to stop. They had come straight from day care and were eager to get home. They did not understand why she could not play with them at that moment. Amy excused herself. The children had to go to bed, and there were preparations for tomorrow.

I felt powerless to help. My heart ached for her hurts and pain. After Amy left, I couldn't forget her question: "Does your church have anything for single moms?" God used that evening to direct me into developing a ministry to single moms.

Types of Support Group Ministries

The support groups you offer single parents and their children must be tailored to their felt needs and to the resources in your own church. There are at least seven types of support group ministries to consider.

1. Newly divorced single parents need the option of a divorce recovery program. This should be structured for a set number of weeks, ranging from four to twenty-six. The average length of such programs is from six to eight weeks. (See chapter 16 for more information.)
2. Children of divorced parents need the opportunity to attend a series of recovery sessions to assist them in working through the grieving process and their negative feelings resulting from the divorce. Widowed single parents and their children can

be helped with their grief recovery with appropriate support group programs (see chapter 16).

3. Support groups that provide fellowship and fun help single parents and their families grow. Ways to provide this are outlined in chapter 17.
4. Churchwide small groups are also helpful for single parents. Even though single parents have limited time to spend on activities other than work and homemaking, many have joined such groups. These go by a variety of names such as cell groups, home groups, home churches, or care groups. If your church has this program, encourage single parents to participate if at all possible.
5. Special support groups are provided by some churches for single parents with special needs such as those recovering from abuse, those fighting abusive behaviors of their own, or persons addicted to alcohol or drugs. If your church does not have these programs, then you should have a list of groups and organizations to which you can refer single parents with these needs.
6. Weekly discussion groups.
7. Single parents and their children can be integrated into existing church support ministries.

In this chapter we will discuss in greater detail the last two types of organized support group ministries.

Weekly Discussion Support Groups

Wendy walked up to one of the seminar speakers at a single parent conference. There were tears in Wendy's eyes but a radiant smile of relief on her face. "Thank you so much for being honest about your own struggles as a parent," Wendy said. "You have helped me so much. I thought I was the only one who felt that way." When she realized she wasn't a terrible person or even unusual because the frustrations of being a single parent got to her sometimes, she could accept herself and her situation more easily.

One of the most important reasons to provide a weekly discussion support group is to help single parents talk about their frustrations, struggles, fears, feelings, joys, and successes. Hearing others express feelings and fears one never dared admit can be a wonderful relief. Or the group can provide a needed look in the mirror that reflects areas of one's life where personal and attitudinal changes are needed. A discussion group allows participants to be consultants one to another as people share how specific problems or conflicts were resolved. Members share knowledge, information, resources, advice, ideas, experiences, insights, encouragement, and helpful Scriptures. Groups pray together and for one another during the week.

Organizing discussion support groups is not complicated. Pray that God will lay this ministry on the heart of the right person to coordinate the discussion support group program.

Basically, the coordinator identifies a list of topics, one for each week, relevant to single parents. Appropriate Scripture passages are found to go with each topic. Then five or six discussion starter questions or sentence completions are written for each topic. Questions need to be open-ended, such as, "What are productive ways to deal with conflicts between siblings?" Sentence completions should invite participants to share: "An important lesson God is teaching me by being a single parent is _____." The coordinator makes copies of the topic, Scripture passages, and questions for the week for each participant.

If more than ten single parents attend, divide the participants into small groups of no more than eight to ten people. Unless all of the members of a small group are extremely shy or reticent, five or six questions or sentence completions should provide a discussion that easily fills an hour and a half or more. (Be sure to set a time to close the evening so the discussion will not go on too long.)

At first a coordinator is all you need, but as the discussion support group program grows, you may want to have a discussion facilitator for each small discussion group. The next step is to provide training in group facilitating for these leaders.

A variation of this discussion support group design is to have a special speaker for the first twenty minutes before breaking up into discussion groups. Or the coordinator could present some key thoughts on the topic of the evening before the small groups form.

It is not unusual for single parents to attend discussion support groups when their families are having a particularly trying time or when a new problem or crisis surfaces and then drop out when life seems easier. Frequently single parents attend sporadically rather than weekly. The important thing is that the group is there when it is needed. If attendance dwindles down to one to three single parents each week, and these are not the same people on a regular basis, you may find that a monthly support group meets the needs of the single parents at your church. However, if two or three single parents attend faithfully, week after week, then check with them before you go to a monthly format. The group may be very important to them, and numbers are not the goal, support is.

Using Existing Support Ministry Structures

This is the model I developed for First Evangelical Church in Memphis, Tennessee, when Amy challenged me to consider the needs of single moms. I chose to establish a facilitating team to integrate single parents and their children into the existing support ministries of our church wherever possible.

Vision

A vision for the ministry must be established before any communication about the ministry takes place. A vision starts with a defining moment in the life of the founder of the ministry—the occurrence in the founder's life that affected the heart and compelled the person to develop the ministry. The defining moment becomes, under God, the motivating force and compulsion to serve others in the ministry. The vision also shapes the paradigm from which the ministry to single parent families will be seen.

Forming the Team

Three months of prayer led us to an elder and his wife who graciously accepted the roles of team leaders. Additional team members were solicited based on the following criteria: spiritual maturity, godliness, faithfulness, availability, teachability, emotional maturity, concern for single mom families, and team compatibility.

I serve on the team as a pastor but not the team leader, and I knew I must not make the mistake of selecting all the team members myself. If you are going to use this model, remember to let the team be involved in the decision-making processes. Ownership of the ministry and team will only occur if the pastor allows the team leaders to make as many of the decisions as possible. Continual consultation by the pastor with the team leader is vital.

In our case, the criterion for selection of the team was the ability to network with other ministries in the church. For example, our present team consists of representatives from women of the church ministry, mentoring, elders, deacons, woman-to-woman mentoring, Sunday school classes, and Wednesday night ministries. Each team member identifies and assesses the needs of individual single moms. Then they connect the single parents and their families with one or more existing support structures in the church.

Existing structures are those organized ministry spheres that are already present in the church. There were several we identified at our church:

elders
deacons
Moms' Day Out
woman-to-woman mentoring
Wednesday family night Bible study
Sunday school
single adult ministry
women of the church ministry
pastoral, professional, and lay counseling

men's small groups
women's small groups
children's and youth ministries
child care pools

You probably have many of these support structures in place in your church from which single parents and their children would benefit.

Our team does not meet on a regular basis. The consensus of the team was that they would meet when pertinent discussions and decisions needed to be made for the progression of the ministry. The lack of structure as to meeting times is very appealing to church members who are already overbooked with meetings.

Conceptual Model

The conceptual model (see fig. 1) is the visual representation that serves as the teaching tool and communication vehicle for demonstrating how the ministry functions. People who serve and are served in the ministry need to see the big picture, which is communicated through a clear conceptual model.

Figure 1. Conceptual model of ministry to single moms

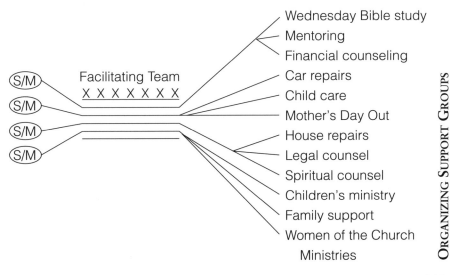

Information Gathering

Gather information and set priorities before beginning a ministry. We contacted three key groups in our church to gather information regarding support structures and suggestions for a ministry to single moms. The vision and conceptual model were presented to each of the three groups. Then each group was asked to give their thoughts and suggestions about a ministry to single parents. The three groups were:

1. pastoral staff
2. representatives of the women's ministries
3. deacons and elders

We also gathered input from some of the single moms themselves. Our program was designed based on the input from these groups.

I have found that elders and deacons generally can add a dimension to information gathering unavailable elsewhere in the church. This dimension is the historical background and cultural makeup of the church. Often staff are not at the church long enough to have a complete understanding of the church's history and culture. Most elder and deacon boards have long-term church members who can help.

Our elders and deacons knew the church needed leadership for a ministry to single parent families. These men approved and gave their full support to the development of this ministry when presented with the conceptual model and information on single parent family needs. In our program the elders and deacons have been an invaluable support for spiritual counsel, wisdom, financial advice, legal counsel, medical or dental advice, business advice, child rearing advice, and many practical needs.

Setting Priorities

Three priorities were set for the development of a ministry to single parent families. The first priority was recruiting a teacher for a mothers' Bible study on Sunday mornings. The Bible study is open to all mothers of the church because our single moms wanted to be in the mainstream of the church. We have found that in our program the attendance remains fairly stable from week to week. Large fluctuations in attendance can have a negative impact on the perception of the success or failure of a program.

The second priority was identifying the child care pools in the church. For us they were: the Moms' Day Out program on Monday and Thursday, Tuesday morning Bible study for women of the church, Wednesday family night, Sunday morning and evening services at the church, and the high school, college, and single adults departments.

Our third priority was soliciting the assistance of the mentoring program offered through the women of the church ministries. Mentoring provides woman-to-woman friendship and spiritual development.

Communicating the Concept

Single parent families and the church need to be informed of a new ministry. We used several communication vehicles: church bulletin inserts and congregation communication forms, pulpit announcements, a brochure for distribution, Sunday school class presentations, and announcements to the elders, deacons, seniors, and women of the church.

Start Small

A new ministry starts the same way a business does—small. A small business starts in your basement or room. When the business grows, it flows over into your living room or dining room. Then you rent a small office. Eventually you hire staff.

A new ministry starts with the people God gives you. You care for them. You shepherd and grow them in the Lord. The ministry grows because you are caring for people.

God is concerned about people. The Lord placed a burden on our hearts for a ministry to single parents. Amy now has something for herself and her family. She can now find support and encouragement at our church.

215

Whatever structure you choose to give to the single parent support group program in your church, ask God to make you aware of the needs, sensitive to the individuals, and responsive to the opportunities to show the love of God.

Rev. Kel Trungian has been pastor to college and single adults at the First Evangelical Church of Memphis, Tennessee (a non-denominational church), since 1992. He has been a pastor since 1983, working in two Baptist churches in Canada. He has an M.Div. from Heritage Seminary, Cambridge, Ontario, and a D.Min. from Trinity Evangelical Divinity School, in Deerfield, Illinois. He has been married to Sherri for twenty-nine years and has two grown children.

21

Counseling Single Parents

ALAN CORRY

Remember the first time you sat down at a personal computer? Did it go something like this? What seemed to be so simple to everyone else turned into a frustrating mess for you. You turned on the computer and tried to follow a simple set of instructions, but nothing seemed to work right. Then you got a self-help, computer-made-easy manual. It might as well have been written in Greek, because nothing seemed easy.

Then a friend came over to show you how to operate your easy, anyone-can-do-it computer. As your friend sat at the keyboard, he or she made the video screen come to life with color, and all the bells and whistles started into motion. Your friend told you everything you needed to know step by step. Every now and then your friend paused to look up and ask, "Do you understand?" Embarrassed to say "no," you replied, "sure." Then your friend proceeded to the next step.

After the lesson, you were overwhelmed with all this new data. You felt even more overloaded than before. The friend left, and you sat back down at the keyboard to try all the wonderful things you had just been told to do, only to realize you had not learned very much. After all, you did not have the opportunity to learn the operations by working through each step yourself. A sense of frustration set in as you turned off the computer, not ever wanting to look at it again.

Many times single parents feel exactly that way when they ask ministry leaders for help with their problems and frustrations in life. Because of our experience and knowledge of the issues facing many single parents, we often can see solutions right away. After a few moments of hearing what they have to say, we have a tendency to tell them what they need to do to solve their problems. Embarrassed to say they don't understand, they reply, "sure," and leave our offices no more prepared to face the issues than when they came.

Our words may be comforting at the time, and single parents may feel better as they walk out the door, but are we really equipping them to work through the complex situations they face as single parents? Even though many people come with the expectation that we will tell them what to do, we actually have a duty to help them discover workable solutions for themselves for dealing with each situation. This teaches the individual accountability and responsibility as well as encourages a strong sense of self-esteem and independence.

This chapter is not about counseling in the professional sense, such as one receives from a trained mental heath practitioner or clinical psychologist. Single parents with needs for professional counseling should be referred to appropriate therapists. Instead, we are talking about pastoral or peer counseling such as one receives from a friend or a person who has knowledge of what one is experiencing. In fact, because of the legal liabilities involved today, some churches no longer use the term *counseling* in their ministries. This may be a wise move. However, because *counseling* is an easily understood term, it will be used in this chapter with the above caveat.

When counseling single parents, you will want to remember that the Holy Spirit is your partner. Always start your day and each counseling session with a prayer for wisdom. Ask the Holy Spirit to assist the single parent in searching his or her heart, thinking clearly, identifying corrective actions or solutions, and making right decisions.

Effective Listening

We often hear only part of a conversation. One reason we have a tendency to tune out what the other person says is because we filter the input through our biases and draw our own conclusions. In essence, we often hear people say what we think they are going to say.

Another reason we don't listen carefully is that we get excited about what we want to contribute to the conversation and don't want to forget what we are going to say, so we mentally shut out the other person's words. Our eardrums are still receiving sound waves, and we are hearing the person's voice inflection, but we are not listening to what he or she is saying. Listening and hearing are two different processes.

The commandment to bear one another's burdens (Gal. 6:2) carried in its very connotation the ability to actively listen to someone with a willingness to pray and lift him or her up before God. Outside of prayer, one of the greatest gifts you can give to another person is the gift of listening—active and nonjudgmental listening. *Active* means to be listening with purpose. Listen to each person as if you have never heard a similar story because each situation is genuinely unique.

As you listen, don't think about what you should say in response, but listen in such a way that you are able to repeat what was said. This does not have to be word for word; you can summarize the words and express the essence of what you understood to let the person know you heard what was said. In addition, as the person hears your summary, he or she can mentally filter the information.

Normally we do not get the chance to hear our own words as someone else understands them. If the reasoning does not make logical sense, then we have a chance to clarify any misunderstandings in the communication. Active listening not only results in people's being heard but also in being understood.

Talk about the Real Issues

What about single parents who will not talk about the real issues? Often people will come presenting an issue that is not the core of the difficulty. We, as humans, have a tendency to avoid that which is painful, and often the real issue is very difficult to talk about. Sometimes people resist accepting responsibility for their part of a situation, so they talk about nonessential things. Time after time you find yourself listening to the same old surface information.

In order to deal with resistance in counseling, you have to be willing to ask probing and open-ended questions. The counselee may need to ponder your question for a short time. Don't be afraid of silence. Sometimes when people take time to think through issues, they are formulating in their minds what they want to say.

The types of questions you ask will depend on the kind of issue with which the single parent is dealing. Your questions should draw a response related to the issue at hand. Seek to bring the conversation into the here and now. For example, if past childhood concerns are brought up, ask the person to state the concerns in current terms. Ask, "What role does that play in how you feel today?" or, "Why do you believe this is affecting your behavior now?"

Another approach is to identify unrealistic expectations or irrational beliefs. Sometimes people's actions are based on faulty beliefs. An example of an irrational belief is, "I must be perfect." We know that on this side of heaven we will never be perfect, but some people operate on the premise that they have to do everything perfectly. Doing our best on any project should be what we all strive for, but doing our best and being perfect are not the same. Being perfect is unrealistic, and trying to be perfect can cause lots of heartache to those who believe they have to reach this mark in everything they do. You might want to challenge them by having them respond to the question, "Why do you believe you have to _____?" and complete the sentence with what they are requiring of themselves. These are just a few approaches you may take in getting single parents to look at what they are saying and see how rethinking their views can change the direction of their lives.

You need to know your limits. If you are not trained to handle serious psychological problems, mental illnesses, or spiritual warfare, refer people with these problems to trained professionals. Have a list of Christian mental health care workers in your community to whom you can refer a single parent for in-depth or crisis counseling.

If a single parent suffers from major depression and talks about committing suicide, take appropriate action. If necessary, contact the police or call 911. Suicide is too serious an issue to go unaddressed. You need to know how you are going to handle a crisis when it arises, because the chances are very good that you will face one at some point in your ministry.

The Most Common Issues Facing Single Parents

Single parents fall into one of several of life's circumstances. There is the single, never married parent who became a parent by having her own biological child or adopting one. There is the divorced parent who may or may not have custody. While some divorced parents share in the custody of their children on an equal basis, most situations are set up with a primary caregiver and the other parent is granted every other weekend and holidays (or some other type of visitation rights if the other parent lives far away). Then there are widow(er)s who became single parents through the death of a spouse. Remember, widowhood is not reserved for the elderly, and the death of a spouse can be as sudden as an automobile accident or may be the result of a lingering terminal illness.

No matter what the circumstance, each of these carries with it the unique challenges of parenting without a marriage partner. Many of the issues single parents need help with are: grief; concerns over custody, visitation, and legal issues; finances; parenting skills and discipline; and feelings of inadequacy. We will discuss ways to approach each of these topics.[1]

Grief

Loss can be the death of a spouse or a divorce that shatters the dream of a happy marriage. The emotion that accompanies a loss is a natural and God-given process of healing. Although there is no one right way for any one person to go through this process, here are some guidelines.

Loss affects people in several ways. At first, numbness usually sets in. Some call it *shock,* and others call it *denial.* No matter what you want to call it, it is the mind's way of shutting down and allowing one to get through the motions of the day before allowing the reality of the event to settle in. It is normal to be in shock or denial in the beginning, but problems arise if a person stays in this mode for a long period of time. Important phone calls don't get made, bills aren't paid, and a dependence on others develops for things that should be handled by the individual.

The next stage of grief is often *anger and blaming others* for the loss. Divorcees often are angry about all of the hurtful and painful things they feel their ex-spouse has done to them. Even widows often feel angry with the deceased spouse for dying and leaving them with all the responsibility. Single parents become angry at the children for not cleaning up their messes or not doing their homework on time. Many Christians become angry at God for allowing the loss to occur.

You may assure counselees that God is big enough to handle their anger. In fact, the Almighty created us with the emotion of anger and gave us some guidelines to deal with our anger (see Eph. 4:26–32). Unresolved anger, however, turns into bitterness and becomes an emotional cancer that eats away at one's whole being. Use biblical truths in your counseling concerning anger and forgiveness.

Sometimes *bargaining* is part of the grief formula. Because we can't easily face the reality of the loss of a spouse (through death or divorce), we try to negotiate. If the spouse is still living, the bargaining spouse may promise to make life changes to be a better partner, to give up objectionable habits, or offer to do or to become whatever the other would want if he or she came back.

With widows there is less of an opportunity to bargain—the spouse is gone forever. But some widowed persons try to strike a bargain with God. "Now that my spouse is gone, please give me . . . make me . . . protect me from . . ." and finish the plea with a major demand. (An example might be "Don't ever again let me lose a close family member.")

When bargaining does not resolve the problem or ease the pain, single parents may go back to anger, or they may move into *depression*. Depressed single parents feel very worthless and lack energy. If the depression is prolonged, it can lead to more serious physical and emotional problems. One of the reasons the depression stage may be overlooked is that while depressed, single parents may retreat into solitude and not feel like doing much, especially talking. It is important to help grieving single parents by holding them accountable and getting them involved in some type of support network. If your church does not have a support group, then you might start one or refer people to a church that does.

The final stage of grief is *acceptance*. The term *acceptance* is often misunderstood. Sometimes you will get a response from people like, "I will never accept this!" Acceptance does not mean being happy or glad about the event but rather coming to terms with reality. Acceptance is an emotional and spiritual state where forgiveness has taken place and one is ready to move on past the pain to rebuild one's life.

Grief is like a journey at sea. Unexpected storms may delay progress, and some people will get shipwrecked along the way, becoming stranded on the islands of denial, anger, or depression. Depending on how long they have been there, some people find a comfort zone on their islands and do not want to leave. As leaders, we may have to send out a rescue team to help these individuals find their way to the shore of acceptance.

Grief is a natural part of emotional healing, but no two individuals will go through the process the same. Be prepared to love each one through it.

Custody, Visitation, and Legal Issues

It is important to understand that unless you are a lawyer, you should not be giving any legal advice. And even if you are an attorney, church policy may preclude you from giving legal advice. So, as a leader in a single parent ministry, you will want to have a list of good lawyers to whom you can refer single parents who need one.

Many of the issues single parents talk about in the area of custody and visitation are of a legal nature. This does not mean you cannot listen and empathize with their concerns. In fact, it might be helpful for them to vent with you in the safety of your office rather than arguing with the ex-spouse or even the children. After they voice their concerns with you and work through their emotions, single parents are more likely to be able to discuss the issues clearly with a lawyer.

You may agree with what the parent plans or wants to do, but watch your words carefully. If you do give advice, you might inadvertently encourage the single parent to pursue something that has a legal consequence, not only for them, but also for you. Just because you feel something is right does not mean the judicial system will rule the same way. Single parents must work through the legal maze with the guidance of a good lawyer.

What about the nonlegal issues concerning custody and visitation, such as the ex-spouse doing things of which the primary caregiver does not approve (e.g., using bad language or letting teenagers watch R-rated movies)? Although the custodial parent may be upset and not approve of the environment the other parent provides, both parents must come to terms with not being able to control what the other does. Help them understand and accept this fact. Then you can assist the one you are counseling in planning ways to discuss the concerns with the other parent and outline what is seen as having a negative impact on the children.

Help the single parent focus on the influence that he or she has on the children, because even a noncustodial parent can have a positive influence. Suggest that the parent talk with the children and explain how certain behaviors displease God, and ask the older children to make choices (such as not watching inappropriate movies) that would be pleasing to God.

Finances

For some people money is always an issue. There is a rule that if someone spends more than he or she earns, there will be financial problems. We all have to live below our income levels if we are to avoid money problems.

For many single parents the amount of money earned does not cover all the extra miscellaneous expenses they face. This is partly because so many couples live on two incomes in today's economy. So when a divorce occurs or a spouse dies, many single parents find themselves having to lower their standards of living to that of only one income. It would be hard not to want to maintain the same spending habits, yet they have to learn to make the adjustments.

Larry Burkett has written a book called *The Complete Financial Guide for Single Parents* (Wheaton, Ill.: Victor Books, 1991). If you do not have a copy in your personal library, you may want to get one. In fact, get several copies so you can give them to single parents.

There are a few things to consider before you start to give financial counsel. One is the temptation to want to personally bail everyone out. Your heart will cry out to the many needs, yet it is best to trust the benevolence committee in your church for this. A second warning is to make sure your personal financial house is in order. It is hard to help someone set up a budget if your own finances are in a mess. (For more information, see chapter 18.)

Parenting Skills and Discipline

Parenting and disciplining are very closely related. *Parenting* is the instruction or teaching of a set of principles by which to live. *Disciplining* is the application of consequences for failing to live according to those principles. The purpose of discipline is to correct unacceptable behaviors rather than to punish. The emphasis of punishment is to make the child suffer for making wrong choices. From the child's point of view, discipline may feel

225

the same as punishment because he or she is being denied something he or she wants; however, the goal of discipline is to teach by experiencing the consequences of one's choices.

When disciplining, parents need to make sure the children know what are the expected behaviors and the consequences of not acting in an acceptable manner. The consequence needs to be clearly linked to the behavior. Unrelated consequences usually fail to teach children to make better choices. (For example, the consequence of not picking up one's toys might be that the toys are not available for play for a period of time.) Discipline must not be administered in anger so that parents do not risk imposing outrageous consequences (e.g., "You're grounded for life!").

Another form of discipline is to reinforce positive behaviors with encouragement and praise. If children only receive attention when misbehaving, they learn they must misbehave in order to get attention. Encourage parents to catch their children doing right things and reward them accordingly.

Feelings of Inadequacy

Some single parents have feelings of inadequacy that may have been reinforced throughout a lifetime of being told they were not good enough. If the ex-spouse had an affair or quickly found a new partner after a divorce, the single parent may also experience feelings of rejection and humiliation. Widowed single parents who were very dependent on their spouses might feel they cannot cope alone. Often single parents try to earn approval from someone (parents, friends, children). All of these things can contribute to low self-esteem.

There are also many other reasons why people struggle with self-esteem issues, and many fears accompany single parenting that can reinforce the negative feelings. One of the most exciting things you will be involved in is helping single parents realize their worth in Jesus Christ. As Christians they have much value to God—something they may not have considered in a long time.

Point out a simple verse like John 3:16 to remind single parents how much God loves them. Show them Psalm 68:5–6, where God promises to be "a father to the fatherless, a defender of widows." Reinforce that God loves and cares about the single parent. Have them read Revelation 3:20. If they have opened their heart to Jesus Christ and prayed to receive him as their personal Lord and Savior, the very presence of God resides in them (1 Cor. 6:19). The presence of God and power of God reside in the people of God. Now that is an awesome thing to consider! Encourage single parents to regularly remind themselves of these facts by writing verses on index cards and putting them on their mirror to read every morning and night. In addition to the verses above, suggest Isaiah 40:10; Romans 8:1, 28, 31; and Philippians 4:6–7.

Encourage single parents to focus on the right things they are doing. Sometimes it is easy to see only the perceived negative things. If they take Romans 8:28 to heart, they will understand that all things work together for good according to God's purpose. That verse does not say that all things are going to be good in their lives, but rather God will work through every event, good and bad, to bring about good for the divine purpose. If they struggle with focusing on the positive, have them read *Disappointment with God,* by Philip Yancey.[2] This should help them see that God is at work in all of our lives. God has a plan and purpose for them, which is to be the best single parents they can.

Ethics in Counseling

When planning for providing counseling services through your ministry, you will need to carefully consider two major issues: the ethics of confidentiality and proper physical conduct. A breach of confidentiality can destroy a person who has come for counseling. Sexual misconduct can destroy not only the counselee but also the counselor's ministry.

Confidentiality

When people share their confidences, they trust you to keep them confidential. Single parents must feel safe to talk about things that are bothering them or things that might be embarrassing or damaging if others outside your office heard. Therefore, at the beginning of your counseling relationship, you must disclose what degree of confidentiality you are prepared to offer.

In some circumstances you may be bound by law to break confidences and report something you hear to the authorities. Only a Catholic priest hearing something in a confessional or a lawyer representing a client have absolute confidentiality rights, so you need to know the laws of your state in this area. If it is clear that the single parent in your office will harm himself or herself or others, or if you discover information concerning the abuse of a child age sixteen or under or some other type of criminal behavior, you must report it or be criminally or civilly liable, especially if someone is injured.

If you are subpoenaed to testify in a court of law or to give a deposition concerning someone you have counseled, you will have to break confidentiality while under oath. It may be wise to have legal counsel for yourself prior to testifying. Also keep in mind that your records are not protected if they are subpoenaed. Therefore, be careful what kind of notes you take. In fact, in most cases, you will find it best not to keep notes. If your memory is short from week to week, ask the single parent to review what was talked about in the last session and remind you what was discussed. Once prompted, you should be able to pick up where you left off.

Sexual Misconduct

Any kind of sexual misconduct can and will hurt all those involved. It will hurt the person who is violated, and if you are married, it will hurt your spouse and your family. It will hurt the church. It will grieve the Holy Spirit and discredit your witness for Christ as well as destroy your ministry and your integrity. The cost of sexual misconduct has a price tag that carries with it the threat of moral and spiritual bankruptcy. Depending on the circumstance, you may be held liable for damages as well as be charged with criminal misconduct if the offense warrants.

The sad thing about most sexual affairs that occur between individuals involved in a counseling setting is that the parties never intended it to happen in the first place. The process of sexual involvement often happens over a period of time as trust turns into seduction. Because pastoral counseling often involves personal conversations that are emotionally charged, an intimate relationship develops between the counselor and counselee. In this safe and protected environment, a false sense of security may develop, leading to feelings of infatuation. The use of touch is compromised, and what was once a gentle hand on the shoulder to console turns into a hug that is anything but safe and platonic.

Mixing the emotional bond and the physical arousal that happens as two people become close is like mixing drinking and driving. You may get by with it a few times while a false sense of invincibility develops, but sooner or later the combination will cause a collision. The more someone engages in this type of tantalizing behavior, the easier it becomes to cross the line of indiscretion and become involved sexually.

What are some safeguards? It is suggested by some professionals that males should never counsel females and females should never counsel males. For some this rule is the best way to avoid any temptation or misunderstanding that might occur. However, this may not be practical for everyone.

Accountability is the most important thing you can do to protect yourself. If you do not have a secretary, you need to let someone know you are in a session. That person does not have to know whom you are seeing or what it is about. If the need arises, keep the door open and turn on a radio in the next room to mute out the conversation coming from your office. Keep your sessions brief (one hour or less) and restricted to regular office hours. Visibility and accountability are important.

Pastoral counseling is a learned skill that when tempered with God-given wisdom can be effective in helping guide an individual or family through some of life's difficult circumstances. As an educator uses different techniques to instruct pupils as they learn new information, a leader will help reveal new approaches to solving the challenges that a single parent may be facing.

It is easy to want to give advice or tell someone what they ought to do. Remember, advice is just your opinion and holds your special biases based on your life experiences. It is fine to voice your opinion and let a person know what you think about a situation provided it is clear that this is your opinion. The main goal is not for you to solve the problems but to equip single parents to be problem solvers themselves.

Rev. Alan Corry has been involved in single adult ministry since 1988 and is currently serving full time at Hickory Grove Baptist Church in Charlotte, North Carolina. He is a graduate of Southwestern Baptist Theological Seminary, having earned M.A. degrees in marriage and family counseling and religious education. He is a licensed marriage and family therapist in the state of Texas and a member of the American Association of Marriage and Family Therapy (AAMFT) and the American Association of Christian Counselors (AACC). He and his wife, Carla, have one son.

22

Establishing Mentoring Programs

CRAIG CASTER

> What good is it, my brothers, if a man claims to have faith but has no deeds? Can such faith save him? Suppose a brother or sister is without clothes and daily food. If one of you says to him, "Go, I wish you well; keep warm and well fed," but does nothing about his physical needs, what good is it? In the same way, faith by itself, if it is not accompanied by action, is dead.
>
> James 2:14-17

Six years ago I was vice president of a large land development company, earning an excellent income, and enjoying the full benefits of the American Dream come true. But something got in my way. Someone took it all away from me—God.

While volunteering as a lay youth pastor, I worked with five foster care teens. It didn't take long to realize how different they were from other adolescents, how cynical and angry, how empty and hopeless. I became convinced that most of their challenges arose from a single missing element in their lives—a father. So I began teaching them what a father should teach his sons.

Soon I found myself waking up in the middle of the night thinking about them, praying for them, and crying for them. God had put a sweet, yet profound, burden on my heart, and I knew I was being called to a new vocation.

About that time I met Miles McPherson, an evangelist who shared his vision to reach at-risk children through mentoring. Miles knew that thousands of kids all over the world come to Christ only to return to their previously self-destructive lifestyles within a year. He believed that unless someone went into these fragmented homes to mentor and disciple them, these children had virtually no hope of sidestepping the life-threatening traps and temptations that lay in their paths.

I decided I wanted to help such spiritually needy children. I wanted to assist those who felt abandoned or unloved, who flirted with breaking the law, who experimented with alcohol, drugs, sex, or violence, and who were drawn into gangs. As I stepped out in faith with God, I faced the terrifying task of telling my partners, wife, and family the shocking news that I was quitting my job. No one needed to remind me that I was right in the middle of building a large home. I was painfully aware that I would have no immediate means of supporting my family. All I knew was that God had given me a vision of a desperately needed ministry.

Even as I proceeded, I had doubts, until one day God gave me a sign that my needs would be met. I was at a pastor's conference in Palm Springs. After a disturbing night of bad dreams and nervous wakefulness, I went to breakfast in an open air cafe. I had just finished my meal when my pastor and a couple of friends approached me and asked jokingly, "Well, is God speaking to you yet?" Just as I was about to respond, a raven flew overhead and dropped a huge piece of bacon on the table in front of me. We stared at the bacon, looked at each other, and started laughing. The implications were too obvious to be true. And then, believe it or not, that morning the conference speaker spoke from 1 Kings 17:6 about the ravens bringing Elijah bread and meat each morning and evening. I no longer had any doubts that God would provide not only for me and my family but also for the ministry. And the Almighty has.

That was the beginning of a powerful ministry, the Family Support Foundation, which has experienced continuous growth over the past five and a half years. Through our foundation many single parents have been provided with a true bounty of spiritual and material bread and meat morning to evening, day after day. We established a mentoring program through which we have matched over 150 adult mentors with children and developed a mentor's manual based on research, experience, victories, defeats, and countless conversations with the ultimate mentor of us all, Jesus Christ. We now mentor both fatherless and motherless families who are experiencing crises in their lives. We receive referrals from the juvenile probation office, city attorney's office, social services, churches, and other community agencies.

While our program does minister to never married single parents and widowed single parents, most of our mentorees have been through a divorce in the family. Children of divorced parents have some unique issues with which they deal. Some ask themselves, "How can these people whom I love so much, and who supposedly love me, split up? If they loved me, would they do this to me? Therefore, they must not love me very much. And if they don't love me, then who does?" Such thoughts can start a chain of deterioration in the child's life. This is true in Christian families but even more true in non-Christian or nominal Christian families. Without believing in their parents' love, without having a life in Christ, and without developing a strong faith, these children feel as if they are free-falling without a parachute. Those aren't my words; they are the words of some of the children we have mentored.

What Is Mentoring?

There are many definitions of mentoring. Some people think it means to show or teach young people vocational skills. I agree. Others believe mentoring is showing kids how to get good grades and directing them toward college. I agree with that also. Still others say it means discipling a child and leading him or her to Christ through the Word. I certainly agree with that. Some people meet with a child three or four times a month to talk or go to dinner or a movie and call it mentoring. Do I agree with that? Yes, of course.

Those are all valuable aspects of mentoring, and few children could fail to benefit from any one of them. But our program is designed to do all of those things. We are more than a traditional Big Brother/Big Sister program. We do more than befriend children at risk. We do more than spend time with them. We deliberately invest in teaching and training children. And as part of our program, we mentor the parent as well.

We take the *whole family* approach to mentoring at the Family Support Foundation. A family is like a mobile. If one piece is out of balance, the entire mechanism gets out of balance.

How Does the Mentoring Begin?

When a young person is referred to our program, we meet with him or her one-on-one. We explain the program, how it works, why a mentor is needed, and the importance of each facet of the program, especially the disciple plan. During this visit we obtain baseline information about the child's emotional state, academic level, relationship with the parents, and personal goals and hobbies.

Whether or not the children referred to us cooperate in the initial interview, their eyes often reveal their hopelessness, especially those without Christ. They're tired. They're hurting. They often feel there's something deeply wrong with them, their parents don't like them, and they are to blame for all of the family's problems. We listen carefully. If we can get them to open their hearts and share their perceptions, we can usually get a tremendous amount of insight about what is really going on in the family. Children have keen instincts.

A few years ago I received a call from a single mother who was crying hysterically. Her thirteen-year-old son was in a lockdown facility in town. He had been in and out of juvenile hall, had threatened a classmate with a knife, had pulled a gun on a family member, and was now under lock and key in a place where his volatile temper could be monitored and managed.

I met with the young man and discovered that his mother had struggled with alcohol abuse all of her life and his father had left when the boy was only five years old. Since then there had been so many of his mother's boyfriends moving in and out of the house that he had lost count. He had witnessed and experienced more violence than he would talk about, and recently his mother's domineering boyfriend had moved into the house and was exercising full physical authority over the boy. His mother gave the man her full support.

During the time I spent with the boy, I shared Christ with him and assured him that there was a reason for everything that happened in his life. I reminded him that he must take some of the responsibility for his actions and that things could change for him, quickly and dramatically. He would need to understand and redirect his anger, learn to forgive his mother, and allow us to establish a stabilizing influence in his life (a mentor). He agreed.

Shortly after he was released from the facility, we matched him with a good mentor. He progressed rapidly in his personal growth. He entered high school and excelled in sports. His mother and her boyfriend came in for parenting counseling, began to apply what they learned to raising her three sons, and discussed getting married. They are truly becoming a family.

This story illustrates the importance of treating the whole family as a single unit. However, not all cases proceed so smoothly.

Some adolescents require more effort and creativity to get them to open up. A method that usually works for me is what I call the "I dunno" approach (because the most common answer I get to several of the questions is, "I don't know"). Many of the children I see think they know what they need to know to survive. Their perception of being an adult is being free to hang out with friends all day, being old enough to have sex any time they want, being tough enough to join a gang, seeing how close they can come to a drug overdose, drinking until they pass out, smoking, fighting, and answering to no one.

So I begin by asking a series of questions, which I suspect they have never answered to themselves. The predictable response is the ungrammatical "I dunno." The conversations go something like this:

"What do you want to do in life?"
I dunno.
"What do you want to do for a living?"
I dunno.
"When do you think you're going to decide?"
I dunno.
"What's adolescence?"
I dunno.
"Let's say you're an adolescent now. When will adolescence end?"
I dunno.
"When do you become an adult? When you're eighteen? Twenty-one? When you get a job? When you move away from home? When?"
I dunno.

At an appropriate point in the dialogue, I begin to change my questions and lead the young person to some answers.

"Who do you know who makes a good living—the kind of living you'd like to make?"
My cousin Billy.
"What does he do?"
Works for the water district.
"And you'd like to work for the water district also?"
Yeah. That would be cool.
"There are a hundred jobs in the water district. Which one do you want?"
I dunno.
"How much money does Billy make?"
I dunno. But he's got a cool car, nice clothes, and a place across town.
"What kind of schooling did he need to get that job?"
I dunno. I think he went to some kind of school. It wasn't college or nothing.

"Wouldn't it be nice to know what kind of schooling you'll need to get a job like Billy's? Maybe he makes eight bucks an hour, but if he would have taken three more classes or gone to school for one more year, he would be making twenty bucks an hour. What would you rather have, the eight or the twenty?"

The twenty.

"Well, wouldn't you like to find out how to get the twenty?"

Yeah. But I don't know no one who . . .

"I do. I know lots of people. And they will help you answer all of these questions."

Most of the kids are looking for help. But before they will expose their vulnerable souls, they need to feel they can trust you. You will need to win their confidence. Your desire to help must be sincere, free of expectations, and neither condescending nor patronizing. Kids can sense if you have ulterior motives, hidden agendas, or unrealistic expectations.

Many of the troubled ten- to seventeen-year-olds who come to our program are so excited to be matched with a mentor that they have already signed the papers agreeing to participate in the program. We still conduct that initial interview. The youngsters need to understand fully the program and what is expected of them. We inform them that the process includes a life skills curriculum and a series of Bible lessons. They cannot enter the program until they agree to do the work and follow our curriculum.

There are also guidelines for parents of participating children. The foundation requires a team effort. The child, mentor, trainers, staff, and parent should all share a specific objective: to introduce or maintain stability in the child's environment. Everyone needs to agree on the philosophy and methodology that will be employed to meet that objective. It is advisable for the mother or father to attend parenting classes, work closely with the mentor, discuss both positive and negative changes in the child's attitudes and behaviors, and adhere to the program guidelines once they've been established.

It is imperative that the parent not punish a disobedient child by restricting him or her from the mentoring sessions. When the child enjoys and anticipates the time with the mentor, the parent faces the temptation to use the sessions as a disciplinary device. Mentoring is not a series of one-time fixes; it is a long-term relationship. It is a healing process. Who would tell a sick child that because he or she misbehaved, he or she can't have medicine today?

How to Recruit Mentors

The most effective way to recruit mentors is to give a short (five- to seven-minute) presentation in church during a worship service, prayer meeting, men's fellowship group, women's Bible study, or any other gathering of the body of Christ. Don't make the talk too emotional or passionate because the human heart is swayed to quick response by rousing speeches or touching stories. The decision to become a mentor must be made with the head and the will so the commitment will be long lasting. Remember it is God who calls and equips people to do the divine will, and those are the ones you want for mentors.

You are looking for prospective mentors whose hearts have already been prepared by God for the task. Ask the congregation how they feel when they see a distraught child walking down the street. Ask them if God is laying kids on their hearts. Then give clear, precise information about the program and what you are asking them to commit to doing. *Commitment* is the key to the success of the program. When the commitment is weak or wavering, the entire mentoring process is at risk of failing. Remember, the goal is to bring stability into the lives of the kids in the program. When you do make presentations, always provide literature on the program and be prepared to take names and telephone numbers of those who are interested.

In addition to making a presentation, you may prepare a bulletin insert to be used several times a year. Or you could recruit mentors by approaching individuals you feel would be effective in the program and asking them to consider becoming involved.

Not that long ago if someone approached a pastor and volunteered to work in the church, the person was usually welcomed enthusiastically. If the person expressed a desire to work with children, he or she would be praised and gratefully put into immediate service. In our blissful ignorance, who among us could have imagined the unconscionable crimes that could be committed within the church itself? Some pedophiles recognized this opportunity and took full advantage of it, and children suffered.

Therefore, though it saddens me, we have had to become cautious about whom we allow to work with our children, especially in a one-on-one type program such as mentoring. You will want to carefully screen prospective mentors before accepting them into your program. Many churches now have an effective system of security and background checks to prevent potential abusers from becoming part of the ministry. Likewise, our foundation has developed a process for ensuring the integrity, character, and commitment level of all our mentor candidates.

Fingerprinting is essential. We have our own fingerprinting machine. In most cities you can purchase one at the police station or at a police supply store, or you can send the candidate to the police station for fingerprinting. In that case, inform the police department that you are sending them someone who will be working with children so they can flag the computer to focus on violent crimes and crimes involving children. If you acquire your own machine, you must follow a procedure dictated by your particular police jurisdiction. In most cases you would complete a form and send it to the appropriate authorities. The report will come back marked "approved" or "not approved"; you are not given any additional information or confidential details.

Fingerprinting is only the first step we take. We require each candidate to complete a mentor application, through which we obtain such valuable information as: work status, education, hobbies, marital status, family status, and criminal record. (A conviction does not automatically disqualify a candidate.

Depending on the offense, a reformed criminal can make an excellent mentor.)

During an interview process, we determine what is motivating the prospective mentor to participate in the program. We try to eliminate anyone who is merely looking for quick, spiritual self-gratification. We also determine the level of commitment. We are looking for people who are responsible, whom we can count on to follow through on at least a year-long commitment to nurture and serve a child at risk. We don't want mentors dropping out of the program. We are entrusting them with a child who needs hope and stability.

Next, we ask for four references. This is very important. Much of our decision is based on what these references say about the candidate. It is amazing how honest these people will be. Even though they are discussing the qualifications of friends, most people rarely lie, embellish, or exaggerate. We ask ten to fifteen questions about the candidate such as:

How long have you known the person?
What is your relationship with the person?
Do you know if the person has been involved in any other ministries? If so, what type?
Was the person consistent and dependable?
Was the person successful in the ministry?

Then we tell the reference what type of position this person is applying for and ask point-blank, "Do you think this person is qualified to do this type of ministry?"

When we have gathered all of the information, we pray about whether to accept the applicant into the program. If we feel led by God to do so, then the person becomes a mentor.

How to Train Mentors

When you have recruited several people to become mentors, you will want to set up a training session to give them a comprehensive description of the program and your expectations of the process and to answer any questions the group may have. I have found that a single three- to four-hour session works best. We reserve a nice room at the church and provide child care if any have children.

Discuss the various ways in which the mentors are expected to train, teach, and disciple the children. Review the Bible and life skills lessons they will be sharing together and any other material you have prepared for them.

When discussing the program in detail, avoid focusing on the worst-case scenarios. While it is true that some children do come with heavy emotional baggage and hardened dispositions, many do not. The time to discuss problem situations is when a particularly challenging child is being matched with a specific mentor.

I encourage you to develop a manual for use in training and monitoring the mentors in the program. The manual we have developed is a concise road map that describes every step to be taken throughout the course of a year. The manual consists of more than one hundred pages, including fifty-five discipleship lessons and a crisis intervention section. The latter includes a list of food and clothing suppliers, hot line telephone numbers to suicide and sexually transmitted disease information centers, and the names and telephone numbers of pertinent social service organizations.

Failure to provide a manual may lead to mentors becoming ineffective and even lazy. It is tempting to merely get together for dinner or just spend time having fun. Food and fun are important parts of the whole program, but they must be combined with academic, vocational, and spiritual activities as well.[1]

How to Match Children with Mentors

Once you have recruited mentors and trained them, you face the biggest challenge of all—successfully matching children with mentors. It's time to think of yourself as a coach in the heat of a championship game. It's fourth down and two. You can't punt. You have to score. The decision is yours. Everyone is waiting and watching. You must decide. Who are you going to send in? Your big fullback? Your quick, agile halfback? Should you run a quarterback sneak or throw a short pass? It's your call, coach!

Everything you have done so far has led to the moment when you match a troubled kid with the perfect mentor. Pray that God will guide you in the process. Use common sense and logic. Use your intuition. Talk with the available mentors. Consider the geographical locations of the homes of the mentorees and mentors. But most of all, let God direct you to the right match. Then make the call.

How to Monitor the Program

Never forget to monitor the mentoring process. Follow up, follow up, follow up. Anything can happen. Mentors will make mistakes, take rejections personally, stay away. Children will have little *hiccups*—as we call the minor setbacks that invariably occur. Parents will sometimes find it difficult to adjust to the new relationship. Everyone will have questions, misconceptions, growing pains. By keeping close tabs on the situation during the first ninety days, and periodically thereafter, you can usually ensure a low mentor mortality rate.

How to Measure Success

If I can get a mentor to meet with a child on a regular basis for a year and diligently work through the prepared curriculum with the child, I believe in my heart the long-range effect in that child's life will be significant. Many of the children may not realize the full effect of the mentoring experience until they reach their twenties or thirties. On the other hand, I've seen children completely turn around in a matter of months. It is an indescribable joy to witness a transformation from raging, constant anger to contentment, peace, and a maturing faith in God.

The Scriptures say we are the light of the world. But what good is it unless we are shining that light into the darkness? We need to mentor troubled children in the church, but we also need to go into the communities around us and provide help, hope, and faith. There is pain all around us. The streets are rampant with drug and alcohol abuse, physical and emotional violence, teen pregnancy, teen homicide and suicide, a growing rate of sexually transmitted diseases, and an increase of youth in detention facilities.

The church must reach out to the hurting world and offer Christian caring. Jesus said, "Whatever you did for one of the least of these brothers of mine, you did for me. . . . What you did not do for one of the least of these, you did not do for me" (Matt. 25:40–45). We must not fail the children or the Lord.

Pastor Craig Caster is the founder and director of the Family Support Foundation in El Cajon, California. Craig has been ministering to families and children for over eleven years as a marriage and family counselor, Bible teacher, youth pastor, and speaker. Through the success of the ministry, God has opened the doors to work with social services, juvenile probation, the San Diego city attorney's office, police departments, and community organizations. In 1997 a federal government report on mentoring youth said the Family Support Foundation mentoring program was one to emulate.

23

Partnering Parents

DOUGLAS JAMES DEES

My definition of grafting is: (1) the process by which nutrients from one root system are supplied to a branch not from that root system; (2) the insertion of a scion into a stock for the purpose of growth of that scion.

One way of ministering to single parents is to become partners in parenting with them. An effective way to partner parents is through a mutual family adoption program, which will be discussed in this chapter. The reason this chapter about adopting families began with a definition of grafting is because the Lord was the one who came up with the idea for adoption in the first place, and grafting is how it is explained in Romans 11:17–24.

In the grafting process a scion (a detached living portion of a plant) is inserted into a prepared section of a larger, healthy plant for the purpose of nourishing the scion to the point of mature fruit bearing. In God's grafting process, we are grafted to the Almighty through Jesus Christ for the purpose of growing us to become more like Jesus Christ each day. A church, then, actually imitates God as some of the families graft, or adopt, each other into their lives for the purpose of nourishing and helping one another grow and become more like Christ each day.

In James 1:27 we are told that pure religion is to visit the orphans and widows. Single adult ministries, and specifically ministry with single parent families, are modern-day applications of that verse. So we should not look at single parent family grafting (or adoption as we will call it from here on) as an option as much as a command. The number of single parent families is growing each day, and so is the need for loving, mutual adoption among families in the church.

This chapter explains how a two-parent family and a one-parent family can adopt each other and become extended families for one another. The three parents become partners in the parenting process through the family adoption program. Both families benefit from the adoption.

Purpose

The highest purpose for matching one-parent families with two-parent families is to create a parenting partnership through which both families are nurtured, grow, and become all that God intends them to be. Many other purposes are satisfied by the adoption process, but the overall purpose of nurturing members to become more like Christ and to become increasingly healthy and productive Christians is always to remain the central focus.

Another purpose for having a family adoption program is the respite it provides for the parents. When either the couple or the single parent spends time alone with all of the children, the other parent(s) can have some totally quiet time for which there is no baby-sitting cost.

Another reason to have a family adoption program is so the children in single parent families get to see how other families actually live. I use the word *actually* because many times children in one-parent families have a somewhat distorted view of two-parent family life since the only time they see other Christian families are at church functions, and we always have our best faces on at church. When they are in a partnering program such as the one we are advocating, the children see that life in a two-parent family has its ups and downs just as does life in a single parent family.

Matching Process

The matching portion of the adoption process has certain parameters that need to be followed to assure as high a degree of quality, relational interaction as possible. Each individual church will need to modify the suggested matching process to make it work well within a particular congregation.

The first thing that is needed is someone who feels that God wants him or her to administer this relational program. From there, the best way to start the program seems to be to just get the word out: "We need two-parent families and one-parent families who would like to form extended families and spend time together."

The process starts when a list of families is developed. From there, you begin a matching process. The leadership of the Holy Spirit is extremely necessary here. There are, to my knowledge, no guidelines that show what age the children could be in either family. There also does not seem to be an age limit for the parents either. Keep in mind though, the energy requirement increases with the number of children. In making a family match, you basically need two families willing to work together for the betterment of each other. I have seen matches that I initially thought were far from perfect turn out to be the best matches of all. Much prayer is needed to ensure positive matches.

Most of the administrative work is done up front. After a potential match is made, there is a first meeting, which needs to be scheduled with the administrator of the program and all three parents involved. At this meeting the parents should discuss the following issues:

1. styles of discipline preferred in the home and how much authority for disciplining the children will be shared with the other parent(s)
2. things both families enjoy doing for fun
3. preferred eating restrictions (such as no snacks between meals or no sugared treats)
4. the children's favorite foods and activities
5. the children's and the adults' hobbies

6. preferred bedtimes for younger children and curfews for older children
7. which friends are approved and which are not
8. any allergies or medical conditions the children may have
9. any medications the children take routinely (insulin, antihistamines, etc.)
10. how much time to plan to spend together and when
11. ways to contact each other at work, home, on a beeper, or car phone in case of emergencies
12. any other areas of concern

You may want to add issues that are specific to your particular setting.

If all three parents think the match will work, then medical release forms can be signed. Figure 2 on the following page gives a sample release form, but you need to check with a local hospital or emergency unit to see if it has all the information required in your state.

At this first meeting the parents will also need to spend time talking about the children and how this partnering/adoption relationship will affect them. This is important because from a molding standpoint, the children will most likely be affected more than the adults.

Once all parents understand and are willing to follow the guidelines, the next step is to just let them figure out among themselves when to get together and what to do.

Guidelines

You need to establish guidelines to follow to ensure the integrity of the program. For the best in spiritual sharing and encouragement, all three of the parents should be believers and involved in the same church. (However, as an outreach ministry, a believing couple could adopt a nonchurched single parent family.) Also, commitment is extremely important. In considering parents for the program, look for stability and longevity of Chris-

Figure 2. Medical Release Form

Child's name _____

Birthdate _____

Home address _____

Telephone _____

Mother's name _____

Father's name _____

Mother's employer _____

Business address _____

Business telephone _____

Father's employer _____

Business address _____

Business telephone _____

Name of responsible person to contact in an emergency if parent cannot be located promptly _____

Relationship to child _____

Telephone _____

Name of physician to call in an emergency _____

Physician's telephone number _____

Medical record number _____

Permission:

_____ has my permission to take my child to the doctor or hospital if necessary for any emergency medical care.

Signed _____

Date _____

The special health condition(s) or allergies my child has is/are:

_____

_____

248

tian commitment as well as commitment demonstrated in other areas of their lives.

It is best to have all parents involved sign a one-year commitment that can be renewed each year. This will give some stability for the children and allow for the development of in-depth relationships. The children of the two-parent family can benefit from learning about commitment, but it is especially important for children in single parent families, who may already feel abandoned by a parent. A short or intermittent commitment on the part of the adults may reinforce in the children's mind that adults are people whose commitments are short-term. They, in turn, may grow to emulate these short-term commitments. That attitude can devastate their future married lives as well as their careers.

You may wish to establish a requirement that participating families have been a part of your church for a period of time so you can get to know something about them before matching them with other families. Or you may feel this is not necessary. But you should carefully screen families because you are being instrumental in bringing people together. Unfortunately, there are those who might want to get into this type of program for the wrong reasons. Most of us have read news stories of abusive adults or pedophiles who have infiltrated church-related children's programs. Screening can significantly minimize that possibility.

Activities

Sometimes the two families will plan weekend activities when they are all together. At other times all of the children go with either the single parent or the couple. The activities the families might become involved with are limitless. The shared activities should not always be something fun (i.e., trips to a water park or fishing); sometimes the activities should be just regular things a family does. There may be days that everyone goes to the woods and cuts firewood for the winter. A yard cleanup day would be good. A trip to the grocery store can be shared. Cleaning out the garage is a great idea. Washing the car (or the dog) can be fun. Just about any activity is appropriate, and most provide teachable moments.

The three parents may want to get a sitter for all the children involved, and go out for a long, casual dinner. Both families may want to take a short vacation together. The sky is the limit for possibilities that life offers for personal interaction. The Holy Spirit can guide families as they plan ways to interact.

Encourage the families to be creative, but remember, in all situations the goal is the deepening of the relational interaction of those involved. Also keep in mind two of the important purposes are to allow single parent children to be involved with a two-parent family and to give the single parent some needed rest. I personally like to see the two-parent family take all of the children at least once every three weeks.

Follow-Up

It is a good idea for the administrator of the program to make a telephone call once a month to check on families. Also, some type of occasion should be planned a couple times a year to get all those involved in the parenting partnership program together: a potluck, a cookout at the lake, a hiking or biking trip, or just a game night at the church fellowship hall. You will be encouraged by attending one of these functions and seeing all the lives that are being changed.

A regular time should be set for informing the church of the program. Though you will have different families come in and go out of the program at varying times, it is essential that you regularly inform the entire church of the program.

Benefits and Drawbacks

There are many benefits and a few drawbacks to the partnership/adoption program. Most of all, a church that has a family adoption process will definitely see God at work and lives changed. The benefits of adoption extend to the single parent, the couple, and all of the children.

The married parents benefit by having a better idea of what it is like to be a single parent, and they receive an enormous blessing just being able to minister to others in a solid, concrete fashion. Their faith may be strengthened as they see God at work providing for the one-parent family.

The single parent also is blessed as he or she helps and ministers to the married couple. The single parent gains parenting partners and an extended family with whom to spend holidays, to visit when the children spend time with the noncustodial parent, and to ease the loneliness of single parenting. There may even be help with some of the difficult physical tasks of maintaining a home.

Another benefit of the program is that all of the children see practical ways of having a relational ministry. The parenting partnership demonstrates to others that you love them. Too much church work is done at arm's length these days, and we do not show our children how important it is to be relationally involved in the lives of others. We must be close enough to people to realize their needs and to be used by God to meet those needs.

One of the most important benefits to the children who live primarily with their mothers is the surrogate fathering this program provides. A healthy father role model can not only teach the children what a father is supposed to be like but also can give them a relationship with a Christian man of whom they can ask some of the hard questions of life. This healthy interaction can then be reinforced by the single parent.

Because children are more likely to grow up believing what is clearly defined for them, the three adults participating in the partnership/adoption program will want to discuss those values which they wish to communicate to the children. What the children learn through this program will, in part, influence how they view life and how they act and react as adults.

We sometimes speak of God as a heavenly Father. How children experience an earthly father often transfers to how they relate to a heavenly Father. If the children of the single parent family have had negative relationships with their biological father, the partnering father can sometimes repair the damage through a loving relationship. Never forget the power of influence from a father to a child.

Single parents may benefit from the family partnership/adoption program by seeing a healthy, functional, loving relationship between the married couple. This may assist them in overcoming distrust or bitterness toward the opposite sex in general, may give them hope that there are such positive relationships, and may provide insights into ways in which they contributed to the failure of their own relationship.

There are, of course, some drawbacks to mutual family adoption. Although there are not many, the ones that exist are tough to overcome. For example, there are times when children know they and their parent are ready to participate in a partnership/adoption process, yet a matching two-parent family hasn't been identified. The children may feel unwanted or left out—like being the last to be picked for kick-ball.

One way to short-circuit that is to have periodic activities where several single parent families participate with several two-parent families and even single adults who do not have children. You need not rely on the partnership/adoption program alone to support your single parent families.

Sometimes partnered families are separated when one family is transferred due to work. However, the children will learn that change is inevitable, and the move will be just another example of that. The families can still call, write, and send birthday and Christmas cards to one another. Having distant caring "relatives" can be a plus during a time of adjustment to a new home.

Timing

When to begin a family adoption program will depend upon the circumstances in each individual church. You don't have to start with fifty families; you might begin with two families who are willing to invest in one another and let the program formalize and grow from there. Don't wait until you have all of the logistics worked out if there is a need and people willing to meet that need. Just start a program. Listen to the prompting of the Holy Spirit as you reach out to strengthen the body of Christ.

Dr. Douglas James Dees is the single adult and college pastor at First Baptist Church in Moore, Oklahoma. He has directed single adult ministries for over fifteen years. He has become a popular conference and retreat speaker and has led retreats for churches and conferences for the Baptist Sunday School Board. He has a heart for helping people understand the theology of relationships. He has an M.Div. from Southwestern Baptist Theological Seminary and a D.Min. from Reformed Theological Seminary. His dissertation deals with the lost doctrine of relationships. He and his wife, Karen, have two children.

24

Planning Retreats, Conferences, and Seminars

BOBBIE REED

*T*his is fun, Mommy," six-year-old Brian said as he grinned up at his mother. They were in the middle of the lake on a paddleboat during free time at the annual single parent weekend retreat at Crista Camps in Poulsbo, Washington.

Marsha nodded at her son and smiled, then concentrated again on working the unfamiliar pedals. Other children and their parents were canoeing, swimming, playing ball games, riding ponies, swinging, and hiking. Sounds of laughter, happy shouts to friends, and calls of "Watch me, Daddy!" filled the air.

Most leaders of single parent ministries have discovered that weekend retreats with the children are a popular activity. Others hold conferences and offer seminars and workshops at the church several times a year.

Weekend Retreats

It is often difficult for the church to provide child care at home for an entire weekend, and often single parents do not have the resources or family members to watch the children. Therefore, a weekend retreat for single parents without their children will draw fewer people than one planned to include the children.

When planning a combined weekend retreat, you will want to provide seminar and discussion time for the adults by themselves with activity time for the children by themselves, activities that include both parents and children, and free time for the families to be together and select from a variety of activities. In order to accomplish this, you will need at least one speaker for the adults and several people to lead activities for the children. Children's activities could include: crafts, skits, music, games, videos, scavenger hunts, art, and Bible stories. Part of the activities would be educational; others would be entertaining and fun. Keep in mind that you will have children of all ages, so you will need separate activities for teenagers and for young children. Some of the teenagers may be willing to assist with the children's activities.

Programs that include both adults and children need to be planned so as to interest everyone. One activity I have found to be fun, attention getting, and insightful is to have family members work together on two collages. Provide used magazines, construction paper, scissors, and glue sticks, and each family makes a collage from magazine words or pictures to illustrate the good things about being a single parent family. They could make a second collage to illustrate the negative things about being a single parent family.

After about thirty or forty minutes of working on the collages (or whenever most of the families have finished theirs), I invite families to come to the front of the room, speak into the microphone, and tell about their collages. The children's comments are often surprising and touching. Parents have often told me they have never heard their children be as open about their feelings about being in a single parent family as when they shared about their collages. The microphone itself adds an interesting dynamic to the reporting process: Some children are shy at first, some virtually yell into the microphone, and others don't want to let go of it when their turn is over.

Other activities that can be planned for the entire group include: starting the day with a group devotional and singing; having families act out skits, do Bible charades, or illustrate Bible verses with drawings or a rebus; scheduling a family talent show; or roasting hot dogs and marshmallows over a campfire.

Free time activities the families can select from are only limited by the retreat facilities and your imagination. Three of the guys from one church brought their four-wheel-drive vehicles and took groups four-wheeling through the mountains. Another group offered water skiing. Outdoor games, water sports, hikes, ball games of all types, and table games are also good choices.

The goals of the family retreat are to provide a time of learning and inspiration for the parents, positive family interaction, and group fellowship. The ministry to the children in this type of setting is usually more educational and entertainment than emotional healing and support, although elements of the latter are present.

A popular choice for single parent family retreats is the Labor Day weekend. If you are not ready to plan a full retreat for single parents and their children, see if you can find one that is being held close enough to your area so single parent families can drive (or carpool) to it. Then advertise the retreat to the single parents in your ministry.

Conferences

Even if you only have ten or fifteen single parents in your church or community who would come to a single parenting conference, you may still want to plan one. If your budget would not allow for covering the cost of having an outside speaker flown in, then you could invite other single adult leaders from your area to join with you in sponsoring the conference and leading the seminars. Or ask individual single parents to each lead one of the sessions. Suggest several topics and give plenty of notice so they will have time to prepare. You may discover some genuine talent in your group for making presentations that are both educational and entertaining.

Plan the topics for a weekend conference to cover a broad range of subjects that are of interest to single parents, such as:

developing self-esteem
helping children develop a positive self-esteem
effective discipline

communicating with teenagers
finding time for everything
coping with the stresses of being in a one-parent family
defining the role of an effective Christian parent

Many churches have found that a single parent conference is not the usual Friday-evening-through-Sunday-morning weekend conference. Instead, it is a Saturday only event that is concluded early enough in the afternoon that the single parents can have time left to do weekend chores and be with their children. Therefore, an 8:30 A.M. through 3:00 P.M. schedule seems to be the most popular.

If you do not want to have a conference geared exclusively to single parents, then at least be sure to have workshop options for single parents in any of the single adult conferences you plan. You might even have a single parent track running parallel to the main conference. This does not require you to plan, organize, and advertise a separate conference but in effect provides an entire single parent conference.

Conferences are educational, inspirational, and renewing as single adults take time to get away from the normal routine to reflect, focus on personal and spiritual growth issues, and check on where they are headed based on their current behaviors and choices. One woman shared at a conference, "I realized this weekend that I have been so busy learning to be a single parent and keeping up with my regular routine that I lost track of the importance of having my personal devotions every day. I'm starting tonight to get back to doing that."

If you can't provide a conference, then find out who is having a single parent conference or single adult conference with single parent workshops, and share this information with the single parents in your church.

Seminars

Periodically you will want to provide seminars for single parents. You may choose to do a series of several weekly sessions.

For these you might have a speaker, show a video series, study a book that has a leader's guide, or use a single parent curriculum. (See the resources listed at the back of the book for ideas.)

Another option is to set one night a month to do single parent seminars on different topics. Although several ideas for topics of interest to single parents are listed in the above sections, a good source of ideas would be the single parents themselves. Ask them to provide a list of subjects they would like addressed. Then you review the list and determine whether some topics would be best combined into one seminar and if others would lend themselves to a short series on a related theme.

Other Options

There is a lot of work required to plan a successful single parent family retreat, and although you do your best to keep the cost reasonable, there is an expense to the families. So until you get several families committed to participating, you may have to wait to host a retreat. On the other hand, some groups use the church facilities to have a weekend retreat and the cost is much less. (Of course the activities are more limited also.)

A conference can be a major event or a simple Saturday function with a minimum of planning and expense. Seminars with out-of-town speakers will require planning, coordination, and sometimes major expenditures, or they can be virtually cost free and easy to schedule. For the very small church or ministry, the best option is to network with other churches in the area and host combined retreats, conferences, and seminars, rotating the hosting responsibilities among the churches.

The second option would be to have a separate single parent Sunday school class during the regular Sunday school hour that would address single parent family issues. This would eliminate the need for an additional weeknight or weekend commitment.

The third option would be to sponsor the attendance of one or more of the single parents to a conference or retreat with the stipulation that upon return the information would be shared with other single parents. Admittedly, this option has limited effectiveness.

The fourth option for the very small church or ministry would be to provide a library of as much literature and videos as possible that single parents can check out and read or view at home. Obviously this option does not provide the group interaction, inspiration, commitment, and energy that gathering together with other single parents provides. Therefore, while recommended as a supplement to other types of ministry or as a minimum way of providing information, it is not the option of choice.

One of the reasons for having retreats, conferences, and seminars is that it is a scriptural concept for those who have walked the journey and learned from their experiences to teach others. Paul wrote that older men and women ought to teach younger men and women and that there is a responsibility for church leaders to teach (Titus 2:1–15). Therefore, you will want to provide educational opportunities for the single parents in your ministry.

Bobbie Reed was a single parent for ten years, has been an author, consultant, and speaker in the field of single adult and single parent ministries since 1974, has authored thirty-three books, and is assistant director of the Network of Single Adult Leaders. She holds a Ph.D. in social psychology and a D.Min. with an emphasis in single adult ministry.

25

Sponsoring a Single Parent Housing Complex

SHARON THAYER
AND BARBARA HUGHLEY

The House of Hope in Cedar Falls, Iowa, is a single parent housing complex that grew out of a vision for a unique outreach for the single adult ministry of the Nazareth Lutheran Church in that city. The original dream was shared by Sharon Thayer, the chairperson of the service committee, and Ella Hansen, the codirector of single adult ministry. But the actual project became much more than they ever hoped for or expected. Today several churches, a sorority group, businesses, and community organizations work together to cosponsor the housing project, which includes the House of Hope (an eight-unit apartment building for women and their children) and Nehemiah House (a five-unit apartment building for single men).

The Dream

In the early 1990s the service committee of the Individuals Together single adult group of Nazareth Lutheran Church explored several projects that might catch the interest of the members. They planned trips to a camp to help with painting and clean-up and discussed short-term missions trips. But the response from the group was disappointing.

In January 1991 Sharon read an article about a project in Des Moines that had been a cooperative effort between several churches. Members had worked on renovating an apartment building to be used for single mothers and their children. When Sharon and Ella shared the idea with the service committee, they were very interested in doing something similar.

Sharon, Ella, and three other interested members of the service committee went to Des Moines to talk with the director, Andy Bales, and to see the project. When they returned, they met with several service agencies and organizations in Cedar Falls. Everyone agreed that safe, affordable housing was a genuine need in the area.

So Sharon and Ella recruited several single adults (including a real estate broker, an accountant, an engineer, construction workers and contractors, and people involved with various jobs and businesses) to form a housing committee. We all began looking for the right building to use for the project, rejecting an abandoned school with asbestos problems, a former funeral parlor, and several other large houses and apartment buildings.

In 1992 contact was made with various ministers and citizens to bring the needs of single parents to their attention and to enlist their support. From this group, the Christian Community Development organization was formed, and it was incorporated as a nonprofit group in 1993.

The Beginning

The first project that was undertaken was renovating a single-family dwelling the city donated to the effort. Grant funds were obtained for the renovation, volunteers did as much of the cleanup and repair work as they could, and professionals were hired to do the plumbing and electrical work. After many, many hours of work, we were finally ready to accept applications from families to rent this house for a year and then be eligible to purchase it for $10,000, which would repay the original grant funds. After reviewing the applications, one family was selected.

In 1993 the city donated another building to the project—this time a five-unit apartment building. Due to the small size of the apartments and a recognition of the needs of homeless men, it was decided that this building would be renovated for housing for single men. Renovation on the building began, and in the summer of 1996 the work was completed.

In the meantime, the dream of a single parent housing complex wouldn't go away. So we prayed that God would lead us to the right building. Soon a woman offered us a building with eight apartments. At first she was going to donate the building, then she decided she wanted to sell it to us for an inflated price. After several meetings with the owner and much prayer, Ella and the woman agreed on a significantly reduced price for the building with affordable payments. We received the keys and took possession of the house October 31, 1994.

Although we knew God had given us the building, it was an awesome undertaking because we had no funding for the project except for some donations from different churches. But additional grant funding was obtained, and the renovation work began.

During this stage there were seven churches involved in the renovation and decorating of the building. Our first idea was to have each church adopt an apartment and do all of the work for it. But not every church had people with all of the needed skills, so the plan was changed. Dick, a retired contractor, agreed to oversee the renovations, and he recruited numerous volunteers in addition to those from the churches. A group of teenagers from one church spent a weekend painting all of the doors of the house. This was a time of daily discoveries of repairs that were needed. Dick and his recruits responded faithfully to each call.

On December 1, 1995, Barbara Hughley moved into the house as the manager, and a single mom moved into one of the apartments just in time to save our insurance coverage. We had been told the insurance would be canceled if the building were not occupied. By early 1996 all eight apartments were filled.

Special Help

Some of the single moms and their children who move into the House of Hope do not have very many clothes, and what they do have may not be suitable for job interviews or attending church in a middle-class or upper-middle-class congregation. One church understood this and did something to help. Several women came to the home to take the moms shopping. Each mother was given fifty dollars to spend on clothes. Then the mothers were invited to the church and were specially honored at a reception.

A Bible school affiliated with another church donated their week's offerings to the project (about one thousand dollars). This money was used to purchase a television, a video player, and several video tapes appropriate for viewing by children.

Some of our best supporters have been the ladies in a sorority who visited the project and saw a need for emergency supplies for the new arrivals who often come with little or nothing. These women made up several gift baskets using large laundry baskets. The baskets include towels, a few kitchen utensils, personal toiletries, dish and hand soap, and several other items to help the single parents get through their first couple of days. The apartments are equipped with dishes, pans, and basic linens, which are inventoried before each single parent family moves in and after they move out. These things stay with the apartment, but the laundry gift basket items belong to the single parent.

The Challenges

Finances are an ongoing problem. Several churches support the project both with supplying volunteers and donating money. Other organizations, such as Bible study groups, the sorority, local businesses, and even a local business college, have been regular donors. We continue to seek grant funds that might be available for the project. And we pray daily that God will meet our needs as promised in Philippians 4:19.

Since the apartment building is very old, there are things that must be repaired and updated. Cosmetically the building is attractive, and the new windows, floor coverings, and yard fence make it nice for the children and their parents and a safe place to live. We continue to battle the old steam heat boiler in winter as it overheats some of the apartments and underheats the rest. On the same day we may have fans operating in apartments with the windows opened wide and space heaters in others with residents bundled in sweaters.

One of the challenges we are struggling to resolve is providing child care. Although some of the mothers have family members who help, most do not. Therefore, child care expenses are significant for those mothers who work or attend school.

The Lessons We Learned

Because we were the Christian Community Development organization, we naturally envisioned having organized Bible teaching in the House of Hope—for example, a Tuesday evening Bible study held each week with outside teachers. Reality turned out to be different than our dreams. There were so many different churches involved in the project that there could be disagreement on what would be taught. Many of the single mothers did not come from a Christian background and had not been involved in church. And because partial funding for the project comes from grants, there are restrictions on the type of teaching or preaching we can do; there are also restrictions against making attendance mandatory. So we have had to keep our religious teaching fairly generic and practical. This was less than we had hoped to be able to do.

As we have worked with single parents and their families, we discovered that we had some misconceptions that had to be corrected. It was hard to accept that some of the women who come from abusive relationships to our safe house later choose to return to their former husbands or boyfriends.

We also assumed the single mothers who moved into the apartments would know how to cook and clean. What we failed to recognize was that many of these mothers come from dysfunctional families. They often have few homemaking skills. We have

264

learned to do regular inspections of the apartments, reward good housework, and educate the residents when necessary.

We thought the young women would be so thrilled to have a nice, clean, pretty apartment that they would automatically show their appreciation by keeping the apartments clean and pretty and by obeying the rules we set for the building. This is what usually happens for the first couple of weeks after a single parent family moves into an apartment. But they soon revert to whatever behavior is normal for them. There can be a change in attitude and a lack of housekeeping efforts. To combat this, we have specific rules for cleaning the apartments and taking care of the building, we make routine inspections, and we involve each of the single parent families in developing or changing the rules when necessary.

Contrary to what we had thought before the project, we learned the welfare checks the single mothers receive are woefully inadequate to cover their basic needs. Fortunately, our supporters bring care packages with soap, diapers, shampoo, cleaning supplies, toilet paper, and other day-to-day necessities that we can use to help the families stretch their incomes.

We have learned to demonstrate Christian compassion and a spirit of forgiveness when one of the women has broken the rules and is facing eviction. If she is deliberately rebellious and uncooperative, we may require her to move out. But in those cases where the mothers are genuinely working at obeying the rules and yet fail once or twice, we are willing to give them another chance. We carefully explain that future failures will be cause for eviction but that we will work to assist them in being successful.

The failures are difficult for us as a board because we ask ourselves, "How could they do that to us?" But we know that most of the mothers are very young and have never been disciplined to live within rules. Therefore, when considering these cases, the board members decide whether we would be better off by working a little longer with the mother we already know or by ridding ourselves of her problems and then perhaps taking on someone with even greater problems. This question causes us to go back and look at our goals. We are here to provide a safe environment in which a young woman can grow and learn, can become self-sufficient, and can learn or improve parenting skills. It is our aim to encourage education.

A pastor once said, "Forgiveness is the fruit of being forgiven." All of us as Christians have experienced God's forgiveness. How, then, can we continue to harbor grudges and erect barriers between ourselves and other people, smugly saying that if they really wanted to they would change. We can't. But we are here to help the change occur.

The Rewards

One of our successes at this time is a young woman who just graduated from high school. She plans to go to the local community college and then on to university.

It also has been rewarding to see the single parents and their families become involved with a neighborhood church on their own. We know it is as a result of all of the practical kindnesses that Christians have shown to these families. When several of the mothers wanted their babies baptized but were too shy to do so in front of the entire church, one of the local ministers provided a private ceremony for them.

The Future

The more we do on our project, the more needs we become aware of in our community. There are women with children who need a more structured environment as they work on parenting skills, drug or alcohol dependencies, and setting new goals for their lives. This may be the basis for a new project. The housing committee has developed a habit of noticing houses and buildings in our area with an eye to considering which one might be the site of a new project.

Those of us who knew and worked with Ella Hansen were saddened by her death in July 1995. Many times we wish we could send a heavenly E-mail message to ask her opinion on one of our controversial issues. We are sure she would know just how to proceed with the yellow house around the corner.

Sharon Thayer raised two teenagers as a single parent. She graduated from St. Francis Hospital School of Nursing in Wichita, Kansas, as an R.N. and has worked in surgery. After additional schooling, she was certified as a registered nurse anesthetist. She completed a B.S. degree in health arts from St. Francis College in Joliet, Illinois, in 1980. When she moved to Cedar Falls, Iowa, she became active in the single adult ministry of the Nazareth Lutheran Church and with the House of Hope project. She serves on the board for the Christian Community Development organization.

Barbara Hughley is the first and only manager to date of the House of Hope. She graduated from high school and worked at various jobs before moving to Iowa where she earned a B.A. degree in psychology and staff development from the University of Northern Iowa in Cedar Falls. She has worked at residential treatment centers and has been a group home director for Lutheran Social Services and a drug and alcohol counselor for Eldora Training School for Boys. She has been at the House of Hope since December 1995.

26

Preparing for Blended Family Relationships

GARY A. SPRAGUE

Some of the single adults in your ministry will decide to get married, and often one or both of the partners will have been married before and have children. In those cases, the goal is blending the former families into a new family, while the reality is often a clashing of the two families' traditions, rules, expectations, and habits. As leaders of single adult ministries, we can help dating partners prepare for successful blended family relationships.

Some of the single parents in your ministry are already fringe members of a stepfamily because their former spouses have remarried. Because developing a working relationship with the stepparent at the other home can be a challenge, some of the ideas in this chapter can also assist these single parents toward healthy blended family relationships.

When providing premarital counseling for single adults (when one or both already have children), there are several ideas you will want to include.

268

Take Time to Build Relationships

There is no set point in a dating relationship at which children should be involved with the dating partner. If children build bonding relationships with the parent's dating partner too early in the process, the kids are more likely to suffer multiple losses because dating does not always lead to commitment and marriage. On the other hand, if the children do not have time to get to know and like the dating partner before he or she becomes a stepparent, there can be problems in the new family. So the best advice you can give your single adults is to involve the children in the relationship building process as soon as there is reason to believe the relationship may be a long-term commitment leading to marriage. Once that decision is made, the wedding should be delayed until the children have become comfortable with the soon-to-be new parent.

Biological parents have time to prepare for a new son or daughter during the nine months of the pregnancy and then develop a relationship with the child as he or she grows up, one year at a time. Single adults who marry a partner with children become instant stepparents of one or more partially grown children. The stepparent has not had a part in communicating values to the children or in shaping their habits, traditions, history, and perceptions of what is acceptable in a family. There are usually conflicts that need time to be worked through together. Wise single adults do as much as possible of this work before the marriage in order to eliminate some of the problems.

Build History Together

Working and playing together builds a shared history as well as develops intimacy and topics of communication. So dating partners who plan to marry and have begun to involve the children in their relationship should intentionally build a history together. They can develop a list of things each person has always wanted to do but never has—from flying a kite to hiking up a mountain, or from attending a baseball card convention to entering something in the county fair. Then they see how many of these things they can do together.

Finding a favorite restaurant and eating there once a month can become a special event for the family. Bringing home and displaying souvenirs (pinecones, seashells, pretty rocks, etc.) from shared activities helps keep pleasant memories alive.

Establishing new traditions together allows children to bond with both the parent and the dating partner. Making flower baskets from construction paper, filling them with fresh flowers, and delivering them to the neighbors on May Day (May 1) was an idea one family adopted as a new tradition.

Do Not Make Comparisons

Although it can be tempting to compare the dating partner with the children's other parent, you will want to remind single parents that this is not wise. The children already will tend to feel a disruption in their family relationships and loyalties. Some can accept a dating partner but do not as easily accept that person as a stepparent with the right to dictate and discipline. Some believe that loving a stepparent is being disloyal to the other parent.

The wise single parent will understand these conflicts and frequently affirm the children's love for the other biological parent. This lets the children know that the parent who is going to be married isn't expecting a shift of loyalty from the other parent to the new stepparent. Single parents will want to avoid making disparaging, bitter, or angry comments about the other parent at all times, especially in front of the children. Paul reminded us to get rid of bitterness, rage, anger, and malice and to forgive one another and be kind one to another (Eph. 4:29–32). This includes former spouses.

Consider Carefully the Living Arrangements

Experts suggest that a new blended family move into a neutral home or apartment rather than into the home of one of the partners. One reason for this is so the incoming children do not cause the children in the home to have to change rooms or share what was once a personal, private bedroom. Also, the person whose home it is will tend to feel that it is still his or her home, and the incoming partner will often feel like a visitor or an intruder. The new partner may want to change the cupboards around while the home owner may resist changing the ways things have been. In addition, it can be very uncomfortable for a new partner to move into a home that was previously shared by a former husband or wife.

Unfortunately, financial resources do not always allow single parents to take the advice of experts in this matter. So counsel your single adults to be aware of these issues and take steps to do what they can to make the home comfortable for both partners. Remodeling, redecorating, rearranging the furniture, repainting, and repapering are things that might help.

One couple who planned to live in the man's home put all of the woman's belongings in the front yard and then moved everything from inside the house to the yard. Together the new family decided where everything would go and what would be kept, stored, or given away. It was a monumental task, but it was well worth the effort because the result was a sense of shared ownership. It was reminiscent of the early church who had a singleness of purpose in their caring enough for one another not to insist on selfishly keeping what belonged to themselves (Acts 2:42–47).

Recognize the Importance of Financial Responsibility

The failure rate for second and subsequent marriages is higher than for first marriages. The two most common reasons for this failure are children and finances. Before entering into a blended family, single adults need to be very open with each other about their attitudes toward money, their debts, their problems with impulse buying, the way they use credit, their ongoing financial commitments, their incomes, their savings, and their giving to the Lord, to others, and to charities. When partners fail to be open and honest with one another, particularly regarding finances, misunderstandings and disappointments develop that cause problems in relationships.

Discuss Expectations

Single adults who are planning to form blended families have a tremendous need to discuss their expectations thoroughly before they marry. The more they can share with each other, the fewer the surprises after the marriage. The more they can settle before the marriage, the less they have to sort out afterward.

The dynamics of discussion before a marriage are different than after the *I dos*. Somehow two single adults planning to be married can discuss expectations and preferences from an equal status. Yet that same discussion after a marriage commitment may not have the same equality if one partner believes (even subconsciously) that marriage gives him or her leverage over the partner. "If you really loved me, you'd do things my way," is sometimes the unspoken belief between spouses.

Things to discuss before marriage include:

disciplining the children
house rules
curfew for older children
eating times
food preferences
stressors
what triggers anger, bad memories, or negative feelings
signals for letting the partner know what one needs or wants
how much alone time is needed
relationships with the children's other parent
daily or weekly schedules
division of chores
special issues involving the children
how conflicts will be resolved
any other topic the couple may face in their new life together as a blended family

Suggest that dating partners pray before each of their discussions, asking that God help them to be honest without being argumentative and to be open to negotiating an acceptable position on each issue. Let them know that an acceptable position might include doing things two ways or having two brands of toothpaste, coffee, or soap.

Form a Parenting Coalition

Sometimes the stepparent is seen as a threat by the children's other biological parent. There may be a fear that the children will come to love the stepparent more than the biological parent. There can be resentment when the stepparent disciplines the children. Differences in values, expectations, and habits result in disagreements. But this doesn't have to be the case.

When parents accept a stepparent as one more adult to assist with supervising and raising the children, a parenting coalition is possible. Children sometimes feel more free to discuss personal topics with an adult who is not a biological parent. The stepparent often fulfills that role. When the children sense there is unity among the parents and the stepparent(s), there is less opportunity for manipulation by the children.

So explain the value of forming a parenting coalition to a dating couple and encourage them to put aside other differences and at least cooperate with one another and the other parent when it comes to issues with the children. Paul's words in Galatians 5:13–15 offer good advice about building positive relationships.

Provide Names of Good Christian Counselors

Tell single adults who are planning for a blended family that they need to decide before they are married who they will go to for counseling *when* they have problems they cannot resolve. Emphasize the word *when,* and point out that you didn't say *if.* All families have problems, and blended families tend to have more than their share because of all of the things that must be blended together. Seeking counseling before a relationship becomes irreparable may be the secret of developing a strong and lasting family.

Demonstrate Hope

Although many second marriages fail, many also succeed. With prayerful planning and a spirit of cooperation and commitment, your single adults can be among those who succeed. Encourage them to plan to be successful by doing all the work they can before the marriage and continuing to cooperate after the wedding.

Gary A. Sprague is the executive director of KIDS HOPE, which runs seminars, retreats, and camps across the country and has begun a national single parent ministry program. He has authored three books: My Parents Got a Divorce *(self-published);* KIDS-HOPE *(Elgin, Ill.: David C. Cook, 1997);* Kids Caught in the Middle: An Interactive Workbook for Children *with Randy Petersen (Nashville: Thomas Nelson, 1992);* Kids Caught in the Middle: An Interactive Workbook for Teens *(Nashville: Thomas Nelson, 1993). Gary received a master's degree in social work from Loyola University of Chicago and a bachelor's degree in psychology and sociology from Trinity College in Deerfield, Illinois. Gary, his wife, Lois, and their three children live outside of Colorado Springs, Colorado.*

27

Teaching Spiritual Disciplines

HAROLD IVAN SMITH

Like millions of other Americans, I sat glued to the television watching the 1996 Olympics in Atlanta. I found the last six miles of the women's marathon particularly intriguing. Once the clear leader, Ethiopia's Fatuma Roba, realized that she was nearing the finish line, her stride became more commanding. Clearly her concentration was focused on one goal: winning the marathon. Then a man began running with her along the sidewalk, holding up the Ethiopian flag and calling encouragement to her. Roba broke into a smile. He ran several blocks, enthusiastically supporting her before dropping back. Then another man, clothed in a jogging outfit that mimicked the flag of Ethiopia, began running beside her cheering. With a radiant smile, Roba won the marathon and a gold medal. The Olympic stadium erupted with applause for her effort.

That should be the role of the church—coming alongside single parents and their children, cheering them, encouraging them, and supporting them in the long marathon called single parenting. It is definitely not a sprint. I often witness miracles accomplished by single parents, yet because we live in a time of enthusiasm for family values, rather than receiving applause for their accomplishments, many single parents feel more as if they are bull's-eyes for arrows of condemnation.

A verse in Acts prods my soul like a pebble in my shoe: "There were no needy persons among them" (Acts 4:34). Reading the context of the words, one learns that this was not simply referring to the financially needy but also to the spiritually and emotionally needy.

However, the spirit of rugged individualism in America these days often offers little more than an occasional "Single parents, God bless 'em!" mentality. When looking for spiritual guidance and direction, many single parents have to virtually ignore the "Do not disturb!" signs posted by some churches. Often single parents experience anger, annoyance, and irritation at the limited or total lack of compassion in many family-centric churches today. Our prized independence leads many single parents down the "I'll do it myself!" path, mumbling under their breath, "Who needs your help anyway?"

Successful single parenting, however, is a partnership with a God who deeply cares about the needs of single parents and their children. I suggest, in the spirit of the opening story, a God who, like Roba's supporters, runs along beside single parents encouraging them. And the church also needs to support and encourage.

Spiritual guidance and direction has a dual focus: one is for the needs of the single parent and the other for their children. It is impossible for the single parent to offer children what the single parent does not have. One single mother, pressured by a child's constant requests for money, pulled open her wallet and demanded, "Do you see any money in there?" Vast numbers of single parents have the equivalent of no money in their spiritual checking accounts or wallets because they have not made spiritual deposits. Sadly, the analogy might be made that the bank is not willing to open accounts in their names. "Two parent families only, please," is the message. As a result, many single parents and their children are spiritually needy.

However, the spiritual disciplines of prayer, Bible study, praise, reflection, meditation, and service are not just for married couples. It is said that during the Civil War, Abraham Lincoln admitted his constant reliance on prayer, noting, "I am driven to it." The same is true with single parents. "I am driven to my knees by the responsibilities and pressures of being a single parent," one father admitted.

My premise is simply that the spiritually healthy single parent pays attention to his or her own spiritual growth and development as well as to the spiritual growth and development of the children. The healthy single adult ministry pays attention to the needs of the single parents who participate in the ministry. We become equipper-encouragers.

The most basic prayer of the single parent is "Help!"—a shorthand God understands. Sometimes the immediate crisis prevents any more words. Realistically, some crises cannot be captured in vocabulary.

When addressing spiritual disciplines with single parents, keep in mind that the two-word phrase "personal devotions" may create instant distress in the minds of single parents. The mental self-condemnation is varied.

> "How dare you claim to be a good single parent and not have daily devotions?"
> "Are you getting up at four in the morning to pray like Martin Luther did?" (Martin Luther had a wife.)
> "Did you read the Bible through last year?"
> "Show us those calluses on your knees from the sweet hours of prayer."
> "Do your ex-spouse, your single adult ministry pastor, and your fellow single adults know about your spiritual anemia?"

Some single adult leaders believe their job is to periodically chastise single adults for a lack of spiritual discipline. However, the minister who wants to be taken seriously must ask, "What kind of spiritual disciplines would I have if I were a single parent?"

So what is spiritually healthy about stumbling into a bathroom before dawn, flipping on a light, reaching for a Bible or a devo-

277

tional book, and reading the portion for the day if accompanied with a "Well, that's done!" attitude? Too many single parents have been shamed into personal devotions.

I prefer that single parents think not of *personal devotions*, but that they experience the *devotional life*. What are the ingredients of a healthy devotional life for a single parent? Prayer, Bible reading, reflection, praise, and formational reading.

Prayer

Prayer may be a significant hurdle for those single parents who are angry at God, their former spouses, the church, pastors, or church people who judged them or who do not welcome them into congregational life. They may reason, "If God had answered my prayer for my marriage to stay together (or had not allowed my spouse to die), I wouldn't be a single parent. So how come God didn't answer my prayer or the prayers of my children?" Such negative attitudes tend to keep some people prayer-challenged.

Many single adults have bedtime prayers with their children and grace prayers at meals, which you as a single adult leader can encourage. However, many rely on panic prayers when the wolf (or the ex-spouse) is at the door, figuratively or literally. Many viciously self-indict: "I know I *should* pray." "I know I should pray *more*." Or, "I know I should pray *better*." Others confess, "I am so tired that I fall asleep praying," or lament, "My prayers aren't effective." Many believers have misguided attitudes about prayer, convinced that the right techniques ensure results.

Tip 1: Encourage single parents to see prayer as a relationship with God. Prayer is about getting to know the Giver of things. This is a liberating concept for the single parent. Given the gospel song's injunction, "Take it to the Lord in prayer," some single parents turn praying into little more than a litany of tattling: "You know my ex is living with a woman . . . my ex is two weeks late with the child support . . . my ex has suddenly become so pious . . . my son is being disrespectful." Some pray with a vengeance that would make the psalmist look wimpish in comparison. "Strike her with boils, Lord!" (See Ps. 9:20 and Ps. 10:15.)

Prayer for some is a litany of complaint: "I don't like the single adult minister." "My car won't start." "The landlord wants to raise the rent next month." Job might be the patron saint of such single parents.

Prayer must be seen for what it is—relationship. Paul wrote, "I want to know Christ and the power of his resurrection" (Phil. 3:10). Paul didn't see Jesus as a cosmic Santa Claus or a glossy catalog: "I want the following stuff. . . ." Help your single parents understand this key point. God is not room service.

Tip 2: Encourage single parents to choose a position. They imitate another's prayer style and then berate themselves when it is ineffective. Kneeling, standing, or lying can all have a place in a single parent's prayer life. However, the position of the heart is more important than the position of the body. I happen to pray better sitting in a comfortable chair. Encourage your single parents to discover a prayer style that is comfortable for them.

Tip 3: Encourage single parents to pray the biblical prayers. The Book of Psalms has traditionally been the prayer book of the Jews and the early church. For centuries, single parents have prayed Psalms 4–13 (whether or not they knew it). The words could well have been written by a single parent. The Psalm prayers offer a jump start on a spiritually cold morning. They prime single parents to pray from their own hearts and needs. Remember these:

"O LORD my God, I take refuge in you" (Ps. 7:1).
"In the LORD I take refuge" (Ps. 11:1).
"How long, O LORD? Will you forget me forever?" (Ps. 13:1).

The Bible also offers other examples of prayers, such as the Lord's Prayer (Matt. 6:9–13) and Jesus' prayers, which include:

"Yet not as I will, but as you will" (Matt. 26:39).
"Into your hands I commit my spirit" (Luke 23:46).

Remind your single parents that Jesus didn't have to pray long prayers, and neither do they.

Some single parents find great spiritual nourishment and strength in praying Jesus' dying prayer: "My God, my God, why have you forsaken me?" (Matt. 27:46). It may be helpful for single parents to notice that in the time of his greatest need, Jesus was not timid, spontaneous, or original. Jesus prayed the psalmist's prayer from Psalm 22:1, thereby modeling for us the prayer of the end of the rope when our brains and souls cannot be original. Prayer can be simply, "Oh God, I am so overwhelmed," and then waiting with God. Isaiah 65:24 says, "Before they [substitute *single parents*] call I will answer; while they are still speaking I will hear."

Dare your single parents to pray the prayers of the apostle Paul, such as:

"What shall I do, Lord?" (Acts 22:10).
"Praise be to the God and Father of our Lord Jesus Christ, the Father of compassion and the God of all comfort, who comforts us in all our troubles, so that we can comfort those in any trouble with the comfort we ourselves have received from God" (2 Cor. 1:3–4).

You can help your single parents adapt the prayer of Paul from *us* to *me* without doing injustice to the text. Also refer them to 2 Corinthians 1:5; Galatians 1:3–4; Ephesians 3:14–20; 1 Thessalonians 5:23; 2 Thessalonians 2:16–17.

Tip 4: Teach your single parents to pray by listening as well as talking. If we talked to our friends in the way we talk to God, most of us would be friendless and lonely. Friends not only talk but also listen. So many people think prayer is about words; some think you have to butter up God or get on the Lord's good side when praying by saying all the right words. Not so. Prayer is also listening—sitting silently and expectantly in the presence of God. In today's vernacular, the psalmist might say, "Shut up and know the Almighty is God" (see Ps. 46:10), or, "Be quiet before the Lord" (see Ps. 37:7). Jesus reminded his disciples not to be impressed with wordy prayers and prayer styles. Jesus might say today, "KIBSP (Keep It Basic, Single Parent)! Talk to me. Listen to me. Wait on my timing."

Tip 5: Teach your single parents to use the prayers of the church. I often pray the prayer Christians have used for centuries, "Almighty God, unto whom all hearts are open, all desires known, and from whom no secrets are hidden: Cleanse the thoughts of our hearts by the inspiration of the Holy Spirit, that we may perfectly love Thee, and worthily magnify Thy holy Name: through Christ our Lord. Amen."[1] Sometimes I change the prayer to first person singular: "Almighty God, unto whom *my* heart is open. . . ." Wonderful prayers can be found in *The Book of Common Prayer;* it is like a minilibrary of prayers. These prayers have been used in the liturgical traditions, but increasingly Christians in other traditions are turning to a prayer book when they cannot verbalize their thoughts and longings.

Although I grew up in a tradition that emphasized spontaneous prayer, I find great help in prayers that have been prayed by my spiritual ancestors and heroes. Dietrich Bonhoeffer, a German single adult martyred by the Nazis, prayed as he faced death:

> O Lord God,
> Great is the misery that has come upon me.
> My cares overwhelm me; I am at a loss.
> O God, comfort and help me.[2]

On another occasion, he prayed:

> O God, early in the morning I cry to you.
> Help me to pray, and to think only of you.
> I cannot pray alone.
>
> In me there is darkness,
> But with you there is light.
> I am lonely, but you never leave me.[3]

Tip 6: Teach your single parents to tell God what it is that they need. They can be confident and specific. God is compassionate and loving. Paul said, "Do not be anxious about anything, but in everything, by prayer and petition, with thanksgiving, present your requests to God" (Phil. 4:6).

Tip 7: Teach your single parents to pray the "Jesus Prayer." For almost the entire history of the church, Christians have prayed, "Lord Jesus Christ, have mercy on me." This prayer is based on the petition of blind Bartimaeus in Mark 10:47, which in turn is based on Psalm 57:1. The Jesus Prayer is best used by finding a quiet place (even if only for a few minutes), tuning out distractions, and simply, slowly saying the prayer one word at a time. Some people inhale on "Lord Jesus Christ" and exhale on "have mercy on me." Seven simple, yet complex, words that invite God's attention. What more could single parents want than Jesus' mercy? An alternative phrasing might substitute the names of the children for the word *me* in the prayer.

As a single adult leader, you can pray for the single parents God has given you in the same manner. "Lord Jesus Christ, have mercy on _____." I call this the *roster prayer*. Pray through your active participant list, pausing long enough to focus on each one by name. You could follow up with a postcard saying, "I prayed specifically for you today," and include an encouraging Scripture verse. That could make a big difference in a single parent's day.

Remember prayer is not about results or technique. The quicker single parents learn and understand this, the less condemned they will feel about their attempts to pray and about their productivity. Prayer is about making time to communicate with God. Prayer offers freedom to say what is on our minds. As J. S. Spong observed, "In our prayers we roam the edges of our human experience and life and give it to God without neglecting our own deepest and most personal concerns."[4] Hopefully your single parents can come to a time when they can pray in complete openness about their lives, past and present.

Bible Reading

Single adults may sing a popular chorus, "Thy Word is a lamp unto my feet and a light unto my path" (see Ps. 119:105), but is that a reality in their lives? One blessing of some contemporary music is that the lyrics are straight from the Bible. So single parents memorize Scripture by singing. This is terrific. Include lots of these choruses in your ministry programs.

Unfortunately for single parents, the technique emphasizers have had much to say on how the Bible should be read and on how much should be read. They imply that only certain practices count. Quantity has often been the rule rather than quality. Many single parents are under the impression that to be truly spiritual they have to read the Bible through, Genesis to Revelation, each year. Nowhere in Scripture is there such a requirement. The technicians are always coming up with a new method: "Read three chapters in the Old Testament and two chapters in the New Testament every day to be spiritual." I would rather have single parents read two or three verses with involvement than two chapters without being engaged with the reading.

To help your single parents truly focus on what they read, suggest they ask questions such as:

What does this verse say?
What might this mean to a single parent situation?
What is God saying to me through this verse?

This is effective counsel to single parents who are time bound. I prefer that Scripture not be read like fast food, gobbling it down without digesting before dashing out the door into the rat race. Scripture is like a fine meal to be savored. Here are some tips for your single parents.

Tip 1: Read Scripture deliberately. Suggest that they begin with either the Book of Mark or James and read slowly, a few verses at a time. Even if they admit to the Lord that they wish there were more time for reading, they can deliberately make time to read a few verses each day.

Tip 2: Ask the Lord to honor their reading. Many of us have a grab-and-read (or skim) attitude. A better alternative is to open the Bible and pause to invite God to meet with us as we read and through what we read.

Tip 3: Take a phrase from the verses. When I teach on prayer style, I like to use Psalm 63:1, "O God, you are my God, earnestly I seek you." I encourage single parents to read that particular verse ten times, emphasizing a different word with each reading: O *God.* . . . O God, *you.* . . . O God, you *are* . . . , etc.

Sometimes words leap out at the deliberate reader, like identifying and enjoying the particular taste of different elements in a salad or meal. Paying attention to those words or phrases is beneficial. Suggest that when this occurs, these words or phrases be jotted down on an index card. The single parent can refer to the words throughout the day if the card is placed in a checkbook, Daytimer, or wallet or posted on a mirror or the refrigerator door. Reciting the words with the children at mealtime, in the car, as one kisses them good-bye, or before bedtime further integrates the phrase or words into one's life.

Tip 4: Put Scripture on tape. The single parent or the children can record a Psalm or other passage of Scripture on tape to listen to during the commute to work or while washing dishes.

Tip 5: Read Scripture with intensity. Sometimes we insult Scripture by our clumsy get-through-it style of reading. With practice one can make Scripture come alive not only for one's self but also for the children. Encourage the single parents to use some of the same dramatic reading techniques for Scripture as they do for the stories they read to the children at bedtime.

Tip 6: Interact with Scripture, particularly the stories in the Gospels. Have single parents read through a particular story silently one time. Then ask them to read a second time using their fingers to point at the lines, and letting words clamor for their attention. Then ask them questions such as, "What is going on in the story?"

For example, the story of blind Bartimaeus sitting by a roadside when Jesus comes near dramatically commands our attention (Mark 10:46–52). Invite single parents and/or the children to act out the Gospel stories. Bartimaeus was not wimpy when he cried out, "Jesus." Rather it was, "JESUS! SON OF DAVID! HAVE MERCY ON ME!" Let the stories of Jesus' life and ministry come alive. Let them zing and sometimes sting.

Was it mere coincidence that the Bible contains stories of prophets' or Jesus' interactions with children and single parents? Take time with single parents to interact with stories such as the following:

the widow's oil (2 Kings 4:1–7)
the giving widow (Mark 12:41–44; Luke 21:1–4)
the widow in the Christmas pageant (Luke 2:36–38)
the single parent whose only son had died (Luke 7:11–17)
the widow with a need (Luke 18:1–8)

Reflection

The word *meditation* has become controversial in many Christian communities. Nevertheless, it is rooted in Scripture and the spiritual habits of faithful believers. For example:

"Now Isaac [a single adult] . . . went out to the field one evening to meditate" (Gen. 24:62–63).
"Blessed is the man who [substitute *single parent whose*] . . . delight is in the law of the LORD and on his law he meditates day and night" (Ps. 1:1–2).
"I will meditate on all your works" (Ps. 77:12).
"Though rulers [add *and my ex-spouse*] sit together and slander me, your servant will meditate on your decrees" (Ps. 119:23).
"My eyes stay open through the watches of the night, that I may meditate on your promises" (Ps. 119:148).

The word *meditation* comes from the Latin word *meditari*, meaning to reflect upon, to ponder, to think about. Meditation upon Scripture responds to the questions, "So what?" and "Now what?"

Meditating on the Word is like chewing as opposed to simply swallowing whole chunks. Some people get "blown about by every wind of doctrine" (Eph. 4:14 NRSV) because they let someone else cut up their meat for them. In Psalm 77:11 the psalmist says, "I will remember the deeds of the LORD." Through meditation the single parent ponders spiritual themes in reference to God and what God has done in the past.

In meditating, one might choose a word such as *grace,* then read a related verse of Scripture, for example 1 Corinthians 15:10, "But by the grace of God I am what I am, and his grace to me was not without effect." Next the person would reflect on the word and what it means to him or her personally. Then perhaps the word would be repeated softly, slowly, then forcefully: "Grace!" The word can be sung. Remember the verse from the song "Amazing Grace"? "'Twas grace that taught my heart to fear, and grace my fears relieved. . . .'"

Meditation can be accomplished during a ten-minute repose in the sun, on a brisk walk, in the shower in the morning, or lying in bed at night after a long day. After all, the psalmist instructed, "When you are on your beds, search your hearts and be silent" (Ps. 4:4).

We meditate by asking the questions: "What does this word, this promise, this characteristic of God mean to me?" "What are the implications for my life or the lives of my children?" Single parents may ask God to freshen up a well-known verse or passage such as Psalm 23 as they meditate.

Praise

One single parent I know has adopted the attitude, "Hallelujah, anyhow!" Praise is a basic component of healthy spiritual survival. David wrote,

> Praise the LORD, O my soul;
>   all my inmost being, praise his holy name.
> Praise the LORD, O my soul,
>   and forget not all his benefits.
>
> Psalm 103:1–2

Wait a minute! Benefits? What benefits do single parents enjoy? Can you say to exhausted, tired, poor, struggling, angry (or you fill in the blank) single parents, "Remember your benefits?" Well, yes! There is always the faithfulness of God to rely on for hope. And considering that there are people in the world who have things much worse than most of us, we can choose to be thankful regardless of our situations. Remind single parents that none of the circumstances of their lives will ever permanently defeat God's plan for them.

Formational Reading

Most of what we read is called *informational* reading. Many single parents miss the opportunity to be transformed by good, solid *formational* reading—what the early church called *lectio divina* or "divine reading." While the Bible is our primary book for spiritual reading, God has also blessed us with a rich heritage of Christ-centered books and resources.

John Wesley encouraged early Methodists to read and apply what they read. Today, too much reading is in one eye and out the other. Single parents moan, "Who has time to read?" Too many approach religious books with the same goal as they do Scripture: Gobble it down and get to the last page. Finish it! Done!

Here are some tips to share with single parents in your ministry.

Tip 1: Ask God to bless the reading to their spiritual growth. Whether it is Swindoll, Lucado, Reed, or Schiller, contemporary Christian writers have some insights based on Scripture that can make a difference to single parents in their pilgrimage. Encourage them to read wisely and widely.

Tip 2: Read attentively. Paying attention to what one is reading is essential. This may mean reading in a comfortable place or going back to reread a passage. Reading attentively lets one store up quotes for a weary day.

Tip 3: Wonder periodically as they read. Give the single parents questions to ask themselves as they read Christian literature. Questions such as, "How does this impact me as a single parent?" "How does this impact my children?" "If I took this message to heart, how would I have to change my life?"

Tip 4: Let the reading warm their brains and their hearts. Teach single parents to savor what they are reading and let the message of the writer reach to the inner self to trigger personal growth and to heal personal pain.

Tip 5: Look for encouragement. Suggest that as they read they look for something that could be written down and given as an encouragement to one of the children or to another single parent. "Have I got a quote for you!" can be like a boomerang. What one gives away may return to bless the giver.

As a single adult leader, you can also prepare and periodically update cheat sheets for single parents. These are ready references in Scripture for immediate help. Corrie ten Boom called them her "First Aid Course," emergency Scriptures "which I apply to a [spiritual] wound until I can look up the rest of the Scriptures which will bring further healing."[5]

You might collect suggestions from your single parents so they have ownership of the project. Prepare a top ten list of promises for single parents. Do promise-grams to your single parents. Laminate the help lists for the inevitable challenges of single parenting. For example:

When others fail you, read Psalm 27.
When you are worrying, read Matthew 6:19–34.
When you are in a headlock with the blues, read Psalm 139.
When your faith needs stirring, read Hebrews 11.
When you need fast courage, read Joshua 1.
When you are making a deposit on a condo in Bitterville, read 1 Corinthians 13.

On my computer I rely on a wonderful device called "Shortcut to Word Perfect, Windows." I click on the icon, and I am immediately connected to the program. The laminated lists are such a device for single parents and their children to immediately connect them to the wisdom of God's Word.

A Devotional Life

There are no gold medals for the spiritually disciplined. But the spiritual disciplines do, if practiced intentionally and deliberately, train, encourage, and comfort us en route to Christian maturity. They are to a single parent what oxygen is to a runner.

The spiritual disciplines are not something that one uses to impress others. They are resources to help all of us (including single parents) become the best we can be. The devotional life is a cushion to fall back on when tired, when we fail, or when we lash out at one of the children.

As a leader, you can help your single parents *lead a devotional life* rather than just *have devotions*. But you must pay attention to your own spiritual disciplines so your bank account is flush. The next Fatuma Roba could be heading your direction today. God can use you to help single parents win the marathon.

Resources for Ministry

It is great to know good books to recommend, although many single parents cannot afford to buy them. So I advise leaders to order multiple copies of helpful books with a commitment to give them away. Do a project to raise money to buy these books. Place copies in the single adult lending library. Use a book like Richard Foster's *Prayer: Finding the Heart's True Home*[6] as a study book for six weeks or a retreat for single parents. Use books for awards. (See the Spiritual Disciplines section of the resources list at the back of this book for a listing of books I recommend.)

Harold Ivan Smith is an author, speaker, and researcher who has written more than twenty books on single adult issues. He has a D.Min. in spiritual formation from Asbury Theological Seminary and a D.Min. in pastoral care from Luther Rice Seminary. His latest book is Holy? Who Me? *(Nashville: Abingdon Press, 1997).*

28

Praying Faithfully

YVONNE KARLIN

"Pray continually; give thanks in all circumstances, for this is God's will for you in Christ Jesus."

1 Thessalonians 5:17–18

Recently I attended a single adult ministry leaders meeting, and I was surprised our time together did not start with prayer. We sang worship songs and greeted one another, but something was missing in my heart. Things just didn't seem to come together for the emcee or speaker either. I mentioned to another leader that I missed having opening prayer and was told, "We know God is here, so we don't really need to open in prayer, do we?" In a word, "Yes!"

It is our privilege and responsibility as leaders to always recognize from whom comes our strength, wisdom, power, abilities, creativity, insight, and even safe arrival at a meeting. If we fail to pray together as leaders, we may also fail to pray with our single adult groups.

We must not take God for granted! Even though we know the Lord is always with us, we need to take time to formally acknowledge the presence of the Almighty. God does not want to be taken for granted any more than one of us would like to be. God desires our devotion. In 1 Timothy 4:11–13 Paul tells Timothy to teach the things Paul has taught him. In this way Timothy would be an example for other believers in his speech, life, love, faith, purity, and reading of Scripture.

God promised never to leave us (Matt. 28:20); we should promise never to leave the Lord out of our lives and our thoughts. Of all the definitions of prayer I've read and heard, my favorite is: "Prayer is the practice of the presence of God." I don't remember where I heard this, but it spoke to my heart. I believe God takes prayer very seriously, and as leaders and teachers, we have a responsibility and the joy to demonstrate to single adults how to make prayer an integral part of their lives.

James 3:1 says that those who teach will be held to a higher standard. Therefore, we must teach more than the definition of prayer, more than a set of rules or regulations for prayer, and more than Bible stories about prayer. Paul urges us to not worry about things but to present our prayer requests to God with thanksgiving, demonstrating our confidence that our prayers will be answered (Phil. 4:6).

The challenge as leaders is to make prayer a practical but personal experience and an expression of our relationship with the Lord. This means that before we can show others how to pray, we must have an effective personal prayer life ourselves. When prayer becomes an integral part of our own lives, anyone watching us will see us praying throughout the day in a variety of situations. They will note that God is glorified in our words, decisions, actions, and relationships.

Why Do We Need to Pray?

There are many biblical reasons we pray. Some of these include:

to obtain help	Psalm 46:1
to communicate with God	Psalm 69:13
to worship the Almighty	Psalm 103:1
to delight the Lord	Proverbs 15:8
to change our attitudes	Matthew 5:44

to follow Jesus' example	Matthew 21:22
to increase our faith	Mark 9:24
to grow spiritually	Luke 6:28
to bring glory to God	John 14:13
to ask for what we want or need	John 14:14
to give thanks to God	2 Corinthians 9:15
to obey the divine command	1 Thessalonians 5:17
to intercede one for another	1 Timothy 2:1
to exhort one another	Hebrews 10:25
to seek guidance	James 1:5
to release our burdens	1 Peter 5:7
to confess our sins	1 John 1:9
to obtain forgiveness	1 John 1:9

When ministering with single parents, leaders can share that prayer is *expected* of Christians, *exemplified* for and by Christians, and *easy*.

Prayer Is Expected of Christians

Throughout Scripture we read that God's people are expected to practice the presence of the Almighty and to communicate with the Lord—to pray. For example, Romans 12:12 urges us to be "faithful in prayer." Colossians 4:12 gives us an example of Epaphras who labored faithfully in prayer. We read that God wants to hear from us in Matthew 21:22, Mark 11:24, and many of the Psalms.

In Matthew 6:5–7 Jesus gave some guidelines for praying. Notice when reading those verses that Jesus said *when* you pray, not *if* you pray. Next Jesus gave a sample prayer, which today we call "the Lord's Prayer." But the clear inference in this passage is that we are expected to pray to God.

Joyce always prays for empty parking spaces close to the store's exit doors when she goes shopping, and God usually provides them. Joyce also always remembers to say, "Thank you, Lord." Some people may think parking places are too trivial to ask of God, but Jesus said in John 14:13 that we are to ask God for anything because our gratitude for answered prayer gives glory to the Almighty. Joyce has learned the secret of praying for everything, whether monumental or trivial. Her walk with God has grown increasingly personal and intimate as her prayer life has deepened.

Prayer Is Exemplified for and by Christians

A group of single adults from my church meets for lunch after each Sunday morning worship service. One Sunday I led the group in the usual short prayer at the restaurant before we ate. During the meal our waitress came over and thanked us for praying. She confessed that she had been feeling bad that she had not been able to attend church that morning. When she saw us praying, she bowed her head and sent a prayer of her own up to God. The natural act of thanking God for our food had blessed the waitress. I don't think she understood that by sharing her story, she blessed us in return.

Scripture tells us to pray continually. That means praying about whatever is happening in our lives. As we teach single parents to develop such an awareness of God's presence that they begin praying as naturally as breathing, their spiritual strength will develop.

A group of single adults went to the beach one evening. One of the women took her cooler back to her car and discovered she had left her car keys in her jacket on the beach. So she left the cooler on the ground beside the car and returned to get the car keys. When she came back to the car, the cooler was gone. It had been a nice, big cooler, and one she had hoped to keep for the other summer outings the group had planned. As she walked back to the beach campfire, she was very upset and was thinking unpleasant thoughts about the person who had stolen her cooler.

When she explained what had happened, her dismay and anger were evident. One of the leaders of the group suggested they pray for the thief. The woman was startled at first, then smiled sheepishly and nodded agreement. Coming together in prayer brought peace to her heart.

First Timothy 2:8 says that we ought to "lift up holy hands in prayer, without anger or disputing." Because we cannot bless and curse in the same breath, we can choose to remain angry or to glorify God through praying for those who have offended us. "Bless those who curse you, pray for those who mistreat you" (Luke 6:28).

One way leaders themselves can be examples of people who pray is to pray on the spot. Three weeks before her wedding, a friend of mine sprained her ankle. She was worried about being able to walk down the aisle and to dance the first dance at the reception. Some of her other plans weren't working out well. She was tense and upset, and she asked me to remember her in my prayers. I asked if she'd like to pray right then. She said she would, and we did. She felt the stress relieve and peace permeate her confusion and frustration. She praised God.

When people tell you of a situation in their lives that is causing them pain, fear, or uncertainty, rather than promising to pray for them later, pray right then. You may continue to pray for them over a period of several days, but that first prayer is best if done on the spot.

Sometimes logistics or distance prevents us from actually getting together to pray. But that doesn't mean that group prayer cannot be accomplished.

A group of single adults and I were planning a New Year's Eve celebration. At one point it seemed that Murphy's Law had gone into effect and anything that could go wrong had gone wrong. Because each committee member's schedule was filled, the only time we could meet was on Saturday. But there were several decisions that needed to be made before the weekend. So I called all of the members saying that at nine o'clock in the evening we would have a joint prayer session. Wherever we were (at work, on the road, in a store, or at home), we would each pray for guidance and wisdom for the committee decision makers. We did just that.

The next Saturday at our regularly scheduled meeting, we shared about the unusual prayer meeting. Each of us had felt the power of the Holy Spirit as we gave our decisions to God. It was a wonderful experience for all of us. We had found a new way to have two or three gather in Jesus' name (Matt. 18:20).

294

Prayer doesn't have to be formal, complicated, a production, at a special time, or in a designated place. We must be willing to pray anytime, anywhere, for whatever we need.

Prayer Is Easy

It is easy to teach single parents to pray if we make prayer a natural part of our gatherings. Here are a few ways that single parent ministry leaders have built prayer into their ministries:

1. Open and close every gathering with prayer. Sometimes the leader prays, or at other times different single parents are asked to lead in prayer. This provides not only an example of prayer but, for some, an opportunity to practice prayer.
2. Have weekly prayer partners. During each Sunday session, invite the single adults to write their names on slips of paper and place them in the center of the table (for small groups) or in an offering plate (for larger groups). At the end of class, each person draws a slip of paper. During the week everyone prays for the person whose name they drew. This activity can be a secret prayer partner or not, depending upon the desires of the group. If there is no secrecy about whose name was drawn, then individuals may telephone, send cards to, or go out to lunch with the person for whom they are praying. In this way, they can learn more about the prayer needs of the person and pray more intelligently.
3. Print and make available prayer request forms. When single parents have special prayer request needs, they can fill out a card and turn it in to one of the leaders of the single parent ministry. These prayer requests are then shared with the ministry team, who spend an hour a week praying for the individuals in the ministry and their specific prayer requests.
4. Take snapshots of each member of your single parent ministry. Then have each person write his or her name and three prayer requests on the back of the picture. The photos are then placed into individual envelopes, and each single adult is given an envelope. They commit to praying for the indi-

vidual whose picture is in the envelope for the next two months. These pictures can be placed on the mirror in the bathroom, on the dashboard of the car, or on the refrigerator. They will serve as reminders to pray for the person. By getting in the habit of praying for someone on a daily basis, single parents find that the Holy Spirit works in their lives and trains them to be more aware of the needs of others.

5. Select Scripture verses (such as Rom. 8:35–39 or Eph. 3:16–20) to be used as a daily prayer by the single parents. Change the verses each week or two. During one of your weekly gatherings, invite people to share how the verses of the week have impacted their lives.

6. Have praise opportunities during your gatherings. When you worship God by singing and praying, don't forget to worship with praise also. Invite single parents to share about ways in which God has been faithful or has answered prayers during the week.

7. Assign prayer partners for a six-month period. Ask which single parents would like to become prayer partners for this period of time. Match those who do into pairs. They can get to know one another, pray together, and will most likely develop a deeper Christian relationship than they had before the experience.

8. Form a prayer chain. Collect the names of all of the people who will make a commitment to pray for others when they are called. Organize the chain so that when a prayer request comes into the church or to the single adult leader, one person makes calls to five predesignated people who will each make five more calls (resulting in thirty-one people all praying for one request). If your group is very large, you might have several different chains, or add another 125 people by having the twenty-five people called by the first five people each call five additional prayer warriors. You will want a way to provide feedback about the answer to the prayer or the outcome of the situation about which they were praying. This not only encourages commitment to the prayer chain but also gives God glory as people share what the Lord has done.

9. Have a weekly prayer meeting either in a home or at church. Let people know that the meeting is open to anyone who needs prayer or who wants to pray for others.

10. Hang a prayer request bulletin board in the room in which your single parents gather most frequently. Encourage people to write their prayer requests and post them on the bulletin board. Read the requests and pray for them yourself and invite others to do the same.

11. Develop a prayer discipleship program for new Christians or those who feel their prayer lives are not effective. Involve mature believers as the disciplers.

12. Have a prayer retreat where most of the time is spent in personal devotions and praying alone or in groups. Keep the lectures to a minimum. Make the retreat a personal experience with prayer. Prepare individual study sheets for participants that give them Scriptures to read about prayer, questions to respond to about their prayer lives, and some good quotes from Christian authors about prayer. Discourage frivolous conversation during the retreat.

13. Have a series of prayer seminars that focus on different aspects of prayer such as adoration, thanksgiving, intercession, and petitions.

14. Do a series of lessons on great prayer warriors such as Praying Hyde, Corrie ten Boom, Ruth Graham, John Wesley, and many others.

15. Invite a different single parent to share a prayer testimony for the group each week. This allows the single parents to see God at work in the lives of fellow single parents, and not just in the lives of leaders.

16. Read some of the prayers that have been written for worship services and ask the group to respond to what is said or meant by the prayers.

17. Print some of these prayers in your weekly newsletter.

In writing to Titus, Paul told him to set an example for other believers by doing what is good. His teaching was to show integrity, and his demeanor and speech were to be above reproach (Titus 2:7).

Why Do We Love to Pray?

Prayer is the source of our strength. Through prayer, we maintain our awareness of God's presence. With prayer, we receive God's direction, wisdom, and affirmation. By prayer, we can change our negative attitudes toward others or about circumstances. Prayer helps us confess our sins and purge our hearts before God to ensure our fellowship is joyous. In prayer, God shows us the divine perspective; we can relax knowing that even when we don't understand, we can trust in God's faithfulness.

Prayer is one way of walking the talk and talking the walk. When the whole image and person fit together and are consistent, it is called integrity. As a person and as a leader, I want the integrity that I find only through a life of prayer, of practicing the presence of God.

Yvonne Karlin has been active in single adult ministry for eleven years, served as director of single adults at Magnolia Wesleyan Church in Santee, California, and has been a member of the Network of Single Adult Leaders since 1991. As a single parent, she raised two children from the time they were ages four and two. She is now a grandmother. Yvonne has been a radio announcer for the last twenty years and has had the number-one rating slot for the last eight years with her program "Kicksy Love Songs" on KYXY in San Diego.

Resources for Ministry with Single Parents and Their Children

Blended Families

Bustanoby, Andre. *The Ready-Made Family*. Grand Rapids: Zondervan, 1982.
Juroe, David J., and Bonnie B. Juroe. *Successful Step-Parenting*. Old Tappan, N.J.: Revell, 1983.
Reed, Bobbie. *Merging Families*. St. Louis: Concordia Publishing House, 1992.

Counseling

Fagerstrom, Douglas, ed. *Counseling Single Adults*. Grand Rapids: Baker, 1996.

Divorce Recovery

Flanagan, Bill. *The Ministry of Divorce Recovery*. A set of three video tapes for use in developing a divorce recovery ministry. Available from NSL, P.O. Box 1600, Grand Rapids, MI 49525.
Hart, Archibald. *Healing Adult Children of Divorce*. Ann Arbor, Mich.: Vine Books, 1991.
Morgan, Andy. *Divorce Recovery*. A set of video tapes for use in an eight-week divorce recovery program. Available from NSL, P.O. Box 1600, Grand Rapids, MI 49525.
Reed, Bobbie. *Life after Divorce*. St. Louis: Concordia Publishing House, 1993. This book has leadership instructions for using the book as a guide for weekly sessions.
———. *The Single Adult Journey*. Anderson, Ind.: Warner Press, 1992. A thirteen-week curriculum with reproducible handouts. Also available from NSL, P.O. Box 1600, Grand Rapids, MI 49525.
Smoke, Jim. *Divorce: Surviving the Shock*. A fifty-five-minute video tape that answers frequently asked questions and outlines ten survival steps for those going through divorce. Available from NSL, P.O. Box 1600, Grand Rapids, MI 49525.
———. *Forgiveness*. A thirty-five-minute video tape available from NSL, P.O. Box 1600, Grand Rapids, MI 49525.
———. *Growing through Divorce*. Eugene, Oreg.: Harvest House, 1985.

Financial Issues

Burkett, Larry. *The Complete Financial Guide for Single Parents*. Wheaton: Victor, 1991.

Grief

Smith, Harold Ivan. Web site: http://www.planetconnection.com/friendgrief and E-mail: friendgrief@mindspring.com

Organizations

The Dougy Center is an organization for helping people work through grief. The Dougy Center, P.O. Box 86852, Portland, OR 97286. (503) 775-5683.

Network of Single Adult Leaders is a ministry dedicated to equipping and encouraging single adult ministry leaders to more effectively reach single adults with the good news of Jesus Christ through the church. Information is available by writing to NSL, P.O. Box 1600, Grand Rapids, MI 49525. (616) 956-9377.

Rainbow Connection provides over four hundred books, videos, and audiocassettes dealing with loss, death, dying, bereavement, comfort, and hope. These are available by obtaining a free catalog from Rainbow Connection, 477 Hannah Branch, Burnsville, NC 28714. (704) 675-9687.

Parenting

Authelet, Emil. *Parenting Solo*. San Bernardino, Calif.: Here's Life Publishers, 1989.

Cynaumon, Greg. *Empowering Single Parents*. Chicago: Moody Press, 1994.

———. *Helping Single Parents with Troubled Kids*. Colorado Springs: NavPress, 1992.

Eastman, Meg. *Taming the Dragon in Your Child*. New York: Wiley, 1994. This book is about anger management.

Faber, Adele, and Elaine Mazlesh. *How to Talk So Kids Will Listen and Listen So Kids Will Talk*. New York: Avon Books, 1982.

Gaulke, Earl H. *You Can Have a Family Where Everybody Wins*. St. Louis: Concordia Publishing House, 1975. This is a scriptural companion to Thomas Gordon's *Parent Effectiveness Training*. New York: Peter H. Wyden, 1970.

Gordon, Jeenie. *Turbulent Teens of Panicking Parents*. Grand Rapids: Revell, 1997.

Hannah, Jane, and Dick Stafford. *Single Parenting with Dick and Jane*. Nashville: Family Touch Press, 1993.

Holt, Pat, and Grace Ketterman. *When You Feel Like Screaming: Help for Frustrated Mothers*. New York: Ingram, 1988.

Peters, Ruth A. *Who's in Charge?* New York: Ingram, 1990. This book is about discipline.

Reed, Bobbie. *Dear Lord, I Can't Do It All! Meditations for Single Mothers*. St. Louis: Concordia Publishing House, 1994. Out of print, but available from author by writing P.O. Box 2087, Chula Vista, CA 91912.

———. *Single Mothers Raising Sons*. Nashville: Thomas Nelson, 1988. Check church libraries for this book as it is out of print.

———. *The Single Parent Journey*. Anderson, Ind.: Warner Press, 1992. This is a thirteen-week curriculum with reproducible handouts. Also available from NSL, P.O. Box 1600, Grand Rapids, MI 49525.

Richmond, Gary. *Successful Single Parenting: Going It Alone*. Eugene, Oreg.: Harvest House, 1989.

Whiteman, Thomas. *The Fresh Start Single Parenting Workbook*. Nashville: Thomas Nelson, 1993.

Single Adult Ministry

Fagerstrom, Douglas, ed. *The Baker Handbook of Single Adult Ministry.* Grand Rapids: Baker, 1997.

Hart, Archibald D. *Children and Divorce.* Irving, Tex.: Word, 1989.

———. *Growing Up Divorced.* Ann Arbor, Mich.: Vine Books, 1991.

Reed, Bobbie, and John Westfall. *Building Strong People.* Grand Rapids: Baker, 1997.

Schiller, Barbara. *Just Me and the Kids.* Elgin, Ill.: David C. Cook, 1994. This is a kit that includes videos, leader's guides, and participant guides for both children and their parents.

Sibley, Linda Kondracki. *Confident Kids.* Cincinnati: Standard, 1997. This is a terrific curriculum for children and parents, and it includes one unit of several lessons on coping with loss and grieving. For more information on Confident Kids Support Groups, contact Sibley at 330 Stanton Street, Arroyo Grande, CA 93420 or E-mail to confidentkids@juno.com/

Spiritual Disciplines

Biersdorf, John E. *How Prayer Shapes Ministry.* Washington, D.C.: Alban Institute, 1992.

Bloom, Anthony. *Beginning to Pray.* New York: Paulist Press, 1970. You may be able to find this out-of-print book in used bookstores.

The Book of Common Prayer. New York: Seabury Press, 1979.

Edelman, Marian Wright. *Guide My Feet: Prayers and Meditations on Loving and Working for Children.* Boston: Beacon Press, 1995.

Fischer, Kathleen, and Thomas Hart. *A Counselor's Prayer Book.* New York: Paulist Press, 1994.

Foster, Richard. *Prayer: Finding the Heart's True Home.* San Francisco: HarperSanFrancisco, 1992.

———. *Prayers from the Heart.* San Francisco: HarperSanFrancisco, 1994.

Huebsch, Bill. *A New Look at Prayer: Searching for Bliss.* Mystic, Conn.: Twenty-Third Publications, 1992. This book is in a free prose, easily read format and is very single parent friendly.

Van de Weyer, Robert, comp. *The HarperCollins Book of Prayers: A Treasury of Prayers through the Ages.* San Francisco: HarperCollins, 1993.

Weems, Ann. *Psalms of Lament.* Louisville: Westminster, 1995.

Widowhood

Brothers, Joyce. *Widowed.* Thorndike, Maine: Macmillian, 1991.

Convissor, Kate. *Young Widow, Learning to Live Again.* Grand Rapids: Zondervan, 1992.

Fitzpatrick, Carol L. *A Time to Grieve, Help and Hope from the Bible.* A Barbour Book. Uhrichsville, Ohio: The Lockman Foundation, 1995.

Lewis, C. S. *A Grief Observed.* San Francisco: HarperCollins, 1966.

Manning, Doug. *Don't Take My Grief Away.* San Francisco: HarperCollins, 1984.

Notes

Chapter 2: *Being a Never Married Parent*

1. "Four Out of Ten Unmarried Women in Their Thirties Have Had an Illegitimate Child," *World,* 25 May 1996, 23.
2. *USA Today,* 6 August 1996, 5A.
3. "Real-Life Murphy Browns," *Single Adult Ministries Journal* 10, no. 98 (1993): 2.
4. Harold Ivan Smith, *Reluctantly Single* (Nashville: Abingdon, 1994), 118.
5. Marcy Mullins, "What's on Your Mind?" *USA Today,* 6 August 1996, 5A.

Chapter 3: *Surviving a Divorce with Children*

1. Judy, quoted in *Single to Single,* Douglas L. Fagerstrom, ed., (Wheaton: Victor, 1991), 325.
2. "Of interest . . . ," *Single Adult Ministries Journal* 13, no. 4, Issue 117 (July/August 1996): 2.
3. Jim Smoke, *Growing in Remarriage* (Grand Rapids: Revell, 1990), 19.
4. Tom Vermillion, *Hate Divorce, but LOVE the Divorced* (Abilene, Tex.: The Single Life Institute, 1990), 5.
5. M. Scott Peck, *The Road Less Traveled* (New York: Simon and Schuster, 1978), 15.
6. Gary Richmond, *Successful Single Parenting: Going It Alone* (Eugene, Oreg.: Harvest House, 1990), 23.
7. Marsi Beauchamp, quoted in Richmond, *Single Parenting,* 25.
8. Carolyn Koons, "Children of Single Parents," in *Singles Ministry Handbook,* ed. Fagerstrom (Wheaton: Victor, 1988), 66.
9. Ray Maloney, "Ten Ways to Raise Terrific Kids," *Reader's Digest,* October 1986, 148.

Chapter 4: *Coping as a Widowed Parent*

1. Kate Conissor, *Young Widow: Learning to Live Again* (Grand Rapids: Zondervan, 1992), 128.

Chapter 5: *Solo Parenting as a Married Person*

1. Eugene Williams in a personal interview with the author in September 1996.
2. Bob Stevenson in a personal interview with the author in September 1996.

Chapter 6: *Relating to a Former Spouse*

1. Lewis B. Smedes, *Forgive and Forget* (New York: Pocket Books, 1986), 39.

Chapter 7: *Teaching Christian Values*

1. For more ideas, see Bobbie Reed, *501 Ways to Teach Your Children Values* (St. Louis: Concordia Publishing House, 1998).

Chapter 8: *Raising Teenagers*

1. Kathy Mills, radio program guest on *Focus on the Family,* date unknown.
2. Jeenie Gordon, *Turbulent Teens of Panicking Parents* (Grand Rapids: Revell, 1997), 62.
3. Ibid., 62–63.
4. Ibid., 65–66.
5. Ibid., 100.
6. Josh McDowell, *Why Wait?* (San Bernardino, Calif.: Here's Life Publishers, 1987), 79.

Chapter 10: *Finding Joy*

1. Charles R. Swindoll, *Three Steps Forward, Two Steps Back* (Nashville: Thomas Nelson, 1980), 74.
2. James Dobson, *Love Must Be Tough* (Dallas: Word, 1983), 13.

Chapter 12: *Living in a One-Parent Family*

1. George Masnick and Mary Jo Bane, *The Nation's Families 1960–1990* (Boston: Auburn House, 1980).
2. Ibid.

Chapter 13: *Having Special Needs*

1. "Never Marrieds Are One of the Fastest Growing Segments of U.S. Adult Population," *Single Adult Ministries Journal* 13, no. 116 (May/June 1996): 1.
2. Richard Estrada, "Viewpoint," *Dallas Morning News,* 23 Aug 1996, 35A.
3. Doug Easterday, "Child or Companion?" *Single Parent Family Magazine,* June 1996, 25.
4. The following resources are helpful when ministering to children of divorced parents:
Rainbow Connection provides over four hundred books, videos, and audiocassettes dealing with loss, death, dying, bereavement, comfort, and hope. The titles are available by obtaining a free catalog from Rainbow Connection, 477 Hannah Branch, Burnsville, NC 28714.
Hart, Archibald D. *Children and Divorce.* Irving, Tex.: Word, 1989.
Schiller, Barbara. *Just Me and the Kids.* Elgin, Ill.: David C. Cook, 1994. This is a kit that includes videos, leaders' guides, and participant guides for both children and their parents.
Sibley, Linda Kondracki. *Confident Kids.* Cincinnati: Standard, 1997. This is a terrific curriculum for children and parents, and it includes one unit of several lessons on coping with loss and grieving. For more information on Confident Kids Support Groups, contact Sibley at 330 Standon Street, Arroyo Grande, CA 93420 or E-mail to confidentkids@juno.com.
5. Ken Brumley, minister to single adults at Green Acres Baptist Church in Tyler, Texas, in a personal conversation with the author, January 1998.

Chapter 14: *Struggling for Control of Their Lives*

1. Judith S. Wallerstein, Shauna B. Corbin, and Julia M. Lewis, "Children of Divorce—A Ten Year Study," in *Impact of Divorce, Single Parenting, and Step-Parenting on Children,* ed. E. Mavis Hetherington and Josephine D. Arasteh (Hillsdale, N.J.: Erlbaum, 1988), 197.
2. Ibid., 211.

3. Irving R. Stuart and Lawrence Edwin Abt, eds., *Children of Separation and Divorce: Management and Treatment* (New York: Van Nostrand, 1981), 27.

4. Sara McLanahan and Gary Sandefar, *Growing Up with a Single Parent* (Cambridge: Harvard University Press, 1994), 41.

5. Greg Cynaumon, *Helping Single Parents with Troubled Kids* (Colorado Springs: NavPress, 1992), 22–28.

Chapter 15: *Demonstrating Scriptural Christianity*

1. George Foot Moore, *Judaism* (Cambridge: Harvard University Press, 1944), 164, 416.

2. Meyer Berlin and Josef Zevin, eds., Harry Freedman, trans., *Encyclopedia Talmudica* (Jerusalem: Talmudic Encyclopedia Institute, 1974), 427–31.

3. James Strong, *The Exhaustive Concordance of the Bible, Dictionary of the Hebrew and Greek Words* (Nashville: Abingdon Press, 1994), 13.

4. Merrill F. Unger, *Unger's Bible Dictionary* (Chicago: Moody Press, 1957), 814.

5. Berlin and Zevin, *Encyclopedia*, 297, and Francine Klagsbrun, *Voices of Wisdom: Jewish Ideals and Ethics for Everyday Living* (New York: Pantheon Books, 1980), 173–75.

Chapter 21: *Counseling Single Parents*

1. For more information, see Douglas Fagerstrom, ed., *Counseling Single Adults* (Grand Rapids: Baker, 1996).

2. Philip Yancey, *Disappointment with God* (Grand Rapids: Zondervan, 1988).

Chapter 22: *Establishing Mentoring Programs*

1. Our manual is available upon request to any person or organization who wishes to use it. For more information or a copy of the mentor's manual, write to Family Support Foundation, 698 West Main Street, El Cajon, CA 92020, or telephone (619) 590-1901.

Chapter 27: *Teaching Spiritual Disciplines*

1. *The Book of Common Prayer* (New York: Seabury Press, 1979), 323.

2. Robert Van de Weyer, comp., *The HarperCollins Book of Prayers: A Treasury of Prayers through the Ages* (San Francisco: HarperCollins, 1993), 73.

3. Ibid., 72.

4. J. S. Spong, *The Easter Moment* (New York: Harper & Row, 1980), 209.

5. Carole C. Carlson, *Corrie ten Boom: Her Life, Her Faith* (Old Tappan, N.J.: Revell, 1983), 26–27.

6. Richard Foster, *Prayer: Finding the Heart's True Home* (San Francisco: HarperSanFrancisco, 1992).